THE MYSTIC SINNERS

AN UNTOLD STORY OF TANTRA

PROYASHI BARUA

Readomania

Readomania Publishing
A division of Kurious Kind Media Private Limited
908, Vishwadeep Building, District Centre, Janakpuri,
New Delhi – 110058
books.readomania.com
email: contact@readomania.com
Facebook: facebook.com/iamreadomania
Twitter: twitter.com/iamreadomania
Instagram: iamreadomania

First Published in 2019 by Readomania

ISBN: 978-93-85854-84-2

Typeset in Palatino Linotype by Shine Graphics
Printed at Thomson Press (India) Ltd.

Readomania

India has traditionally been the land of storytellers and a lot of us have an inherent skill of creating good plots, good stories and good narrations. With a little encouragement and support, many more authors will be widely read and attain a place in the sun. This is the essence of *Readomania*—an initiative that nurtures emerging stars of the literary world.

It would not be an exaggeration to say that *Readomania* is the talent hunt in fiction. It goes a step beyond by not just identifying the talent but also nurturing it and showcasing it to the world. In the process, we have created a powerhouse of content.

Readomania has four principal interest areas—traditional print publishing, online library of short stories and poetry, literary events and products.

The print publishing works towards delivering good quality content to the readers. We publish good authors in meaningful anthologies, novels and works of narrative non-fiction. Our books stand out for their perspectives, the plots, the language and most importantly their ability to enrich lives.

Take a break, read something nice, write something beautiful. Read our books or visit us at www.readomania.com and enjoy a whole new world of literature.

To my nephew, Rivaan. I want this book to forever remind him that I love him the most in the world.

Prologue

It was 6 September 2012. A boat was ferrying across the Tunga river in Karnataka. Maya Chatterjee drew her arms to her nude breasts in an attempt to avert the salacious scrutiny of Prem Kumar Shastri who was seated at the other end of the boat. Beads of sweat erupted on the contours of her nude body and the breeze did little to stem the tide of sweat. Her head was lowered in embarrassment. Long tresses that cascaded to her navel translated to armour. *'Armour for a battle against fate in which I need to win,'* Maya resolved.

Around midnight the boat meandered between banks abounding in vegetation. An owl screeched. 'It is hurt and going to die,' Shastri said abruptly. 'There is glory in killing and dying for a cause. Everything is possible on this earth but one has to submit reason to faith.'

'But you said that these jungles are alien to poachers and tantrics! So who could have hunted the owl?' Maya quizzed.

'Tribal bird catchers. They are at home with the venom spewing cobras and are unaware of the secret Kaal Bhairav Temple and the curse surrounding it,' Shastri promptly interjected.

His elaborate description of the river route and the surrounding forests, at the start of the journey, had apprised Maya of every experience that she might undergo. She was sure that the presence of bird catchers was definitely not a detail which this pot-bellied man with piercing eyes could have omitted.

Before she could voice her apprehension, he steered the boat to the edge of the bank. It halted on the shallow waters and he disembarked with one hand clutching the hull. As the boat steadied he signalled Maya to get out. After she got out unquestioningly, Shastri reached for a coarse bundle of rope under his seat and tied the boat to the nearest sturdy tree.

Pointing his little finger upwards, Shastri darted towards a thicket. 'I will be back soon,' he shouted. As his voice receded, Maya furtively glanced around. Silhouettes of plants were visible in the fractured moonlight that filtered through the lush canopies of tropical trees. Unclad and anxious, she realised that she was entirely at the mercy of a man who she could not trust yet she was relying on him for a miracle that would save her husband. The events of the last forty-eight hours started racing back and forth in Maya's mind and made her delirious. Finally, her mind settled on a fateful moment.

It was the twilight of September 4 when Maya dialled Shastri's number. He answered on the first ring.

'Haan ji, behenji, hum aapke seva main tan, man aur dhan se haazir hain. Aap hume seva ka avsar denge to hum aapko nirash nahi karenge, (Sister, I am available at your service with all my body, mind and wealth. If you give me an opportunity to serve you I shall not disappoint you)' he implored and commanded at the same time.

'My husband has been falsely implicated in a corruption case. I have heard that you are capable of miracles and so am hoping that you will do something that will clear everything against him,' Maya pleaded.

After a stifling silence, Shastri answered in a flat voice, 'My powers are allowing me to see the problem. Your husband has karmic enemies who are trying to defame him. There is only one way to defeat them…but am not sure if it will be acceptable to you.'

'What is that way? I need to know it right now.' Maya could now hear the man breathing on the other side and somehow it made her uncomfortable.

'As I see it you will have to make some penances connected to water and reptiles. You will have to cross the Tunga river and visit a sacred Kaal Bhairav Temple barefoot that is infested by deadly snakes. Only a few know about the existence of this temple and the curse that surrounds it.'

'And what is that curse?'

'Well, barring full moon nights, if a man ventures near the temple unaccompanied by a woman, he becomes impotent.' Maya could hardly breathe as he continued. 'Also you will have to leave your most valuable piece of jewellery in the middle of the river for the river gods.'

'I shall abide by whatever you say,' she answered, wearily.

'Then I suggest you reach Mattur at the earliest. We need to complete our mission before the weekend for your penances to bear the maximum fruit.'

'You will be accompanying me?'

Shastri let out a throaty laugh. 'My powers combined with your efforts will work this miracle. Actually, there are a few other things that I have to tell you but not over the phone.' He uttered the last sentence in a whisper and rattled on, 'I will message you my address. But you must promise that you will not speak about this mission to anyone. Speaking about it will jeopardise the outcome.'

'I understand.'

There was a click at the other end as Shastri disconnected.

Maya was unable to sleep that night. She had never ventured anywhere without her husband. *'I am sure I shall be able to manage the journey to Mattur but what shall I tell Alok?'* she wondered.

By morning she had thought of a plan.

'Alok, a school friend of mine is visiting Shimoga with her family. She will be there till this Friday and is insisting that we meet,' she announced at the breakfast table.

Alok was busy scrutinising some official papers. The strain of the past months was creasing his normally jolly appearance.

'So, can I go? Sheela is returning to the US soon and we won't be able to meet for the next ten years,' she insisted.

'What are you saying?' Alok was more attentive now.

Maya repeated her request.

'You can take the car and leave for Shimoga tomorrow morning. I shall request the driver.'

'I know how difficult it is for you at this stage to place any official request. I shall be fine travelling by bus.'

A strange expression crossed Alok's features. Maya's heart was pounding. Given his protective nature, she was sure he was unconvinced.

'I think you are right. Surely, your friend will receive you in Shimoga.' He smiled slightly.

'Alok has been so stressed that he isn't really his usual self,' Maya told herself.

Throughout the bus ride, Maya fervently hoped for the success of her mission and clasped her palms in prayer. It was two thirty in the afternoon when the bus wheeled into Shimoga. Maya hailed an auto to her destination that was eight kilometres away.

A clammy breeze started blowing as it sped along the areca nut tree-lined road to Mattur. Maya clutched her knapsack. The heaviest and costliest piece of her jewellery—a four-inch-wide armlet in solid gold was carefully tucked among the few clothes that she was carrying.

At Mattur, the auto negotiated its way between clusters of small brick houses, straw sheds housing cattle and goats, and statues of gods and goddesses before halting near a flight of steps that led down to a pond. As Maya handed the fare, the driver looked at her with suspicion and some concern.

'*Now there is no turning back*,' Maya assured herself as she started descending the steps. The pond was fringed with trees. On the right edge was a small brick house sheltered by a tree that had a knotty trunk. Painted an ugly blue, the house looked a little eerie.

Maya rapped at the door. A short man with a full head of hair opened it within seconds. She hesitantly stepped inside. A mop of waist-length hair hung on a nail and there were posters of Goddess Kali everywhere. The man motioned her to sit on a low bed and settled himself into a charpoy, gazing at her.

There was a sting on her abdomen. Maya jolted back into the present and realised that it was a wasp. Before she could react to the searing pain, Shastri reappeared from the thicket.

'One can't ignore nature's call,' he said as he fiddled with his dhoti.

'When are we reaching our destination?' Maya asked as they walked alongside the river.

'In half an hour,' the tone of the reply was clearly rude.

'Do I need to throw my armlet in the middle of the river while we are returning, after performing the penances?'

Shastri nodded.

The forest on the adjoining banks had thickened. Maya's thoughts returned to her time in Shastri's house.

Sensing her nervousness, the man introduced himself, 'God will bless your friend Tanushree for directing you to me. I have been successful in all the cases when people like you have faced disappointments with other tantrics. There is nothing that cannot be achieved through tantra *shastra*. I don't want to exaggerate my importance but I have the combined blessings of Maa Kali and Bhairo Baba,' he continued, adding, 'Sister, if you have faith, my powers work hundred percent. If you doubt me then you are making things difficult.'

Maya managed a smile. 'I am confident that you shall restore my husband's honour and I shall be eternally grateful to you.'

'Then I am convinced that you will unquestioningly abide by what I have to tell you yet. According to the texts, every woman who offers her most valuable ornament to the river gods after paying homage at the shrine of Kaal Bhairav, receives a perennial shower of blessings. She and her loved ones are forever wrapped in his benediction. But there is one condition. She has to go nude to the shrine.'

Maya could not believe her ears. 'This is something that I cannot do in a million lifetimes!' she declared.

'It is also my duty to tell you that once a woman decides to pay homage at this shrine, she should follow the code and go ahead. Else, she and her family are bound to face adverse consequences.'

'But you never told me about the code…or the ramifications of not following it,' Maya pleaded. 'Besides, our scriptures say that a woman can appear nude only in front of her husband.'

'I have told you several times before that I shall be able to help you only if you have unflinching trust in me. I can already see that dwindling, so I won't stop you from returning. But…,' he contorted his brow.

'But what?' Maya demanded.

'I am worried about your husband now as I know how fatal the consequences will be.'

Only the whirring sound of the fan was audible while Shastri disappeared into the other room. When he reappeared, he was holding a fistful of ash.

'I was trying to see if there is something that I can do for your husband when the Lord unleashes his wrath on him. Unfortunately, I won't be able to save him.'

Maya was sweating profusely. Kohl started trickling down from her eyes in a straight line, smudging her fair face.

'It is true that our scriptures say that a woman can appear nude only in front of her husband. But you are doing this only for him,' Shastri consoled. 'Besides, I will not look at your body after you disrobe. We shall go to a secluded part of the bank, well past sunset. You can undress there in the cover of bushes.' Shastri's voice was beginning to have a strange effect on Maya.

Against her will she muttered, 'As you say.'

'I am glad you understood the ramifications of going back.' Shastri's voice was triumphant.

Maya had no recollection of the next few hours. She started feeling drowsy and everything seemed like a blur.

'Did I doze off? I didn't realise I was so exhausted with the journey.' She sat up on the low bed to face Shastri. It was 9 pm and he was squatting on a mat encircled by incense sticks and tiny mounds of ash and herbs, lost in a trance.

Maya noticed that Shastri's skin was glistening and a woody odour had blended with the puffs of mogra smoke. An empty bottle lying around told her that the tantric had dabbed sandalwood oil on his body.

'The auspicious time for our mission has started. I can already feel the mystic pull from Bhairav*ji*,' he muttered in a hoarse voice and stood up.

They walked in silence along the deserted village lanes. Strangely, Maya was now minus the turmoil that she had experienced throughout the evening. After walking for another ten minutes, during which Shastri gave a graphic description of the river route, they reached the riverbank. A frail-looking boat was moored at one corner.

Shastri climbed on the boat and motioned Maya to go behind one of the massive trees and undress. It was too dark to see each other clearly as the clouds were shrouding the almost potent moon and stars. It took some time for Maya to disrobe. She appeared before Shastri concealing her chest and pelvic region with her knapsack.

Shastri noticed that she was now minus her watch, wedge sandals, gold chain and thin gold bangles. Only her tiny diamond ear studs remained.

The hissing sound of snakes jolted Maya back to the present.

'On full moon nights, the five-headed serpent that guards Kaal Bhairav's shrine comes to the river,' said Shastri. He was steering the boat to the edge as they had reached their destination.

As he started uncoiling the rope to moor the boat, Maya felt a pain coursing through her stomach. Ignoring her discomfort, she followed Shastri among the trees and overgrown grass. An owl let out a blood-curdling screech as they stepped into a clearing.

The Kaal Bhairav Temple was fully visible now. Built of black stone, it had carvings of the deity across its entrance.

Snakes of various sizes were gliding on the grass. Without thinking, Maya dashed behind Shastri inside the temple.

To her surprise the inside was nothing like a regular temple. There were no bells and the shrine was not visible in the darkness. With her right palm on the wall for support, Maya followed Shastri.

Soon, they started descending some steps. After reaching flat ground, Maya saw that the entire space was illuminated by a couple of rusty oil lanterns. A snake hissed ferociously but they continued and turned to the right. A terrifying yet magnificent-looking statue of Kaal Bhairav was mounted on a shrine canopied by a five-headed serpent.

Shastri squatted before the shrine and uttered some mantras. The serpent stopped hissing. He then opened a bag and took out an array of incense sticks, parched grains, a dead fish, a bottle of liquor and an assortment of powders. After carefully arranging everything and lighting the incense sticks, he looked at Maya and blurted, 'Sit down and keep repeating after me.'

Maya started trembling as Shastri took out a booklet and straightened the creases on its yellowed pages. He read out a line from the booklet and paused for Maya to repeat. This continued for about forty-five minutes. It was getting claustrophobic as the fumes had no outlet. There was a stench of cheap alcohol and decayed fish all around.

Abruptly, the reading stopped. Shastri got up and started blowing into the powder mounds. Soon, the entire space was shrouded with a grey veil. Maya felt dizzy.

'Follow me,' croaked Shastri as he retraced his footsteps through the temple. Clutching at her knapsack she complied.

After a few minutes, just as they were about to step out of the entrance door they heard the deafening sound of a gunshot. Despite her stupor, Maya could decipher the silhouette of a bird dropping from the sky a few yards ahead of the temple's entrance. Within seconds there was a growing cacophony of savage voices and metal. Her vision started blurring and she lost consciousness.

a rescue and a flashback

A light flickered before Maya's eyes as she started regaining her senses. The morning rays of the sun filtered down through a banyan tree. As she saw the loose, knee-length shirt covering her, she remembered the horrific events of the previous night.

'How did I come here and who clad me?' she wondered anxiously.

Then, she saw a log house perched between the sturdy branches of two massive trees. A bamboo ladder stood under its verandah. A man of average height started climbing down. He had a solid-looking pair of binoculars slung around his neck. The man walked up to her and extended his right palm.

'Hi, I am Arvind Kamath. You had some misadventure. But luckily, I found you,' he sounded sincere. 'This is my longest shirt. So, I covered you with it. I have a few trousers and shirts that will probably fit you,' he continued, pointing to the log house.

Maya sat motionless at the base of the banyan tree.

Arvind bent down to help her up to her feet and flashed a gentle smile. 'Freshen up, change into something more comfortable, and have some tea and poached eggs. I promise you that you will feel better,' he said in a gentle voice.

Almost in a daze, Maya wobbled up the ladder and stood on the verandah. The door of the only room was swaying with the flow of the river breeze. Once inside, her eyes settled on an open closet that had rows lined with jackets, trousers, shirts and men's underwear. Grabbing an indigo baggy shirt and trousers, Maya dashed into the tiny bathroom and latched the door as securely as she could.

Somehow, the spotless sanitary fixtures made her feel very unclean. All this while her mind had been wrestling to drive out all assumptions of the time during which she had been unconscious. As she shut her eyes and stood under the shower she could see graphic images of Shastri ravaging her body.

As her finger tips reached between her legs, her torment dwindled. There were no telling signs of semen! She realised there was no foreign odour or marks anywhere on her body either. *'And the bastard had massaged himself with sandalwood oil…so is it possible that he did not…'* Maya could not pronounce the dreaded word even silently!

As she dried herself with a towel, she sensed a dull ache in her shapely breasts. *'So, probably he had only molested me and fled with my knapsack,'* she comforted herself.

Within ten minutes, she had descended the steps.

Arvind passed a plate of brown bread and poached eggs as she sat on a rug that he had spread for her. 'I must say that the clothes are sitting really well on you.'

The sun had disappeared into a mass of gathering clouds. Anticipating a storm, a flock of birds were returning to their nests.

'That is a blue-tailed bee-eater,' Arvind informed as he noticed her looking at an unusual bird.

She turned to face him with an inquiring expression.

'I am an ornithologist. I work for the WWF and incidentally feature in the hit list of some of the most wanted bird poachers.'

'Oh okay,' Maya spoke for the first time.

In the silence that followed, Arvind tilted his head and smiled. 'And now let me tell you how I found you last night... After midnight some poacher had fired at a tawny owl...tawny owls are endangered owls that live on river banks and they are a catch for poachers and tribal bird catchers...' Arvind stopped his narration and started fiddling with his camera.

Maya was sure that he could hear her heart beating... finally, she would know something about the time that she was unconscious!

'I rushed in the direction of the gunshot. I must have run for about a few minutes when I reached a spot from where I could see the bird lying lifeless. Through my binoculars I could see that this spot was a few yards away from the right outer wall of the Kaal Bhairav Temple. Half a dozen tribal bird catchers carrying oil lanterns had surrounded the corpse. I must have been less than half a kilometre away from this spectacle for I could hear the men uttering a consecration hymn as they encircled the bird. After fifteen minutes, they carried the bird away....'

Arvind turned to Maya and saw that she had turned pale. 'While I was watching this I noticed a human silhouette crouching among the trees adjoining the left portion of the temple. For some time I thought this was the poacher but then I realised that a poacher armed with a gun will not be so intimidated by the tribals. I could see the man inching away into the thicket. I assumed he was going in the direction of the river. Soon, he had disappeared.'

Maya's heart had almost stopped beating.

Arvind looked at her before gulping some water. 'After the tribals had disappeared, I ventured in the direction of the temple. I had an uncanny feeling that I would find something there...and presto, I was right! At the entrance of the temple I could see a woman sprawled on the ground...,' Arvind realised that it was unnecessary to describe the further sequence of events.

Maya was now sure that the theory she had formed in the log house was right. Shastri had not been able to rape her! Her mind occupied itself with other worries—all her money and ornaments were in the knapsack. How would she return to Bangalore? Also, her saviour deserved to know why she was lying nude and unconscious at the doorstep of a temple at an unearthly hour. How on earth could she explain that?

For the next ten minutes, Maya watched Arvind taking shots of the bee-eater that had perched itself on an uprooted bark. Something told her that if he kept talking about his work she would be spared the ordeal of explaining the horrific chain of events that had led her here.

'It will be interesting to know more about your work,' she said, meekly.

Almost as if he had read her thoughts, he smiled and nodded. 'I understand that you want to go back home. I am going to row you back to Mattur after sunset. But I assume you don't hail from there. Are you from Shimoga?'

'Bangalore. And I shall be grateful if you can please put me on the bus that goes from Shimoga to Bangalore.'

'I shall escort you on your bus journey. It is important that you are safe now,' his voice resonated genuine concern. 'And, maybe it will be nice if I have a name to address you.'

'Maya. I am Mrs Maya Chatterjee.'

'Happy to have made your acquaintance, Mrs Chatterjee, but I shall call you Maya,' Arvind extended his hand for the second time.

For the next six hours, Arvind regaled Maya with fascinating stories of his work. 'I have always maintained a low profile. Not even people inside WWF know my itinerary in the wild. So it leaves me baffled whenever these poachers trail me to the jungles. But I have been lucky so far to have escaped them,' he concluded.

Maya managed a shallow smile. Despite the heaviness that had entrenched itself into her heart, she was enjoying Arvind's company.

Throughout the afternoon, there had been a spell of torrential rain. It finally ceased at around 4.30 pm.

'Sometimes good luck can make a great difference. If the rains had continued, it would have been impossible to take you back safely to the shores of Mattur,' Arvind remarked as he readied the boat.

As soon as Arvind's steam boat came to life, Maya fell silent again. The ornithologist realised that she was drawing painful comparisons with the journey that she had undertaken, probably a couple of nights ago.

They reached the banks of Mattur within an hour and half. Within minutes they boarded a taxi to Shimoga and reached their destination just in time to catch the night bus to Bangalore.

'So, you will manage the way to your house?' Arvind asked her for the fourth time and forced a five hundred rupee note into her palm as they stood at the Bangalore depot.

She nodded in a daze.

'Give me your number,' he urged.

Maya looked at him for a while before giving her number.

'I don't know what I can do to repay this kindness. And, I don't really know if we shall ever meet again,' she smiled sadly as they were about to part ways.

'I was just being another human being. And something tells me we shall meet again,' was the cheerful reply.

As she hailed a cab to her residence, something told Maya that from that moment on, she would have to endure her grief all alone. And this was exactly what happened for she could not bring herself to confide in Alok about her enormously embarrassing ordeal.

Initially, Alok had been engrossed in his own problems to notice that his wife had become a lot more subdued. Clearly isolated in her grief, Maya had started becoming delirious. She would wake up in the middle of the night screaming in anguish and would frequently talk to herself in the course of the day. After several such episodes, Alok, who had never bothered to understand this behaviour change, admitted her in a rehabilitation centre.

It was 26th February 2013. Tears streamed down Maya's cheeks as she looked out into the ten-acre garden from her bedside window. She was housed in the ground floor of a mental rehabilitation centre of Bangalore.

A nurse frisked in with a tray. 'Mrs Chatterjee, you need to finish your porridge. Medicines can't be given if you don't eat,' she instructed.

The nurse kept chattering, mostly to herself throughout the ten minutes that she was in the room, changing the bed linen and bathroom towels.

'Mrs Chatterjee, your husband loves you and so he has spent much in getting you a private ward. You must cooperate with us for your recovery, for his sake,' she announced before marching out.

Her words about Alok kept echoing in Maya's head, making her cringe. For the entire month and a half that she had been in this asylum, she had been introspecting about their relationship and had always ended up with uncomfortable questions.

'Maybe I am missing something. Maybe our time together was not so superficial,' she consoled herself. She gazed out of the window and into her past.

'I had spotted a rainbow in the evening. Our marriage is bound to be lucky for each other,' Maya whispered coyly as Alok lifted her brocade veil on their wedding night.

'I don't believe in these superstitions but I do believe that I am a very lucky man to have married a beautiful woman like you,' he gushed while proceeding to unclasp her ornaments.

Maya smiled. 'But you were insisting on matching our horoscopes.'

'I only said I am not superstitious. I never said I don't follow convention or rules.'

'Mrs Chatterjee, it is time for your weekly injection,' the compounder interrupted her thoughts.

'These injections are doing nothing for me. I told you before and am telling you again—I am just fine. Please let me go home.'

The glum-faced compounder walked up to her side with his surgical apparatus. After he left, Maya shifted uncomfortably on her bed to ease the pain and looked out of the window. She closed her eyes and made an effort to transport her consciousness to the first three years of her marital life. The silhouette of a house with a lawn loomed against the backdrop of the morning sky.

'I am glad you have worn green today. Green is auspicious for Wednesdays. Your meeting with the Divisional Forest Officer is bound to be favourable,' Maya told Alok after breakfast.

'Well, if he is convinced about my research proposal, there is a good chance that we shall soon be posted to Dehradun. Life there will be easier for you compared to this.'

'I am happy with anything that is good for your career. And I am anyway getting used to the Sundarban suburbs.'

'But three years of this place, right after tying the nuptial knots, isn't exactly the best thing. I feel guilty that your shopping sprees are so few. Besides, you hardly socialise on your own.'

Maya felt a longing for the structured life that she always had. She missed the official parties, weekly outings to the nearest town and the elaborate meals that she used to supervise in her kitchen that had a retinue of servants. Alok had qualified as a loving and considerate husband in her social circles. But did her heart resonate with these adjectives? Right then, she wasn't sure.

Maya's mind transported her to the fateful afternoon of 11th February 2012; an afternoon of copious rain.

'Memsaab...Memsaab, something terrible has happened. We dashed into a speeding Bolero. We...' the voice at the other end of the landline started trailing as her head started spinning.

'How is Sir?' she finally blurted.

'We rushed him to the village hospital. The doctors there are now transporting him in an ambulance to a hospital in Kolkata.'

'We are driving down to Kolkata immediately.'

'But the car is dented. And I too have some injuries. I have been given first aid.'

'But I have to go! Krishna Da, can you please arrange for someone to take me immediately,' she pleaded between sobs.

'I will ask my brother to drive you to Kolkata. He will take you in Saheb's Jeep,' he answered after a brief silence.

All throughout the ride, Maya kept praying for Alok's recovery.

'Filter coffee and *poha,*' a voice brought her back to the present again.

'I don't want any.'

The man wheeling the trolley of refreshments left the room without another word. Maya tried to drive out the painful memories of the two whole days that she had spent outside the ICU for Alok to regain his consciousness.

'It is said that there is light after the darkest hour but in our case the darkest hour has only preceded a never-ending nightmare. Or is this nightmare only mine? Alok has never bothered to come and see me,' she wondered with a heart throbbing with pain and regret—regret for being overly superstitious and blindly trusting an astrologer who happened to be her childhood friend.

'But what else could I have done to help Alok? And Tanushree? Why did she cheat me and land me in so much peril? Did I miss some vital clue to the impending betrayal when I walked into her chamber that day?' she asked herself almost harshly. And then, the dimly lit corridors of a dilapidated building in Salt Lake surfaced in her memory.

She had been surprised to see a receptionist sitting in front of her friend's chamber. The girl gestured to Maya to sit on a sofa while jotting appointments over the phone.

After about fifteen minutes, Maya was ushered in. The chamber had an olive green door at one end. Piles of hard-bound books, birth charts, a couple of talismans wrapped in red cloth, and some paper pouches cluttered the desk.

Tanushree looked different from her school days. Dressed in a garish salwar kurta, she looked domineering.

'Sit,' she instructed Maya in a flat tone. Her expressions were soulless. 'Have you brought his birth chart?'

'His mother has misplaced it and I didn't think it was right to bother her with it, at least not for the time being. I can tell you the exact timings of his birth.'

Tanushree started etching a horoscope on an A4-sized paper. Finally, she looked up and said, 'Well, *Rahu* in the fifth house is now in a phase of severe affliction. *Ketu* too is not in a favourable position. In such a situation, harm from enemies is inevitable.'

'Alok is a man of honour. He could have endured any other adversity but not this humiliation! His enemies have done everything they could to implicate him. Now even the top officials are convinced that he has accepted a bribe from some poachers. They are blaming him for the dwindling count of spotted deer and Indian Rollers,' Maya looked distraught.

'It is sad when our own planets go against the very things that we hold so sacred. And how is his health now?'

'There had been a rupture in his intestine and that required him to undergo a surgery followed by bed rest for two months. He just resumed office and now this has happened.' Tears started welling in Maya's eyes.

Tanushree's look softened. 'Don't worry, Maya. I am training under a renowned Kali *sadhak* of Kolkata. I shall take my guru's counsel and solve Alok's problems.'

She got up and disappeared behind the green door. After some time, an odour of camphor started enveloping the room. Tanushree reappeared holding a folded paper tied with a red string.

'Keep this in your purse for twenty-one days. On the twenty-second day, set fire to it in a closed room. Collect the ashes and flush them in the toilet.' Maya took the paper and put it inside her purse. Something in Tanushree's voice told her that she should not be questioning.

'Take these as well,' Tanushree handed two small yellow paper pouches. Smear a little powder under your husband's pillow every night, for the next twenty-one days. And on the twenty-second day, take the remaining amount in your palm and blow it in the direction of the rising sun.'

'Everything will sort out after three weeks?' Maya questioned, anxiously.

'This is just one part of the remedy. I will be able to tell you the second part only after consulting my Guru*ji*. But yes,

I can assure you that after everything is done the problem will be solved.'

As she stepped out into the road and hailed a taxi, Maya felt an ease that she had not experienced for long.

For three weeks, she meticulously followed Tanushree's instructions with surging faith.

'I have done exactly as you had said. What are the next steps?' she inquired over the telephone.

Tanushree answered after an uncomfortable silence. 'Alok is undergoing *Kaal Saarp Yog*. The ramifications of this *dosha* are particularly deadly in his case. And hence my Guru*ji* has advised a *mahayagya* of Kali Maa.'

'So when do I need to do it?'

'You can't participate in the final ceremony. There are some tantric rituals involved in it. The *mahayagya* will happen at my Guru*ji*'s house on the night of *Amavasya*. I will only be assisting him.'

'So, you will give me the *vibhuti* after it is over. And that will solve everything,' Maya emphasised on the second sentence.

'Yes, and you have to give me thirty-five thousand for the ingredients.'

Maya was shocked at the astronomical amount. 'Thirty-five thousand?'

'This *mahayagya* requires several kilos of black turmeric, herbs and rare intoxicating substances. Besides, we need at least five varieties of fish and meat. Quantities of each variety will run into several kilos. Then there is liquor, several kilos of rice and lentils.'

'Can I buy them for you instead of sending the money?'

'Well, you will not be able to source most of these ingredients. These are not retailed in the most obvious shops. I am only trying to ease your burden.' Tanushree finished with a sarcastic laugh.

'I will send you a cheque,' Maya answered flatly.

'You needn't send any cheque because you will have to come to Kolkata exactly three nights before the ritual to carry out one preliminary part of it. You will have to collect an urn of ash from a cremation ground at midnight. I shall tell you which one after you arrive.'

A shiver ran down Maya's spine. 'Let me know the exact dates,' she blurted and disconnected.

Maya remembered the foreboding darkness of the spooky cremation ground in Tollygunge Road. It was early July. Monsoons had flooded almost all the by-lanes of Kolkata. After alighting from her taxi in a deserted lane, she walked amidst mud and slush for almost twenty-five minutes to reach her destination. Neem and mango trees lined the oblong cremation ground.

'After you collect the ash, you will receive a signal from the spirits that roam the place. It can be anything—a piece of cloth dropping from nowhere or an unexplained flash of light. Our *mahayagya* will only be successful if you receive the sign,' Tanushree's words kept echoing in her mind as she scurried in the direction of the cremation pyres.

As she bent down at the silent pyres, droplets of rain water trickled down from the trees around, almost alarming her. Maya thought it was the sign and almost in a daze secured her bounty and scurried out of the gates. But for a long time afterwards, she had recurring nightmares and would wake up in the middle of the night half screaming and half crying, 'I have finished the most challenging feat of my life!'

'When will all the charges against Alok get resolved? I cannot see him depressed any longer,' Maya inquired two days after the *mahayagya*.

'Within forty days,' Tanushree assured.

During the painful wait, matters only got worse. Alok was suspended from service.

'Just wait for another week. Forty days will be over and positive results will start showing,' Tanushree consoled Maya who had anxiously called her after hearing about the suspension orders.

Unfortunately, Tanushree's prediction turned out only partially right. Alok was reinstated in service but after a demotion. He was transferred to Bangalore.

'Is there any way in which things can become what they were six months ago?' Maya asked between sobs over yet another phone call.

'I can't hear you properly. Let me call you back,' her friend replied.

The call came after half an hour.

'I just spoke to Guru*ji* about Alok's situation and he said that his problems have not ceased because his horoscope is also afflicted by *Pitridosha*. However, there is one man who can help you without fail—Prem Kumar Shastri. He lives in Mattur village which is very close to Shimoga. He is one of the most powerful tantrics alive.'

'How can I contact him?'

'Let Guru*ji* talk to him. If he convinces him to help you, consider yourself blessed.'

Maya closed her eyes and tried her hardest to drive out all recollection of her ordeal. She finally opened them, looked at her phone and thought, 'I haven't heard Alok's voice for so long!'

And right at that moment, it started ringing. She fumbled to pick it up, her vision blurred by tears.

'Alok! I am so happy that you finally called...,' she fell silent when the voice at the other end greeted her. It wasn't Alok.

'Maya, this is me. Remember?' The voice was male and brimming with cheerfulness. 'I am your friend from the jungles.' There was a throaty laugh.

'Arvind? What a pleasant surprise!' Without knowing why, Maya felt happy after a long while.

'I am in Bangalore. And I need to meet you. A friend of mine is making a documentary on tantrics, to expose their nefarious ways and I thought you should share your experiences. He will maintain anonymity. Think about it, Maya, this is also a way in which you can avenge the injustice that you suffered.'

There was a long silence.

'And you are not alone. He has a close friend, Kamakshi. She used to work as a copy writer in an ad agency and has also suffered like you.'

'Can I meet you, Arvind?'

'I was about to ask you where. Is it okay if I come home?'

Maya started weeping. 'I am at an asylum. Silver Crescent,' she finally replied between muffled sobs.

'What?' Arvind sounded genuinely astounded.

Maya quickly narrated the events of the last few months.

'I am coming tomorrow. I know the people who own the place. Keep everything packed. I am taking you with me to Mashobra…to be with Ranbeer and Kamakshi.'

Without asking any questions, Maya said, 'I shall wait for you.'

friendships in mashobra

The management was apprehensive about releasing Maya and letting her go with Arvind, despite the fact that he happened to be a close friend of the owner's son.

'How do you know her?' They grilled him.

'I had rescued her when she had lost her way and entered a jungle. The rest of the picnickers had left...this was several years back and we have been friends ever since,' he persisted.

'Whatever it is, we can't let her go anywhere without her husband's consent.' The head supervisor was adamant. However, when numerous calls to Alok went unanswered, his stance changed.

'You are taking her to Mashobra...to be in the company of some friends?'

'Yes. You already have all my coordinates. I am giving you the number and address of the place that I am taking her to. All you need to do is give it to Mr Chatterjee when he comes. Maya will be only too glad to be in his custody,' Arvind said, assertively.

The supervisor was checking the accounts register. Alok had not even cared to clear her bills for the previous month. He let out a sigh and finally said, 'But you will have to clear all the bills and sign an undertaking.'

Arvind nodded.

It was nearly 6 pm when they reached Mashobra after a couple of days. Oak and pine trees, covered with frost, lined the driving stretch to Rosewood Cottage, which would be their home for some time. Built on a hillock, it was a pretty, two-storeyed bungalow.

'Was there a lot of congestion on the highway?' A thin, white-haired man greeted them on the steps of the verandah. Maya and Arvind stretched their palms to shake hands.

'Maya, this is Ranbeer,' Arvind introduced the two.

'Darling, your room is next to Kamakshi's on the top floor. Freshen up and we shall all meet for high tea.'

Maya could not decipher the look in Ranbeer's eyes.

The inside of the cottage was prettier than the picturesque bungalow. A wooden ceiling complemented the brick red-and-cream walls of the living room. As Maya started climbing the winding rosewood staircase to the first floor she felt a sense of homecoming.

'I love the orange and red décor of my room,' she told Arvind and Ranbeer when she joined them after a refreshing hot water bath.

'That is the sunset room on the top. I have the sunset room on the ground floor. Offers a splendid view of the valley,' Ranbeer replied, pointing to some pictures on his sophisticated SLR. 'I am making a photo diary of sunsets.'

Just then, a dusky woman in her early thirties walked towards the table.

'Kamakshi, our friends are waiting to meet you.' Ranbeer stretched his arm in her direction.

'Hello, Kamakshi! I'm Arvind and this is Maya.' The ornithologist kept staring at the woman even after he finished speaking. With sensual lips, smouldering eyes, an aquiline nose and perfect cheekbones, she reminded them of the Bollywood actresses of the seventies.

'Hi!' Her greeting lacked any shade of emotion. For some time the conversation froze as the waiters started bringing in food.

The rest of the evening was spent around the fireplace. The two men had an animated conversation on birds and filmmaking. While Maya heard everything enthusiastically, Kamakshi looked preoccupied.

Suddenly, Kamakshi was alert, 'I just saw someone moving…outside the window.' She pointed to one of the side windows.

The men dashed across. 'There is nobody,' Ranbeer said after straining his eyes in the darkness.

'I think we should call it a night,' Arvind said abruptly, looking at Maya. 'I think Maya wants to retire to her room.'

'I am okay sitting here for a little longer,' Maya bit her lip as a surge of blood coloured her cheeks.

Ranbeer and Kamakshi could see that though the lady had consciously avoided Arvind's earnest gaze, his concern had touched her as she cast a lingering side glance at him.

Finally, after an uneventful hour, the quartet proceeded in the direction of their rooms.

Arvind tapped Maya's shoulder as she trod on the first step of the staircase and said, 'I asked the housekeeper to send a hot water bag to your room.'

'Thank you, Arvind,' Maya responded with a shy smile and hurried up the staircase.

'Blizzards are predicted for the next three days,' the manager of Rosewood Cottage announced as they walked into the dining area for breakfast the next day.

'We wanted to go to the apple orchards near Kufri. Would have been a nice change for the girls,' said Ranbeer. Turning to them he added with a twinkle in his eyes, 'We've been snowed in but we can still enjoy indoors.'

'It is going to be a boring day,' Maya thought to herself.

'Actually, it will be great to stay indoors and discuss our plans for the documentary. I have some thoughts on it already,' Ranbeer immediately added.

For the next three hours, the four huddled in front of the fireside in the common living area. Ranbeer turned out to be more interesting than any of them had imagined.

'I was tired of my family business. So, I escaped to Italy after my thirty-fifth birthday. And ever since, my life has been one beautiful escape—escaping everything that ties the flight of my spirit.'

'And what did you do there?' Maya was clearly amazed by this bohemian man.

'I spent years in the countryside, documenting the idiosyncrasies of people through my paintings and photographs. I made a living by selling these from a small shop on the outskirts of Milan.'

Seeing the spellbound expressions around, Ranbeer laughed and said, 'I had interned with the famous photographer Raghu Chawla, in my twenties. But painting has always been my first love.'

'And how did you get started with documentaries?' Maya quizzed.

'An art gallery owner from Rome once visited my shop. He asked if I would be interested in making a collage of my photographs and display it in his gallery. I agreed. The collage caught a lot of attention. I gave two interviews to the press. Around this time a renowned European documentary filmmaker contacted me to work with him.'

As Ranbeer paused to light a cigar, Maya concluded that the man was not above bragging.

'And, of course, that was a turning point of your life.' It was Kamakshi who spoke this time. 'I have been so trapped with myself all these months that I never bothered to ask about your life. Not once after I rented the room on your terrace,' she added in a soft voice.

Ranbeer tapped her forehead and said, 'I understand how tough it has been for you.'

There was an awkward silence. '*What possibly could be her story?*' Maya started wondering. And the next thought was, '*I too will have to share my story.*' Strangely, it did not make her uncomfortable.

'Well, many of Ranbeer's documentaries have featured in international film festivals.' Arvind informed. 'So when he approached me some months ago saying that after sometime he wants to make a documentary on my work, I was honoured.'

'You are India's most celebrated birdman, after all. And I will be grateful if you stop embarrassing me.'

After lunch, conversation lulled as the men realised that discussing the documentary on tantrics would not be easy for Maya and Kamakshi. Ranbeer cleared his throat and made a start, 'Well, I met Kamakshi three months ago. But I had decided to make this documentary much before. I have a friend called Merlin. She is a French researcher and I had met her in Banaras last year. Merlin had come across some people who had suffered at the hands of tantrics. Ever since I heard these stories I have been planning this documentary.'

'But Ranbeer, when we spoke last September, you wanted to make something on forensic investigations!' Arvind exclaimed.

'Your memory gets foggy whenever you return from the jungles,' Ranbeer retorted in half-jest and half-sarcasm. 'I shall be shooting a large part of my documentary in Banaras. Another friend of mine knows a very learned priest there. This priest is against occult malpractices and should be happy to guide me.'

'Hmm...after all Kashi is not just India's oldest spiritual destination, it is also a land of mystics—genuine and fake,' Arvind reasoned.

The girls were silent.

'I want to highlight the sheer ridiculousness of tantric practices. And I was thinking that somewhere in the middle of the documentary, we can feature appreances and talk about some of the unfortunate experiences that people have suffered.'

Tears started welling in Maya's eyes. Kamakshi was expressionless.

'If you are uncomfortable, I shall omit this part,' he gently assured.

'The world deserves to know everything through your documentary,' Maya finally said in a voice quivering with emotion. Before anybody could say anything, she painstakingly narrated her ordeal with Shastri and everything leading to it.

'You are a brave lady and a devoted wife. Unfortunately, your courage only put you into senseless danger,' Ranbeer reasoned.

Maya noticed that the expression in his eyes conflicted with his tone.

'Maybe you will feel better if you share everything with them,' Ranbeer held Kamakshi's hand and said rather persuasively.

Kamakshi nodded and gazed into the fireside. 'I too did everything for the sake of love. The only difference is that he was not my husband...but someone else's.' She closed her eyes and let the tears stream down.

'When Raj and I met at a party seven years ago, I instantly knew he was my soul mate. He was not the best looking man at the party, yet I found him compellingly attractive. And I am sure he felt the same way for he walked up to me and introduced himself. He was an Air Force pilot, posted at Bareilly and was visiting Delhi for some work.' Kamakshi paused.

A wild cat screeching outside the cottage meddled with the silence.

'We had exchanged numbers and started talking almost every day, and before his next visit to Delhi, we were in love.' Then, Kamakshi turned to face Maya and said, 'I could never stop loving Raj...even after he confessed that he was already married to a woman who could never understand him! After his confession, I had tried to break away from him a couple of times. But I was never strong enough to stay away for long.' Kamakshi started sobbing.

Holding a cigar, Ranbeer stepped out of the living area. It was clear that he had heard the sequence of events leading to the break-up several times before.

'Our bond that had strengthened with the passage of time started souring when he got posted to Delhi, three years ago.' Kamakshi smiled a little sarcastically and continued, 'For I could never understand why despite being in the same city our meetings had to be far apart.'

After wiping away the tears that were welling in her eyes she proceeded, 'I had told him a zillion times that we could always part on a graceful note if he ever felt burdened with the weight of our relationship. But he had always dismissed the prospect. At the same time, he was super cautious of hiding our relationship from Natasha. He couldn't afford a situation in which he had to divorce her and lose custody of his only child.'

Before Kamakshi could continue, Ranbeer dashed into the room. 'There is someone...' He was panting and pointing his finger towards the French windows that opened to the rear lawn of the cottage.

Kamakshi's Ordeal

'What? Who?'

As Arvind questioned, they realised he could be the same person that Kamakshi had seen the previous evening.

'I was smoking in the verandah when I felt like someone was slinking into the grounds. Initially, I thought my imagination was playing up. But after a few minutes I heard a muffled cough and decided to investigate. I walked towards the sound and saw someone stealthily walking past our window.' Ranbeer was now standing in front of the French windows and lifting a portion of the curtain.

'Was the man eavesdropping on us?' Arvind muttered almost to himself.

'Might not be that dramatic,' Ranbeer replied. 'I have heard from the manager that petty thieves often frequent the grounds.'

Before anyone could say anything the manager entered the living room to rekindle the fire. 'We are running short of firewood as several logs were stolen last night from the backyard. Our security guard has taken ill so the thief might be back tonight to steal our chickens. However, he will be out of luck as we have fenced the area today with barbed wire.'

As everyone settled back into their chairs, Kamakshi picked up the narrative again.

'I refused to understand his compulsions for not spending enough time with me and started having bitter fights. Actually, it was all my fault for he never retorted.' Fresh tears rolled down her cheeks as she struggled to retain her composure.

'Well, it was a complicated relationship and obviously his frequent non-availability exhausted your patience.' Ranbeer edged close to his friend and offered her a handkerchief.

After sipping some water, she resumed, 'Every morning Raj used to wake me up with a phone call. But one morning of last September he hadn't called till 10 am. Worse, he did not answer my call or respond to my messages. I had a particularly bitter fight the previous evening and for the first time he had answered me back. So, I was all the more anxious to patch up.

Then I sent him a string of abusive messages. How was I to know that he was unwell and resting at home, his phone was on silent mode and with his wife who, of course, read everything?

I don't know the exact sequence of events for Raj and I never spoke privately after that. But yes, I guess she humiliated and taunted him with my messages, forced him to ring me from a public booth and ask me to come to one of our usual meeting places.'

There was an awkward silence.

'I guess we would have parted for good that day even if he had come alone. But it would not have been an acrimonious parting. The rancour of that day will continue to haunt me till I live.

Seeing her accompany him, I felt angry, sad and betrayed at the same time. Actually, I had felt insanely helpless and wanted to spoil Natasha's victory. And so, without thinking, I told her everything that I never should have. At the end of what clearly was the most stressful hour of my life, she knew every sensitive detail about our six-year-long relationship.'

Kamakshi started crying uncontrollably again. It took her several minutes to compose herself. 'I wanted one last meeting with Raj that would allow me to say everything that will remain unsaid. I could have then moved on in peace,' she added, sadly. 'But, he changed his number and deactivated his email. Since I did not know his address, there was no way in which I could contact him.'

'And then?' Maya prodded.

For the first time, Kamakshi looked hesitant. She resumed after Ranbeer looked gently in her direction. 'Then I lived in a painful daze for months. Everybody around me had started sensing my depression. One day, my maid told me about a mystic from South India who had come to live in a dilapidated farmhouse in Chattarpur. According to her, this woman was endowed with supernatural powers and capable of obliterating every grief. Sunita insisted that I visit her once. Initially I was apprehensive, but after a few days she said something which melted my inhibitions. Vasanthi *Amma* was genuine and therefore unlike the frauds, never advertised her powers in newspapers. I decided to meet *Amma* and meticulously jotted down the directions.'

Kamakshi let out a deep sigh and resumed, 'The farmhouse where she lived with a small retinue of helpers was nothing like I had anticipated. Heaped with mountains of rubble, sacks, boxes and cartons, the compound resembled a construction site. I noticed that many of the sacks and cartons were tightly sealed and a bluish white powder-like substance littered the grass.'

'And how did *Amma* look like?' Arvind was curious.

'I never got to see *Amma*. She used to sit behind a curtain in the main hall of the building while meeting her clients. There was a shrine outside the red curtain with at least twenty brass idols of the goddess, her many incarnations.'

'And then?' Maya prodded.

'To my surprise, without my telling her anything she knew everything about me. That I had come to her because of heartbreak and that my name starts with the letter K. She recounted incidents from my past with surprising precision of dates.'

Ranbeer smirked and said, 'The bitch must have done her homework with your maid!'

'Well, she told me that from my energies she could see all the sins of my previous lives. These sins were causing my misery and to make penances I would have to offer two serpents in solid gold at her shrine. She specified that each serpent would have to weigh half a kilo.'

'And you actually got them made?' Arvind was aghast.

'I thought she was my last hope. So, I exhausted all my savings and got them made, to be offered at her shrine on the day of the full moon.' Kamakshi's voice sounded both helpless and sad. 'I will never forget that cold January night. *Amma* commanded me to enter the adjoining room after placing the gold serpents on the shrine. As I entered I was transfixed by a beautiful blue statue of Goddess Tara adorned with a garland of marigolds. The room was shrouded with incense fumes and a short, ugly man was chanting some mantras. After a few minutes, my senses became a bit foggy. The man beckoned me to come closer to the statue. My legs instantly complied.' Kamakshi stopped to catch her breath.

Maya started patting her back. 'After uttering some mantras the man asked me to kneel down. Soon, I realised that he was unbuttoning my cardigan and... Before I could react, he was running his dirty hands mercilessly over my breasts. And just as I tried to push him away he did something that I could have never imagined!'

'What?' Maya's eyes were protruding in horror.

'He ran a blade across my forehead and smeared his finger with the blood. Between my screeches I heard him saying that my penance is complete as I have offered my blood to Tara Devi.'

'And where was that *Amma*?' Arvind demanded.

'I was too traumatised and rushed out of the house. I did not stop running till I got to my cab that was parked outside. The driver was aghast too see blood trickling from my forehead and despite my resistance administered first aid from a box that he kept handy. Since I was sobbing hysterically, he realised it was pointless asking me about any details and drove me back home in silence.' Kamakshi looked exhausted.

Nobody spoke for the next half hour as Kamakshi stared blankly at the dying embers in the fireplace grate.

'Didn't you think of registering a police complaint against that woman?' It was Arvind who finally broke the silence.

'Not that I didn't think of it but it seemed cumbersome. I knew I would have had to recount all the details that led me to Vasanthi in the first place.' Her flat voice spiked with anger when she mentioned the con mystic.

'And I know how very embarrassing it is to face people while telling them about your ordeal with a tantric.' Maya drew parallels with her experience.

'Don't know how true it is but I am told that there are no clear laws in our country to convict tantrics,' Ranbeer said.

'Wonder why we cannot use our common sense and keep away from these savage rascals.' Arvind was angry.

'Because sometimes our problem can be so overwhelming that it defies all common sense,' Maya mumbled almost to herself.

'I will have a quick shower and order a light dinner in my room. I have a splitting headache and need to rest,' Kamakshi announced, abruptly.

The others realised that they too needed to retire to the solitude of their rooms. While her narration had saddened Maya and Arvind, Ranbeer wanted to reflect upon the mystery behind the intruder in the lawns. Something told him that stealing firewood was not the motive.

In the next few days, the documentary filmmaker tried to lighten the women's mood by narrating stories about Banaras.

'You will love Merlin and Baccha. Everyone at Banaras addresses Merlin as Meera. There is always so much to learn from her. Baccha Yadav, my friend and owner of Everest Café and an adjoining guesthouse where we shall all be staying, is a sweetheart. He has this habit of forgetting important things and then remembering them at unexpected times.'

Maya smiled. 'So when are we reaching Banaras?'

'As soon as I hear from my crew.'

The next five days passed peacefully. The snow was starting to melt.

'I am going to Delhi, day after,' Arvind announced. 'Have to reach the jungles of Madhya Pradesh for a research assignment on egrets.'

Maya felt a pang in her heart. The thought that he might remain completely incommunicable while in the jungles saddened her.

Almost as if he had read her thoughts, he asked in a more relaxed tone, 'And, when are you guys reaching Banaras?'

'By next week. My crew is reaching Delhi this Tuesday. We shall proceed together on Wednesday. I have already informed Meera,' Ranbeer replied.

Once Arvind departed for Delhi, the manager handed Maya a sealed envelope. She retired to her room to read the contents. It was a small note inscribed in Arvind's clear handwriting:

> *Maya, I have instructed the management of Rosewood Cottage not to reveal the details of your next destination to Alok Chatterjee. And I want you to keep this a secret from our friends.*

The note went on to reveal a lot more about Arvind and what he thought of her, making Maya very happy.

banaras

It was six in the evening and the sky was shrouded with a mask of crimson and purple clouds. Meera was sitting by the window at Mystic Flavours Café. Situated on a hillock, this café offered an expansive view of Assi and the adjoining ghats. The sight of priests scurrying along with their ritual paraphernalia among the milling crowd of tourists and vendors filled her with an inexplicable calm.

'*Te quiero*,' she heard a Spanish lady say to her child at the adjoining table. Meera smiled at them. The little boy waved in her direction. Then, he seemed confused and brought his hands together into a namaste. While Meera's hazel eyes reflected her Caucasian origin, her complexion was darker than other foreigners. She could almost pass off as an Indian.

Though her mother was French, her father had been half-Indian and half-African. Meera had been very attached to her father and after losing him at the age of twelve, she had kept him alive by reminiscing on the mythological stories from India that he had narrated. A few years later, her mother re-married and started a family but Meera grew up missing her father.

To keep herself connected with her deceased parent, Meera started reading about India. Although she had never visited India, she felt an unexplained connection with the country. Finally, last spring she flew down to New Delhi and visited Rajasthan, Kerala, Lucknow and Banaras, and there had been no turning back since then.

Meera's thoughts turned to Ranbeer and she smiled at the memory of their first meeting at a Holi party that Baccha had hosted at Everest Café for Indian and foreign tourists.

A local guide that she had met at Dashashwamedh Ghat had apprised her about the party. In the days that followed, their friendship had steadily grown. When Ranbeer understood her need to establish her roots, he suggested the possibility of undertaking some course connected to India. Eventually, she decided to pursue her higher studies in traditions of Hindu worship and applied to the Oxford Centre for Hindu Studies.

The waiter arrived with the bill and she paid absentmindedly. The telephone conversation, which she and Ranbeer had the previous night, was playing on her mind. 'I hope Maya and Kamakshi find solace here. After all, Banaras is probably the only place on earth that can somehow free people of their grief by suffusing it in its mysticism,' the thirty-year-old researcher ruminated.

After stepping out, Meera headed towards the market area. She had to make a choice—of either going to Harishchandra Ghat to watch an ascetic, who came there every Tuesday after moonrise to perform some dangerous feats or returning to the guesthouse. At her guesthouse, she could observe the young priest who would spend the evening reclining on a cot on the terrace of his dilapidated two-storeyed house. She chose the latter as she realised it was a Monday.

As she entered the guesthouse, Baccha waved at her and shouted from the dining area, 'Madam*ji*, I heard that Ranbeer is coming day after, with two lovely ladies.'

Meera smiled at him and started climbing the stairs. She was aware that Baccha had a crush on her that made him go the extra mile in ensuring that she had a comfortable stay in Banaras.

The Ramnagar Fort situated on the outskirts of Banaras was Meera's next research destination. Gopal Sarai, the librarian of the Centre for Vedic Studies, accompanied her. Sarai was an authority on the socio-cultural factors that had influenced the composition of the Vedas and Meera often consulted him for her research work. Sarai also shared a proximity with the director of the Oxford Centre for Hindu Studies.

The officials in charge of Ramnagar Fort were unwelcoming when they learnt that Meera was a researcher. They turned more apprehensive when she disclosed the topic of her research—missing and forgotten religious manuscripts of the Vedic Age. The only highlight of the trip was a visit to the Yash Kashi Temple that was in walking proximity of the fort. As they paid their obeisance at the massive Shiva Linga, the *pujari* told Meera that a visit to the Vishwanath Temple is incomplete if one does not follow it up with a visit to Yash Kashi.

'Yash Kashi grants wish fulfilment,' he had informed as he touched her forehead with his *chandan*-soaked finger.

It was around four in the afternoon when they returned to the main town. The sun had mellowed and the two strolled to the river bank.

Sarai had always noticed the élan with which Meera went about her work despite the fact that her accent and mannerisms were visibly different from the locals.

'Is Meera your real name? In your academic records it is Merlin,' he abruptly asked after they had settled themselves on the steps of Rana Mahal Ghat.

Meera laughed as a man playing a flute passed by. 'Well, once me and my friend Ranbeer had met a *ravanahatha* player on the footsteps of this very ghat. I wanted to master the exotic-looking instrument. The man conceded to teach me and said everyone should call me Meera from then on as Meerabai used to play on her *ravanahatha*.'

Sarai merely smiled. He handed a blue book to Meera and said, 'I have never lent this reference book to anyone.

In fact, it has never even been part of our library. I will be in Delhi for a few weeks as I have some important work. We shall meet once I am back.'

That evening, soon after the Ganga *aarti* concluded, Meera scampered to Raja Harishchandra Ghat. It was Tuesday and the ascetic would be there. She had seen him performing fierce *sadhanas* every Tuesday, in the past month, and resolved that today she would follow him to his dwelling. One of the more solemn ghats of Banaras, Raja Harishchandra Ghat, was always milling with people. Meera was surprised to find it unusually deserted that evening. The ascetic too had not arrived. For a minute she thought of returning to the guesthouse. But she quickly dismissed the thought and climbed about ten steps to sit and wait for the mystic.

Closer to the river edge, a few *chandaals* were rummaging the ground. Soon, the ascetic appeared. Wearing only a red loin cloth he strode purposefully to the brink of the river with a *trishul* in one hand and a blazing cauldron on the other. A cobra and *rudraksha* garland slung from his neck.

Meera strained her eyes to capture the details of his rituals. The halo from the full moon helped. Placing the *trishul* and cauldron on either side, the man bent near the river edge and cupped his palms to collect the sacred water. His back was towards Meera and she realised that he was chanting mantras, for he remained motionless for some time. In time, he stood up, holding the cauldron and *trishul* in either hand, walked around in a circle. Orange flames sprang up to define the circle. He bore the *trishul* vertically, on the ground encircled by the disciplined flames and put the cauldron near it. His bony structure soon contorted into a hatha yoga pose.

As the ascetic continued his *sadhana,* his lone audience was both terrified and mesmerised. The conclusion was even more spectacular. He extinguished the fire boundary by swallowing the flames. Finally, he caught the cobra around his neck and brought its raised hood within inches of his tongue and—the cobra spilled its venom on his tongue. Meera knew that this marked the end of his ritual and got up to trail him.

And then something happened, which Meera could never forget for the rest of her life—her legs refused to comply with the signals of her brain and she was conscious of a magnetic field around her that was restricting all movement. As she stood helplessly, she could see the six feet plus frame of the ascetic strutting along the ghats. Finally, he became a tiny speck in the distance. When her legs started coming back to life, the ascetic had completely disappeared.

'This ascetic is undoubtedly endowed with psychic powers and had been aware of my plans of trailing him. He had frozen my movements by dint of his special powers. This is probably my first personal encounter with a tantric,' an aghast Meera reasoned. It took her a little while to compose herself and descend to the ghats.

As she collected her keys, Baccha noticed that she looked dazed and unusually tired and shouted after her, '*Khana room main bhej denge aur baad main* filter coffee.' Along with the meal tray Meera noticed that he also sent a note reminding her of the morning boat ride—they would depart from the ghats exactly at 4.50 am in order to witness the sunrise near the Manikarnika Ghat.

Ferrying on the Ganga at daybreak translated to an enchanting experience. Fumes from cremation pyres, sounds of temple bells and people taking their morning dip in the river revealed how life, death and spirituality are omnipresent dimensions of this town.

'Madam*ji,* you looked hassled when you returned last night. All okay?' Baccha inquired.

'Not really. I had a rather scary encounter with…with a tantric last evening,' she said.

The boatman, who had been humming on a tune, fell silent.

'Ranbeer is coming here to make a film on tantrics. Maya and Kamakshi have suffered so much at their behest. I too have heard of their tactics from a few people around town. I don't understand why the judiciary of this country does not have laws to convict this savage breed of humanity!' Meera questioned, passionately.

'Well, tantra is actually sacred and is practiced for the upliftment of mankind. There is a community of Aghori tantrics on the outskirts of Banaras that cure medically incurable diseases including leprosy. Sadly, there are very few genuine tantrics left in this world. About ninety percent of tantrics in the country are imposters. And this is precisely why tantra is getting a bad name,' he clarified.

At that moment they crossed the Manikarnika Ghat and the Kashi Karvaat Mandir. Alluding to the lopsided structure, Baccha explained, 'The temple had swayed during an earthquake that occurred several hundred years ago. A very revered tantric had stopped it from crumbling by using his special powers. There is another major feat by tantrics that modern India can never discount. During the Chinese aggression, a community of Aghori tantrics had performed a *yagya* in Madhya Pradesh and almost immediately, the progressing Chinese troops miraculously retraced their steps.'

Meera slowly recounted her experience of the previous evening. Baccha and the boatman were well aware of the existence of this fierce man in Banaras.

'He is believed to be the seventh descendant of a very pious Aghori tantric who lived in Banaras in the late sixteenth century. After becoming an Aghori tantric, this man had estranged himself from his family. And for almost six subsequent generations there was nobody like him in his family. But Limar Singh, who was born in the seventh generation, had an uncanny resemblance with his far removed Aghori forefather. He demonstrated strange powers from his childhood—he could heal terminally ill people with just a touch. Finally, at the age of seventeen, he disappeared. His parents are dead and his siblings have sold their ancestral property and left Banaras. The tantric you encountered yesterday, Madam*ji*, was Limar Singh who has returned to his hometown after severe penances in the Himalayas,' narrated Baccha.

'How are people so sure that this very ascetic is Limar Singh?' Meera quizzed in disbelief.

'His identity and purpose was revealed only recently by a clairvoyant,' Baccha replied.

'And who is this clairvoyant?' Meera asked.

'He is an old man who resides in the main town. His predictions and remedies have never gone wrong. Madam*ji*, by meditating upon the late afternoon and early evening sun rays, this clairvoyant is capable of ascertaining the precise reasons that are responsible for the challenges that plague the people who come to him. Somebody had asked him about this strange ascetic. It had taken him quite a while to meditate upon the question and see the answers.' Baccha explained.

'And what exactly is Limar Singh's purpose?'

Baccha exchanged a quick glance with the boatman before replying. 'He is here to find and guard a sacred text of the Aghori tantrics. A text that got lost in the passage of time, probably during the period when the British rulers were waging a war of intolerance against the practitioners of tantra and sacred places of practice. Written by one of the most powerful Aghori tantrics of this country, nearly ten centuries ago, this text is hidden somewhere in Banaras. According to the clairvoyant, this fact was revealed to

Limar Singh by Lord Shiva after he finished thirty long years in exile, lost in meditation.'

'You said it is hidden in Banaras. Who hid it and why?' Meera was curious now.

'This text contains powerful mystic formulas that can usher unprecedented positive changes in the world. It is believed that it also contains a formula to reverse the ageing process. However, the formulas have to be implemented in totality and precision, or the effects can be heinously malefic. Therefore, there is an understood but unwritten code surrounding the text—it cannot fall into the hands of evil or semi-literate tantrics.'

Meera was speechless. *'Oh how I hope that the clairvoyant is right. Limar Singh's discovery of this text will translate to an enormous fillip for my thesis. The academic world only knows that certain Vedic texts are missing and some have been forgotten. The fact that there is an undiscovered text will be quite a sensational breakthrough…and I might acquire unprecedented recognition even in the global research fraternity,'* she thought to herself as a tingling sensation coursed through the nerve endings on her fingers.

Baccha scratched his head. 'I don't remember who but someone told me that the tantric who authored this text had lived a very mysterious life.'

'You mean the clairvoyant?'

'Not the clairvoyant. I don't remember who.'

'What else did the clairvoyant say about the text?'

'That this Aghori had lived an extraordinarily long life and that at the time of his death he had given this text to a trusted disciple of his. The text was hidden by a descendant of this disciple, maybe about a hundred years ago. Apart from the direct descendents of this trusted disciple, nobody knew about the existence of this text in the last ten centuries,' Baccha informed.

'You said that someone told you that the author of this text had lived a secret life. So probably even at the time when it was written, a thousand years ago, nobody knew about it. So in a way this text has not been discovered,' Meera inferred.

'Yes, only a secret Aghor community knew about it. He had told me this...I seriously can't remember who.' Baccha had a crestfallen expression.

'So, has he found the text? Does the clairvoyant not know where it is hidden?' Meera asked.

'No, the clairvoyant does not know. And the people of this town only wanted to know about the mystic. His preoccupations are of little interest to anyone here,' was the nonchalant reply.

As the boat set its course to reach Shivala Ghat, Meera was lost in thought. '*What if the ascetic failed in his mission of finding the sacred text? What if it was already in wrong hands?*' she wondered. As the boat reached its destination, a third question quickly coursed through her mind—*What if the undiscovered text also throws light on some unknown facts about Vedic literature? My research paper might need to address many more complexities than I am prepared for. For all I know, I could be nominated for an award. Also, it is likely that Ranbeer and his friends discover more about tantra and tantrics, than they are already prepared for while shooting their documentary.* Something told her that the focus of her research would change and that the script for the documentary would need to be rewritten.

Gauripradа

As they hurried up the steps leading to Shivala Ghat, Meera reminded Baccha that he had to arrange a meeting for Ranbeer with the head priest of Vishalakshi Temple. Ranbeer, Maya, Kamakshi and a three-member production crew were reaching Banaras in a few hours.

'I am not sure whether Gauriprada will agree to meet. And even if he does, he might not answer questions related to tantra,' Baccha shrugged his shoulders. Looking at Meera's dismayed face, he added, 'It will be a challenge for me to convince Gauriprada to talk. But Madam*ji*, I will do it.'

When the group arrived, Ranbeer and Meera exchanged a hug.

'I am so happy to see you and so sorry that you lost your father last October,' Meera told her friend in one breath.

Turning towards Maya and Kamakshi, she introduced herself with a warm smile. Of the two, Maya looked more resilient, she observed.

After the guests retired to their rooms, Meera had a conversation with Baccha. 'Are you sure that Gauriprada knows enough about tantric malpractices that can guide an entire documentary? And will he speak against all the tantrics of Banaras?'

'Madam*ji,* he will speak once I assure him that Ranbeer will never disclose his identity. Gauriprada*ji* is a learned priest who is against blind occult practices. After he understands the intent behind Ranbeer's documentary he will be happy to volunteer information,' Baccha assured.

Meera looked sceptical. 'He might also have to accompany the crew to some forbidden places. That might jeopardise his anonymity. Would he be willing to take the risk?'

Baccha's optimism was surging. 'While shooting, we should all be in disguise.' There was a brief pause after this dramatic suggestion. 'After all, secrecy is important not just for Gauriprada but for everyone who is assisting the documentary. Because...' he left his sentence unfinished and for the first time looked worried.

Just at that moment, there was a shrill ring on the dining room intercom. Baccha picked up the receiver and started jotting room service orders for lunch and rushed in the direction of the kitchen.

A feeling of heaviness had started creeping into Meera's chest, after hearing Baccha's last word. Thinking that the river breeze would dispel it, she decided to go for a stroll on the ghats.

In the following days, Everest Café was at its liveliest best as interesting people started frequenting it to meet Ranbeer. Baccha had managed to convince Gauriprada effortlessly. The priest would also assist them in identifying the locations for shooting.

'What exactly did you tell him?' Meera asked.

Baccha arched himself near her ear and whispered, 'I said Ranbeer*ji* has been commissioned by the government to make this documentary and that secret security agents will oversee the protection of everyone involved. I also told him that he will be rewarded for his assistance. And Gauriprada will not miss any opportunity to qualify for the trustee post of the new temple complex on the outskirts.'

Meera was speechless. 'Why did you lie so much? And this means he was far more reluctant than what we anticipated.

Did you ask him why he is so apprehensive? I mean it looks like he is already very scared.'

Baccha dismissed her questions, saying, 'Why are you worried, Madam*ji*? We should only be concerned with the outcomes.'

'Either Baccha is exaggerating his efforts or Gauriprada actually knows a lot about these dark practices. Knows enough to put his life in danger!' Meera thought.

A few evenings later Meera, Maya, Baccha and Ranbeer ambled towards Godowlia Chowk to meet Gauriprada. Kamakshi opted to visit Shivala Ghat instead and write her diary.

After negotiating patches of cow dung that littered a dimly lit lane, the four reached Gauriprada's house.

'Do not knock. I will hear you coming and unlatch the door. None of my neighbours should know that I am helping you,' the priest had instructed Baccha that morning.

As the door started unlatching, Meera and Ranbeer cast a glance around to see who the neighbours were. They could only catch a glimpse of an ascetic clad in a yellow robe.

'Well, I don't know how to thank you for agreeing to help me with this documentary,' Ranbeer blurted out the moment the priest appeared.

Gauriprada studied him a little suspiciously before gesturing to the group to come inside.

'It is useless to get entangled in the matters of people and things that have no bearing on our lives.' Gauriprada's first sentence as they proceeded to sit on the worn-out rugs spread across the floor was unexpectedly brusque.

'Our friends have grievously suffered at the behest of tantrics. This documentary can fetch justice for Kamakshi and Maya if it manages to expose all the dark practices of this savage breed of mortals,' Meera said, passionately.

Hearing her, Gauripradа turned a little friendlier. 'The genuine practitioners never take advantage of people's misfortunes.'

As Gauriprada finished speaking, Ranbeer cast an admonishing glance at Baccha. Were they supposed to convince Gauriprada all over again?

'You have to agree that today the genuine ones are outnumbered. What's worse, since occult practices are performed in secrecy, most crimes go unreported. This documentary shall be a step towards preventing these crimes,' Meera persisted.

An uncomfortable silence ensued. It abruptly broke with Gauriprada's throaty laugh. 'I can see that you are disturbed...and now I see two duties ahead of me.'

'And what are these?' Maya asked.

'I will help your friend to film the ploys of the imposters. But it also becomes my sacred duty to educate you about the sanctity of this timeless practice. After all you are in Kashi, Swami Ramananda's sacred abode. I cannot inflict any unrest on his great soul by not enlightening you on the truth of tantra.'

'You mean the truth about its purity? I am beginning to conclude that there can be nothing sacred about it. Perhaps in the olden days people were too simple to understand that tantra is nothing but illusion. My guess is that evil men had fabricated their own cunning formula to create this illusion and trick people. And over the years these formulas came to be perceived as sub-sects of tantra.' Maya finished sarcastically.

Gauriprada smirked. 'Tantra is nowhere near illusion. In fact, it is mankind's oldest technique of questing for the absolute truth. Besides, it is common sense that every fake object or phenomenon is inspired by the original. Just like fake diamonds are inspired from real diamonds.'

'And, of course we have the real diamond right before us. Limar Singh!' Ranbeer said, quickly narrating Meera's experience with the ascetic.

'So, you actually had the intentions of following Limar Singh to his dwelling? He could have even burnt you to ashes! Anyone who hampers his cause or troubles him will invoke the wrath of Bholenath,' Gauripradа retorted.

'Well, aren't you going to help us trail him for the documentary? I mean although we cannot actually trail him, there must be some way of keeping tabs on his activities. After all, we can't exclude him especially because he has come to Banaras for such a fascinating mission. He is probably one of the rare genuine tantrics left in the twenty-first century,' Ranbeer insisted.

'There is no way in which we can monitor his activities without his knowledge. And anyway, it would have been a futile exercise. Apart from his Tuesday ritual he does nothing but meditate. I heard that once he visited the home of a Brahman family to bless them. This family has for generations revered Lord Shiva and erected a large temple resembling the Shiva Linga inside their compound. People say that Limar Singh had entered it and enhanced its aura.'

Ranbeer looked unconvinced.

Gauripradа closed his eyes and continued, 'Besides, I don't think it is right to allude to his mission in your documentary. It might not be right to expose his mission to the world, at least until it is accomplished.'

'But you just said that my documentary has to be balanced. Don't you feel you are contradicting yourself?' Ranbeer tried hard to conceal his irritation.

'You are not going to film only the frauds. I am going to show you the places where the descendents of the original Shaiva and Vaishnava tantrics practice their austerities even today,' Gauripradа replied with authority.

'I heard that the Vaishnava tantrics of Banaras had corrupted their original practices in the fourteenth century.'

Ranbeer's words startled everybody. None of them had expected the documentary maker to know anything about tantra beyond the surface level.

'So, you know about this speculation? Well, it is just that—a speculation. Some decades ago, a section of the local people of Banaras had believed this theory but it is not true.'

Maya who had been hearing everything intently was very intrigued. 'What then is the truth?'

'Banaras has always been the stronghold of Shaiva ascetics and tantrics. Till the beginning of the fourteenth century, they were largely the dominant sect. The Vaishnava sect started growing, with Ramananda's arrival in the fourteenth century. Around that time, Islamic invasions of India were rising. Ramananda started incorporating people from the lower folds of society into his sect to prevent them from converting into Islam. The speculation is that some of these people were only attracted to the tantric order of the Vaishnava sect. To put it simply, they were not interested in the austere life of normal ascetics. Well aware of the mystical ecstasy enjoyed by tantrics, they started their own experiments with tantra after borrowing from the basic principles of Vaishnava tantra.' Gauripräda paused to drink his ginger tea.

'And so that is how the original practices got corrupted,' Maya mumbled almost to herself.

'It is a baseless theory. In fact, some even stretch the speculation further saying that many *totkas* and mantras of the Vaishnava tantrics got mixed with the Islamic *totkas*.'

Baccha finally asked Gauripräda, 'So you will help my friend, right?'

Gauripada nodded. 'We will start on the approaching *Amavasya* night.'

'We are indeed indebted. And now we will take your leave,' Ranbeer replied as he and the others got up.

'Everything that seems perfect in this world is not perfect. Likewise not everything that appears tarnished is completely tarnished. You will all experience this truth after the documentary is made, maybe even earlier,' Gauripada said as he led them out.

As the four hastened their pace towards the ghats they could hear the muffled sounds of oars splashing the Ganges—oars of the few boats that had chosen to venture on a ride well past the time of the Ganga *aarti*.

Maya was contemplating on Gauripada's parting words and realised that the events of the past months merited introspection into all her notions of good and bad, including her beliefs. 'Maybe there is a purity about tantra. Something that can only be experienced by the ones who genuinely devote their life to understanding it,' she reasoned. Instantly, the agonising memories of September 6 surfaced and she concluded, 'No matter what Gauripada says, the unfortunate truth is that all tantra is fake and practiced with evil intentions.'

On the other hand, Meera was engrossed in one thought—how did Ranbeer manage to have such an informed conversation with Gauripada? From whatever she and everyone else knew, Ranbeer had never believed in this practice and therefore, after his decision to make a documentary, he had not bothered to research on the subject.

'There is nothing about this heinous practice that deserves academic attention. I am just going to film the malpractices happening under its name and make my discovery.' He had told Meera a couple of days ago.

'Discovery?' Meera had been surprised. Ranbeer had ruffled her hair and laughed it off.

A man mumbling to himself jolted her back to the present. Dressed in a silk kurta and Kolhapuri *chappals*, his appearance was nothing like the regular tourists and pilgrims. There was a strong whiff of sandalwood perfume as he ambled past them in a daze.

'I have seen this spectacle before. I don't remember where though. Who is he?' Meera asked Baccha while her gaze remained fixed on the man.

'He is Arshad Singh, the grandson of Brij Bhooshan Singh, one of the richest feudal lords of Bihar in the days of the British Raj. Brij Bhooshan Singh came to Banaras in the pre-independence era to immerse his father's ashes. Already married and father to two teenage sons, the flamboyant man fell in love with a young woman. His family had opposed his relationship but he eventually married her and settled here. He started living in the haveli that his ancestors had built. In the auspicious month of Shravan, this haveli used to be home to several generations of this feudal family, when they would come here on pilgrimage. Arshad Singh, Madam*ji*, is Brij Bhooshan's second wife's progeny.'

'I have heard of this man. In fact, tomorrow I will be attending a musical night at the public gallery near his haveli. I believe it is in the same compound.'

'People say that Arshad Singh is a borderline schizophrenic. There are times that he is normal and times that he is nutty. He often disappears from Banaras for long stretches. Some people say that Arshad's family is cursed. In every generation, mishaps have occurred. There have been accidents and mental and physical ailments.'

'What else do you know about him?' Maya asked.

'Arshad interacts with only a handful of people. Gauripradа is one among them. They have become thick friends recently. Arshad has inherited his grandfather's flamboyance and is a connoisseur of arts and music. Some people even say that he has knowledge about the ten tantric *mahavidyas.*'

Ranbeer at once became alert. He tilted his head and asked, 'Does this man live in the haunted haveli with the *Naga* sanyasi? And is he the same man who pays homage at the Dhumavati Temple every single day of the monsoon months.'

'How do you know about the rumour that the haveli is haunted?' Baccha was surprised. 'People believe it is haunted because every year on *Ram Navami,* moaning sounds emerge from it. And for the rest of the 364 days, it is guarded by the *Naga* sanyasi.'

'*Ranbeer has never mentioned this haunted haveli. Very strange considering that he talks to me about everything and everyone in Banaras,*' Meera thought.

At that very moment, a transvestite draped in a gaudy sari started descending the steps of Bhosale Ghat. Her anklets made a clanging sound. Ranbeer took out his camera and adjusted the flash to photograph her. The light revealed the most interesting part of her appearance—her forehead adorned with a *chandan tilak* comprising of three vertical stripes.

'It is believed that these transvestites are part of the Rasik clan. Very few of them are left in modern India,' Baccha elaborated. '

'Who on earth are Rasiks?' Meera wondered aloud.

'You heard Gauriprada mention the Vaishnava saint, Ramananda. His followers are called Ramanandis and Rasiks are a small section of the Ramanandis. They pretend to make love to the deities of their choice at night. They often emit cries of ecstasy and longing,' Baccha answered, sheepishly.

Meera's curiosity was expanding with each discovery that was happening in this mystic town. She resolved that she would ask Baccha about the haunted haveli and *Naga* sanyasi but in private.

attack at shivala ghat

Amavasya was now a week away. Everest Café had translated to a fresh lease of life for Maya and Kamakshi. 'Rosewood Cottage was nice but somehow I love the chaos here better,' Kamakshi told Maya one evening while they were sitting on the second-floor balcony that overlooked Shivala Ghat.

Vendors were trying to persuade tourists. Three hooded men were walking towards the farthest edge of the ghat. Kamakshi focused her attention on the activities of the vendors while Maya strained her eyes to follow the hooded men. They halted after sometime, looked around and gestured to the sole boatman on the bank. He came up to them and handed a small packet. To Maya's surprise, one of the men concealed the packet under his kurta.

It was time for them to get dressed for the evening as Meera who had effortlessly become their friend would be taking them to the musical event organised at the public gallery near Arshad Singh's haveli.

As the women dressed in colourful kurtas walked along serpentine alleys sandwiched between squalid buildings, Meera remarked, 'Everything here, including the people, is more than a hundred years old.'

Maya and Kamakshi understood that the old-world charm of the town transcended to people and places, irrespective of their chronological age.

The conversation shifted to Ranbeer.

'Is he your best friend, Meera...I mean, in India?' Maya asked.

'Well, he is one of my closest friends. I think he is closer to Kamakshi than me,' Meera laughed.

'And why do you say that?' Kamakshi was embarrassed.

'Last year when I told Ranbeer about how I had met some people who had narrated gory experiences with tantrics, he had said that something so primitive should not even be discussed. But after hearing your experiences he is inspired to make a documentary on the subject!'

'Really?' Maya exclaimed. 'I clearly remember that he told us that he had decided to make this documentary after he heard you.'

There was an awkward silence. 'Do you know what N stands for in Ranbeer's name?' Kamakshi abruptly asked. 'I mean his full name is actually Ranbeer N Ahuja. I had seen this written over a folder lying on his desk...a folder that probably contained his academic certificates.'

'No, I don't. In fact this is news to me! And you never asked him yourself?' Meera inquired.

'I did. But strangely he did not answer and changed the subject of conversation almost immediately.'

By now, they had entered the bustling market place and walked on silently.

'Where are we going?' Kamakshi finally asked a little wearily.

'To meet Rustom for our passes. He arranges musical events and nights, and is very resourceful. On a couple of occasions he has regaled Baccha's guests by organising musical evenings at Everest Café too.'

Finally, they reached a market and halted before a tumbledown looking three-storeyed building. It reminded one of Mughal architecture minus the grandeur. The paint had paled beyond decipherable limits.

As they started climbing the staircase that started at the edge of the ground floor verandah, a musty smell greeted them. They also noticed an intermittent trail of powder. 'This smells familiar,' said Kamakshi as she bent down to gather the bluish powder on her fingertips.

'Familiar? How?' Maya and Meera exclaimed at the same instant.

'Well, this is the same odour and the same bluish powder that pervaded and littered the grounds of Vasanthi *Amma*'s farmhouse.' The answer came in a barely audible pitch.

'What?' Maya was clearly taken aback for she stared at the powder trail with a tense expression for a good few minutes.

'Are you sure?' Meera mumbled.

Nobody could say anything for a while. They resumed their climb after a while.

Meera rapped on the third floor door. 'He must be offering his namaz,' she said, casting a glance at her watch. 'We have to wait.'

After about twenty minutes the door opened and a tall man with shiny black, shoulder-length hair appeared. He ushered them to a wooden charpoy and settled himself on a mat.

'Rustom, this is Maya,' Meera introduced her friend by putting her hand on Maya's shoulder. Rustom nodded his acknowledgment. 'And this is Kamakshi,' she continued turning to the younger woman.

'Namaste, Kamakshi*ji*,' the man said in a husky voice.

Rustom was inscrutable. He was polite but fairly brusque; his first-time visitors discovered during the course of their conversation.

'So what brings you to Banaras?' he looked at the two Indian women and inquired.

'They are Ranbeer's friends and have come with him for some documentary work,' Meera replied.

'Meera, let them introduce themselves,' the man said in a half-offended tone. 'Will you tell me what this documentary is all about? And where are your husbands?' He narrowed his eyes and gazed at them.

While Kamakshi started fumbling, Maya replied confidently, 'This is a documentary about how people have suffered at the behest of tantrics. We have known Ranbeer for years and also happen to know firsthand experiences of people who have been victims. Therefore, we are assisting him in the research'. Everyone noticed that she avoided the personal query.

'Well, it is unwise to tamper with religion,' Rustom answered almost emphatically.

'This is not tampering with religion. The objective is to expose something that has unduly taken a license for wrongdoings in the name of religion,' Kamakshi clarified.

The atmosphere became tense.

'I think we should go now, it is already 8 pm,' Maya interrupted.

'Yes, we should as the *shayari mehfil* at Arshad Singh's haveli begins at 8.30 pm,' Meera added.

'Okay,' Rustom said in a nonchalant voice as he got up to lead them downstairs. A little reluctantly, he handed them the passes.

The three women walked on in silence. Meera noticed that Maya was fidgeting with her phone. She looked hassled.

'What is the matter, dear?' Meera inquired.

'Alok wants me to return home immediately. He probably does not have a clue about where I am but definitely knows that I am not in the asylum. He has probably just found it out as he has been calling constantly and has also sent a text,' Maya replied and switched off her phone.

'So, isn't that good news?' Kamakshi was surprised at Maya's reaction.

'No, it isn't,' Maya replied, blankly. 'He is livid at Arvind for rescuing me from the asylum and is going to lodge a police compliant against him! I can well understand what is happening...Alok must be trying to contact Arvind on the number that he doesn't use while he is in the jungles. From the message I can make out that Alok has already contacted Rosewood Cottage. They haven't disclosed our whereabouts and hence he is furious.' Maya remembered how before leaving for Madhya Pradesh, Arvind had bribed the manager and told him to mislead Alok about her whereabouts.

'When these men realise that we are no longer in their control they start flapping to control us again,' Kamakshi smirked.

'Do you want to go back to him?' Meera asked, gently.

'No!' Maya was emphatic.

Tall walls marked the boundary of the sprawling lawns. The architecture of the gallery was a mix of colonial and contemporary influences. Most of the guests and performers had already arrived and were strolling around the lawn. Some were musicians carrying instruments and some probably were *shayars*.

The interiors were opulent. An unlit chandelier hung from the ceiling of the massive lobby while low volt electric bulbs ensconced in wall-fitted glass shades illuminated the space. There were at least a dozen divans and sofas upholstered in silk and brocade. Paintings of men and women, mostly depicting ancient and medieval Indian social and religious customs, covered every inch of the walls.

Kamakshi was fascinated by one painting that was strikingly different. The forehead of a feminine face was adorned by an unusual symbol. It was an inverted pyramid set inside a round flower. On the three edges of the pyramid were three tiny symbols that were difficult to decipher. Only the colours were clear—yellow, black and white.

'Don't you think the bindi is disproportionate to the rest of the face?' she asked Maya.

'Yes, somehow it also looks a little elevated compared to the rest of the painting.'

From the rear windows the three girls could see fountains against the backdrop of fairy lights. About five hundred yards away, was the haveli—dark and desolate. Meera strained her eyes to see if she could spot the *Naga* sanyasi. Soon the gallery was reverberating with the medley of musical instruments and classical songs. But Arshad Singh was conspicuous in his absence.

Meera noticed that Kamakshi looked distracted throughout. 'What are you thinking about?' she asked.

'That painting is familiar...,' she answered pensively.

'You might have seen something similar to it somewhere else. Why should you be thinking so much about it?'

'I don't know why it is making me think so much but it is.'

Just at that moment Baccha joined them. 'That was painted by Arshad Singh's great-grandfather or some ancestor. I am not very sure how many generations old it is. Some people say that it is a replica of a piece of sculpture that the family owns. Probably the sculpture exists inside the haveli. But nobody would know as it is forbidden territory.'

Meera gasped. 'This Arshad Singh is quite a character. You mentioned about that *Naga* sanyasi. What are *Naga* sanyasis like?'

'Madam*ji*, do not talk about the *Naga* sanyasi in public.' Baccha whispered.

'Why?' The three women demanded together.

Baccha started walking towards the exit door. He obviously wanted to answer once they were out of everybody's earshot. 'All I can tell you is that his existence is known only to the oldest inhabitants of Kashi and these people like to keep a few things private. *Naga* sanyasis are actually warrior ascetics. Gauripradа had once told me that from about the seventh century to the late seventeenth century there were about six organised tribes of warrior ascetics who would help kings defend kingdoms against invasions. Some of them also fought to gain stronghold of religious centres and places of worship. It is believed that Arshad Singh's ancestor, the one who had originally built this haveli, had a faithful warrior ascetic among his retinue of servants.'

'And this one is his descendent? Did Gauripradа tell you not to talk about the *Naga* sanyasi in public?' Maya asked.

'Yes, he did. But this one is no descendant. Sanyasis or ascetics never marry. He merely hails from the tribe of *Naga* sanyasis. These sanyasis started disappearing after the nineteenth century. Today, there are only about two dozen of them. Gauripradа says that they know many secrets about medieval India's religious and esoteric practices.'

'So, Ranbeer should focus on trailing him instead of obsessing about Limar Singh!' Meera exclaimed.

'Why on earth is this one guarding Arshad Singh's haveli?' Kamakshi demanded.

'Just a coincidence that he happens to live in the premises. He was brought to Banaras some years ago by Arshad Singh himself.'

'Why?'

'Remember I told you that Arshad Singh is a schizophrenic and often disappears from town? It is believed that he travels to places of worship on the outskirts of villages and towns. People say that he forgets his identity while travelling. He must have met this ascetic on one of his voyages and brought him along.'

As the three women and Baccha walked back to the guesthouse, their conversation hovered around the eccentric Arshad. 'His parents died when he and his brother were teenagers. A few years later, his younger sibling migrated to London where his father had bought a townhouse. But Arshad stayed on in India, in their ancestral haveli. He owns a lot of agricultural land on the outskirts and gets an annual income from the farmers, which he declines when the produce is insufficient,' Baccha informed.

'Oh, so he must be quite rich?' Kamakshi interrupted.

'Yes, and like you might have guessed, he gets a royalty from the state for this gallery as it is his ancestral property.'

It was nearing midnight, when they reached the flight of steps on Shivala Ghat, leading to the back entrance of Everest Café.

Meera halted midway. 'I will join you after a while,' she urged her friends to carry on.

Before any of them could react she was running down the stairs. They saw her running towards the end of the ghat and could make out the silhouette of an approaching boat.

For the past four nights, Meera had noticed that this motorboat chugged into exactly the same spot of the ghat at 11.30 pm. She had observed from her balcony that precisely at midnight some hooded men would arrive and empty the boat of its contents—a couple of cartons. Today, she decided to understand what exactly was going on.

She halted about two feet away from the spot where the motorboat was moored. The boatman was not around.

After a few minutes, Meera felt a sharp blow on her head. Her vision blurred and the only thing that registered was a knife handle engraved with a mutilated owl. She fell unconscious.

The next thing that she remembered was Baccha sprinkling water on her face.

'Madam*ji*, how did you faint?' he was asking. 'It is one in the night and I realised you have not returned. So I came out looking for you,' he explained in a rush.

Meera was too stunned to reply. Baccha helped her to her feet and they walked back in silence to the guesthouse. Her mind was racing, *'Who could have attacked me? It was a rehearsed blow. Banaras somehow doesn't feel like before. Could some conspiracy be brewing?'*

Something told her that she needed to tell Ranbeer about the attack. She rushed to his room. A light was filtering out from the cracks beneath his closed door.

'Ranbeer!' Meera rapped on the door.

To her surprise the door slid open and the room was empty!

Meera waited for a good half hour before deciding to return to her room. As she was passing the side table, she caught sight of a black-and-white photograph, jutting out from a closed diary. She scrutinised it. A small boy was sitting between his parents. Meera recognised the little boy as Ranbeer. The lady was fair while the man was dark complexioned. *'Unusually dark for a Punjabi,'* she thought to herself.

For a split second Meera was tempted to read the diary. After all it must be containing secrets of the sometimes inscrutable Ranbeer! Just as she was toying with the idea she caught sight of a small, rectangular piece of metal. It was in a mug tucked between a bunch of pencils and pens. She took it out. It looked like a locket. The metal was rusted and had an imprint of a human figure on a chariot on one side. It was hard to decipher whether it was a man or woman.

Just then, she heard a muffled cough outside the door. Anticipating Ranbeer's entry, she hid behind the cupboard with a pounding heart. There was silence for two whole minutes after which she could hear the sound of footsteps in the corridor. It was clear that whoever it was, had gone away.

As Meera put the two objects back on the side table her eyes fell on a book lying in a half-open drawer. It was a spiral-bound book with a transparent light blue cover.

'*He must have photocopied it,*' she thought to herself and then noticed something that sent a chill down her spine. The first page, covered with text, had the same heading as the first chapter of a book she had been reading—a book on neo-classical theories that explain the extinction of symbols and manuscripts from the pre-Vedic and post-Vedic period, which Gopal Sarai, the librarian from the Centre for Vedic Studies, had given her!

She picked up the book and flipped through the pages. Ranbeer had indeed photocopied her reference book, without her permission. Meera instantly understood when and how. Just two evenings back, Baccha had told her that he had spent the entire afternoon checking if the right keys were assigned to each of the twenty guest rooms.

'But why?' Meera had been bewildered.

'Because just yesterday my manager had purchased a fresh bunch of key rings numbered from 1 to 20. And accidentally he put the key of room number 8 in the number 9 key ring. More than half the rooms are unoccupied. So I thought I should ensure that all keys are in order before guests start arriving.'

'Oh, you mean he put the key of my room in Ranbeer's key ring?'

'Yes. Ranbeer had returned to the guesthouse quite early last evening. After collecting his keys, he returned to the reception after an hour to say that his door was not opening.'

'What?'

'Yes, Madam*ji,* I too found the length of time strange and am not sure but I think I saw him going out and coming back from the private rear entrance during this time.'

'He told you that he could not open his room as he had *my* room key?'

'He only said that he could not open his own room. So I took all the keys of the five rooms that are on the first floor to find his right key. I found it attached to your key ring and your key was in his ring.'

Meera had made a mental note to ask Ranbeer about the incident later. 'I am glad I didn't! I would have cautioned him and never discovered this! He must have got the book photocopied within that one hour. But why did he sneak into my room and take it in the first place?' The answer seemed foreboding.

Embroiled in disturbing thoughts, Meera walked out of Ranbeer's room. *'Seeing the new key ring he must have understood that his key was in some other ring. It was smart of Ranbeer to try opening my room after he realised that he could not open his own. So he was waiting for a chance to enter my room in my absence! I must say he got incredibly lucky. And I did tell him about this book. Why did he not borrow it from me?'*

As she undressed, she remembered how Ranbeer had surprised her by having an informed conversation with Gauripradа. *'It is also a little strange that he knows about the Naga sanyasi. And why did he tell Kamakshi and Maya that he had decided to make this documentary after he met me last year?*

Is Ranbeer involving me in this documentary only because he wants to access my research notes? But how can even the most confidential parts of my study be of any use to him? I went to Ranbeer because I wanted him to help me figure out who attacked me and why. But I am not sure if I should be confiding in him at all! What is Ranbir's motive behind this documentary?'

a twisted form of salvation

The frenzy of pilgrims on Shivala Ghat peaked on the morning of *Amavasya*.

'Taking a dip in the holy river is considered particularly auspicious on *Amavasya*.' Baccha appeared behind Ranbeer who was zooming his camera to capture shots of people jostling for space in the crowded waters.

'Gauripradа has said that tonight we will shoot two rituals. One happens secretly in a dilapidated temple. The other happens on the cremation ground after midnight.' Baccha informed.

Meera had not confronted Ranbeer about photocopying her book. Unsure about Kamakshi's proximity with Ranbeer, she hadn't shared her discovery with the other girls either.

Baccha opted to stay back on the first night of shooting. 'Having too many people might be risky,' he stated.

'I am tired and would prefer to sleep,' Maya told her girlfriends.

Meera and Kamakshi exchanged a knowing glance. Maya was obviously expecting a call from Arvind late at night. For the past few nights he had been regularly calling after ten and they would stretch their conversation for a good two hours.

At 11.15 pm, Meera and Kamakshi accompanied Ranbeer and his crew to meet Gauriprada at Vishalakshi Temple. To their surprise they bumped into Professor Bharadwaj, Meera's research guide, near Chet Singh Ghat. Dressed in a khadi kurta and pyjama, he was ambling in their direction.

The professor did not see the group approaching as he was engrossed in a deep conversation on his phone.

'Hello, Professor. Did not expect to see you here at all!' Meera exclaimed.

The professor abruptly disconnected the call and returned her greeting after an uncomfortable silence, 'Neither did I expect to see you!'

The brusque tone took the group aback. They noticed that the professor's eyes were unusually red. They were also acutely conscious of a stench of cheap alcohol.

'He looks confused and strangely very irritated,' Kamakshi thought while Ranbeer wondered why a man like Bharadwaj who headed the department of Sanskrit at Banaras Hindu University (BHU) would settle for local alcohol.

'Bharadwaj Sir, I was trying to get in touch with you this entire week. I had called your direct landline. Your secretary informed me that you had gone to Mysore and will be back only next week. Guess you returned early, as it is only Saturday today,' Meera said, matter-of-factly.

'What was the need to call on my landline when you have my mobile number?' the professor retorted.

'Well, because your phone was either out of network or switched off.' Meera tried to pacify.

At that instant, Bharadwaj's phone started ringing and he disconnected it without even looking at the screen. Before anyone could say anything, Bharadwaj inquired, 'Isn't this Ranbeer and his documentary crew?' Narrowing his gaze on the shooting equipment, he added, 'My, my…it looks like there is some action happening tonight.'

Everyone merely nodded. Meera introduced Kamakshi and deftly added, 'We are actually returning from a shoot.' Though Ranbeer's documentary was a well-known affair she somehow felt it wouldn't be right to apprise him about their immediate course of action.

There was a brief but awkward silence that was interrupted by Bharadwaj's throaty laugh. 'Well, I am sorry I was rude, Meera. It's been a long day and I am heading back to the campus,' he added in a relaxed tone. 'You see I have just finished a long discussion with an overseas researcher who had especially come to Banaras to meet me. Actually, I had to cut short my trip after he called me a couple of days back seeking an appointment.'

'Really?' Meera exclaimed, tactlessly.

Bharadwaj was known to be unapproachable. He had agreed to supervise her thesis after much coaxing from the Director of Oxford Centre for Hindu Studies. Besides, it was very unlike him to cut short his own plans and attend to random requests.

'But I don't quite understand that reaction,' the professor's voice was now clearly spiked with sarcasm. He drew closer, gently tapped the edge of her forehead and added with a shift in tone, 'I guess we are all exhausted and need to reach our beds fast. Conversations can wait. You can call me tomorrow afternoon and we can discuss the progress on your thesis.'

Before Meera could answer, Ranbeer briskly shook Bharadwaj's right palm and said, 'Meera has told me that you have immense knowledge about religious texts pertaining to almost every period of human civilisation. I will be grateful if I can borrow some time from you in the coming days. I actually want to understand...erm...understand about the possible metaphysical influences of certain texts.'

Bharadwaj was taken aback by this candour in Ranbeer's approach. 'I will let you know if I am free,' he answered in a slightly rude tone and started walking away. Meera saw that he had an admonishing glare when her eyes met his.

As they resumed walking Meera wondered why the Professor had behaved so scornfully. She cast a glance at

Ranbeer who read her thoughts and shrugged his shoulders in reply.

Close to Vishalakshi Temple the air started feeling different. For about half a kilometre they became conscious of a magnetic energy field.

'Limar Singh must be around,' Ranbeer remarked and pointed to a human silhouette sitting in an upright position close to the river edge.

Gauriprada was waiting on the temple steps, with a lantern. 'It is only 11.35 pm. The temple is barely a fifteen-minute walk from here so we should start walking after half an hour. The crazy ritual starts well after midnight,' he said.

'You mean to say this ritual is practiced by a con mystic?' Kamakshi searched her vocabulary to coin the most appropriate term for the fake practitioners.

Gauriprada gestured them to sit. 'I think you all need a formal orientation before starting,' he sighed. 'Not every unscrupulous tantric is fake. There are men and women who pose as tantrics and exploit people for money and sex. And then there are real tantrics who use their knowledge for evil goals. Many among them are twisting the ten *mahavidyas*. The second category is profuse in modern India. Actually, tantra has only two objectives—union with the Supreme Being and the good of fellow human beings.'

'So, tantrics are either fake and unscrupulous or genuine and unscrupulous?' Kamakshi demanded indignantly. 'I refuse to believe that it can have any merit. And what are these ten *mahavidyas*?'

'*Mahavidyas* are knowledge pertaining to the worship of ten different forms of the Mother Goddess. This knowledge encapsulates all the tantric rites and formulas. In pre-historic

India, many people upheld the faith that the divine creator is a woman. There is also a myth that the ten incarnations of Vishnu have manifested from the divine feminine. When the Aryans invaded India, the theory of the supreme feminine got subdued,' Gauripradа paused.

Meera and Kamakshi who had been looking at him with rapt attention asked in unison, 'So when did the *mahavidyas* originate?'

'The Shakta cults of India that upheld worship of the divine feminine had only got submerged in the Vedic Age. They had not become extinct. Right from the sixth century, these cults embraced the concept of *Bhakti* as an alternate way to attain salvation. *Bhakti* is nothing but unconditional attachment and surrender to the Mother Goddess. *Mahavidyas* essentially contain the canons of this concept.'

'Tantra at one level is all about expanding consciousness and merging it with the uninterrupted reality of the cosmos. It is all about surrender,' Ranbeer again surprised them with his profound logic. 'So, it is easy to understand the connection of tantrics with *mahavidyas*. . .I mean the genuine tantrics.'

'You mean to say tantra is older than the Vedic period?' Kamakshi asked.

'Much older. It was at its peak in the Indus Valley civilisation. Though there are no definite records, it can be inferred from archaeological and literary evidences that it is a 4,500-year-old tradition,' Gauriprada said.

'From my basic research I know that tantra broadly can be grouped under Shaiva, Shakta and Vaishnava tantra. Which among these is the oldest?' It was Ranbeer again.

'There are different theories on this. Under these sects there are several sub-sects with unique rituals. But this organisation happened only around the middle of the ninth century. Had it happened earlier, a huge calamity would have been averted,' Gauriprada finished.

'What calamity?' was everybody's knee-jerk reaction.

'In those days there were no organised sub-sects, so the tantrics who had authored important texts did not have any dedicated followers who could preserve their work through generations.'

Gauriprada stood up and started descending the stairs. He signalled to the group to follow him. They must have walked for about five minutes when they heard a human screech. 'Where are we?' Kamakshi arched closer to the priest and asked in a whisper.

'Lahori Tola.' Gauriprada informed in a stern whisper.

Meera and Kamakshi instantly remembered that Rustom's house was located at Lahori Tola. A few steps ahead, after negotiating an unannounced bend they spotted a temple on their left. In the dim halo that filtered from the open door they could make out a statue of Kaal Bhairav.

'This is the Dattatreya Temple. Gorakhnathis worship Dattatreya,' Gauriprada hurriedly whispered as he paced on.

Abruptly, Ranbeer halted and shouted, 'Stop!'

'What is your problem? Told you that we can't draw attention,' Gauriprada hissed.

'Can't you see that man?' Ranbeer pointed in the direction of the deity. A shadow was crouching near the shrine. He seemed to be rummaging for something. 'I am sure he is there to steal something.'

Gauriprada glared at him and commanded him to keep walking. Ranbeer complied hesitantly. To their surprise, just as they were crossing the temple the man walked out. He was stark nude. His head was covered with a red cloth and his forehead was smeared with ash and turmeric paste. A light woollen shawl was flung over one shoulder and he sported an unusual waistband studded with metal symbols and letters.

When they were out of his earshot, Gauripradа informed, 'This was your first glimpse of the *Naga* sanyasi.' Meera cast a sideway glance to gauge Ranbeer's expression. It did not reveal anything.

The priest gestured to switch off their torches. They trailed behind him into the courtyard of an old fashioned house that looked uninhabited. A temple was situated at the centre. The door of the temple was fastened and through an open window they could see the halo of lamps. Gauriprada boldly started walking towards it. As they neared the temple a sound similar to the moaning of a savage animal became audible. An unfamiliar smell greeted them. It reminded them of sandalwood, herbs, charred milk, ashes and. . .blood—all at once.

The decibels of their heartbeats multiplied as they crowded near the window. The cameramen adjusted the night-vision cameras. About seven lights ensconced in lanterns hung from the roof. An enormous brass statue of a man and woman in a conjugal position stood at one corner. The walls of the temples were engraved with multiple forms of the Mother Goddess. There was a thin veil of smoke everywhere. Suddenly, there were sounds of footsteps. It was clear that there was an inner chamber and people were now walking out of it to the main area.

'There they are,' Meera could not help whispering as two transvestites appeared. They squatted near a cauldron in the middle of the room. A plump, skimpily clad, middle-aged woman followed by four young women, possibly in their late teens, appeared next. It was a spectacle for the girls were only covered in neem foliage around their bust and pubic parts. They marched towards a mat laid out at one end of the room. The older woman settled herself on the mat and untied her bun. Tossing her open hair she started swaying her head. Soon she was muttering something under her breath, with closed eyes, and after every five minutes she would let out a menacing sound. A dozen claws and nails of animals and birds along with the ends of exhausted incense sticks were littered before her mat. After twenty odd minutes she opened her eyes.

The woman commanded the four girls to sit in a circle before the erotic brass statue while she started a tandav. One by one she caught hold of each one of them and yanked away the foliage covering their vaginas. With deft precision, she sheared a few strands of pubic hair with a mildly sharp object. 'Aren't they getting hurt?' Meera could not help letting out a loud whisper.

The tandav continued. This time the four girls joined in. Finally, after about an hour, the older woman fell on the ground, face down and arms outstretched. As she remained submerged in her trance, the battery of the portable camera started blinking. It was a signal to the group to depart. As they retraced their steps, each of them struggled to make sense of what they had just witnessed. Once they reached Mir Ghat, they sat motionless for almost half an hour.

It was Kamakshi who broke the silence. 'This woman is meddling with the *mahavidyas*. How on earth can the divine Mother ever be happy if her mortal daughters are exploited for her worship?' Her voice was quivering. After a pause she added, 'Well, maybe there are some genuine tantrics after all...but they are all bloody evil.'

Gauripradа tried to ease the tension with his throaty laugh. 'Don't be so...' he was interrupted by a message alert on Ranbeer's phone. 'Did I not ask you to put that on...' he was interrupted again for a simultaneous alert followed on Meera's phone. Neither of them cared to check their messages. They were far too eager to hear Gauripradа's verdict of the ritual.

'Did you really not guess the connection?' Gauripradа quizzed with raised eyebrows. 'You have lived in the West...

so am very surprised,' he was gazing directly at Ranbeer and Meera.

'The ritual is nowhere connected to the ethos of tantra. This is a self-proclaimed godwoman who is responsible for...'

'...for an undercover prostitution nexus? Wait, I think I have heard of her. Didn't know she was hiding in Banaras. Is she the same woman who started Erotic Salvation? I forget her name...Vividha something,' Meera interrupted.

'She is the one and she is tarnishing the name of tantra... using it for her own dirty ambitions. The four young women that you saw are among her many thousands of disciples and the ritual was their initiation ceremony. They have undergone weeks of formal training in tantric sex...a training to alleviate them to be a sorceress of copulation. After the initiation these women are considered demi-tantric goddesses. Any man who has intercourse with them attains moksha,' Gauriprada sighed with disgust.

'How does she train them? Are there any male disciples?' In the light of the torches Meera and Kamakshi could clearly see the lewd gleam in Ranbeer's eyes.

Gauriprada ignored Ranbeer and continued, 'Erotic Salvation is a movement that promises nirvana and enlightenment through sexual activity free from any conditions and code. If you ask me, it is not much different from the hippie movement activity of the mid-sixties.

'Does it involve drugs too?' the youngest cameraman asked.

'It is rumoured that both men and women inject psychoactive drugs before having sex...,' Gauriprada paused.

'Obviously to induce orgasms,' Ranbeer slyly finished.

'Where does this sex happen?' Kamakshi quizzed.

'It happens secretly at the homes of the women members. The movement proclaims that it is the vulva that marks the beginning and end of consciousness. It is through the vulva that a new life emerges and therefore genuine transcendence of the physical and material world is only possible by passing through it.' Gauripada's face was flushed with embarrassment.

'So, this woman is NOT twisting the tenets of tantra. I mean, her ugly rituals are of course not connected even remotely to the sacred canons. Like you said she is only using the name of tantra for her dark ambitions,' Kamakshi sighed. 'If many more people understood the actual essence of the sacred esoteric practises, people like Vasanthi *Amma* and Vividha Devi would be out of business.'

'You have nailed it. With the quest for modernity, a sheer majority of our countrymen have forgotten to study many of our ancient traditions. Tantra is no exception. Most people think it is only a dark and foreboding practice of primitive beings, which is not true. This perception can only change if people start inquiring on the metaphysical aspects of tantra. Obviously, when people are armed with knowledge they don't fall prey to exploiters,' Gauripada reasoned.

'What are Vividha Devi's dark ambitions?' Ranbeer inquired.

'I don't know what exactly the truth is but I have heard that Vividha Devi has already acquired a dedicated following. She receives donations from her wealthy followers and apparently they want to erect an iconic temple in her name to popularise her cult. If this happens mankind is doomed.'

'Why?' Ranbeer demanded.

'This temple will also house a library of books and journals written by the champions of neo tantra who oppose classical indigenous tantra. The original tenets of Shaiva and Vaishanava tantra are anyway misunderstood; the literature prophesied by this cult will erase the understanding that still exists among scholars.'

Seeing the confused expressions, Gauripradа explained, 'Tantra *shastra* is based on the metaphysical reality of existence. It is a holistic discipline and can translate to mankind's progress at many levels. Every discipline has to evolve to keep pace with the needs of the changing times. Unfortunately, this has not happened with tantra and therefore tantra *shastra* is being rejected in the modern world.' He glanced at his watch. They had to proceed for the next ritual.

'I understand what you mean,' Meera said, thoughtfully. 'On the other hand, neo tantra, which is nothing but a sham, a cover for promiscuity has much greater acceptance and followers today as it embraces contemporary objectives. I heard that it is a technique of using sexual energy to heal relationships and undesirable experiences. I guess you are worried that this library will encourage further criticism of classical tantra and it will have no hope for revival.'

Gauripradа nodded. 'It is already 3 am and time for us to move to our next destination,' he announced.

As they started walking, the priest edged close to Meera and whispered into her ear, 'There is something more to that woman and why she and her cult are dangerous. But I will tell you only when you are alone.'

Before Meera could ask him why, Ranbeer who was walking ahead of her stopped abruptly. Had he heard Gauripradа whisper?

She walked beside him and was surprised when he nudged her sharply. 'Did you check your message?' Ranbeer was holding his phone. Meera checked her message inbox. There was a message from an unknown number. It said: *Stop the documentary shoot or face very dire consequences.*

Meera turned white and glanced at Ranbeer's phone. He had received the exact message from the same number!

'Should we tell the others?' Meera whispered.

Ranbeer shook his head and said with a strange expression, 'Can't you see? We really can't tell Gauripradа anything….'

Meera opened her mouth to protest but realised Ranbeer was not entirely wrong. After all they had a tough time convincing Gauripradа to help them. He might withdraw his support if he came to know about the threats!

all about forbidden traditions of worship

The air smelt of decaying flesh at Manikarnika Ghat. As the group started descending the steps they could see a circle of fire. '*Om Maha Kalyai Ca Vidmahe Samasana Vasinyai*,' the seven words of a sacred Kali mantra greeted them as they took positions behind tall piles of cremation wood.

The camera zoomed in on an ascetic clad in a black robe and ornaments of rudraksh beads and marigold flowers. Despite the gigantic knots, his hair reached below his torso. He was squatting on the back of a corpse inside the circle of fire and his eyes were shut.

Severed heads of goats and chunks of red meat encircled the outer fringes of the flame. Bottles of dark liquid were scattered. 'These are all baits for the evil spirits—to ward them away from the corpse. I am not sure which text this Aghori is referring to but I think it is the *Shyamarahashya*,' Gauripradа explained. 'He is performing *shav* sadhana, a much ostracised form of tantra. In ancient times, *shav* sadhana was performed to unite with the absolute power and obliterate the fear of death. Sadly, in this *Kaliyuga*, it is performed to gain control over the soul of the deceased.'

The corpse was outstretched on something that resembled deer skin. Though it was lying on its stomach, its face was contorted and facing the tantric. A symbol had been drawn on the back that was glistening with the sheen of a yellowish brown paste. The mouth was ajar and stuffed with a large betel nut. The feet and head of the corpse had been tied by a cloth rope.

'What are these?' Meera exclaimed as the camera moved around the outline of the corpse. A sea of bluish powder and yellow seeds was surrounding it. 'This looks just like the stuff that was littering Rustom's steps,' Kamakshi remarked.

'Strange things you girls observe.' Gauriprada remarked.

The ascetic was starting to tremble. Abruptly he opened his eyes, stood up, and placing one foot over the back of the corpse took the posture of a warrior in a battlefield. In that position he started reciting the mantra—*Om Maha Kalyai Ca Vidmahe Samasana Vasinyai,* again. This time the entire mantra was audible—*Ca Dhimahi Tanno Kali Prachodayat*—the ascetic belted with rising ferocity.

The dogs that had been feasting on the meat started running away. Soon there was a cacophony of fading dog howls and cat cries. Without warning, a mass of clouds started swirling in the sky and a flash of lightning erupted just above the circle of fire. The Aghor bent near the corpse—its head was now slightly raised! The next five minutes translated to a spectacle that was impossible to forget—for the corpse came alive and started talking. He seemed to be answering every question that the Aghor was posing. At the end of it, he looked pleased and raised his outstretched arms in the direction of the skies. After a loud rumble, the sky became placid. The corpse was lifeless again and the Aghor started decapitating his head with a weapon. 'He is taking out his skull,' Gauriprada informed. The two women looked away.

The Aghor extinguished the boundary and started emptying the liquor bottles. He dug the ground and buried the goat heads and the corpse. As the cameramen started rolling back the equipment, Ranbeer and his friends could see the Aghor was stuffing all his paraphernalia, including the liquor bottles into a large sack. He emptied the contents into the river.

'Did he kill that man?' Meera asked as they were trailing behind Gauripradа in the direction of Shivala Ghat. They were all relieved when the priest answered in the negative. '*Shav* sadhana is performed through the corpse of people who are very poor. Many of these are just left on the cremation ground to rot because their families cannot afford the money for the last rites.'

Gauriprada looked at his watch and declared, 'Right after daybreak, I have to meet a pilgrim in the adjoining ghat to perform his father's last rites.' Turning to Ranbeer, he added, 'I shall tell you everything I know about the origin of this ritual. What you witnessed is slightly contaminated as *shav* sadhana is only performed on full moon nights. But I shall be able to tell you only tomorrow morning...before you go out to talk to the people in this town.'

'Well, it's so gripping that...,' Ranbeer was cut short when Gauriprada interrupted with a wave of his hand and darted in the direction of four hooded men who were sitting on a boat.

'Don't follow me now, I have some work,' the priest instructed, tersely.

A little disappointed, the exhausted group walked towards the guesthouse.

'I doubt that people will be forthcoming about their experiences. In any case, we shall probably hear about second-hand experiences. The ones who encountered tantrics will be too embarrassed to share,' Ranbeer announced when the group had gathered for breakfast the next morning.

Meera cast a quick glance at Maya and Kamakshi. They continued to munch on their toasts without reacting to the insensitive comment.

'Well, in my opinion it is unlikely that the people who are shy to talk to your crew would have shared their experiences with anybody else.' As she finished speaking, Meera realised that there was nothing logical about her argument and that she had only said it to dent Ranbeer's cockiness. Like the others, she too was hoping that their first day of talking to people in the town would translate to interesting insights.

The initial hours were a waste. Most of the people they had stopped on the ghats and market area for a byte had looked at them either with suspicion or amusement. 'Should we just omit this part? People think we are crazy when we walk up to them and say that we want them to share their views on tantra for our documentary,' the head cameraman suggested at lunch hour.

'This part can make or break my documentary. Once the word spreads that a bunch of lunatics are in town to make a documentary on tantra, the ones who are hiding with their experiences shall find their way to us,' Ranbeer answered confidently.

His prophesy was right. In the afternoon as they were strolling on the ghats they spotted a middle-aged man walking towards them.

'I am SR Upadhyay. Can you help me lodge a police compliant?' the man asked when he reached them.

'Against?' Ranbeer and Kamakshi asked together.

'Against Tukaram...he calls himself a *baba,* but he is only a fraud,' the man said in a hushed voice.

Ranbeer gestured to him to sit on the steps.

'My daughter is missing since the past two months and am sure that Tukaram is responsible. Last year she moved in to stay with us as she was on the verge of a divorce. My poor child was...is in depression...so she had gone to that man in the hope of saving her marriage.'

The man gazed sadly into the Ganga. 'Ever since she started going to that man her behaviour became weird. She would be silent for days together or cry hysterically. Since I do not approve of tantrics, she had kept her visits a secret. I discovered everything when I found some small bottles with powders and liquids in her room. I had heard about this man who lives in the market area… apparently he could perform miracles with magical concoctions.'

'How are you so sure about this theory?' Ranbeer came straight to the point.

'She had gone to sleep peacefully on the last night that we had seen her. But in the morning she was nowhere. We combed the whole town, informed our relatives and the police about her disappearance and Tukaram…nobody managed to find her. Finally, our washerwoman told us something that makes it clear that this horrible man is indeed behind her disappearance…'

'What did she tell you?' Meera asked gently.

'Well, many young women who had gone to Tukaram with their problems in the past had also disappeared. Mangla said that she even knows a young man whose wife is missing since the past three years. People of this town say that Tukaram is a black magician and has delivered on the promises to his clients but there is also a rumour that he has only delivered in the case of male and elderly clients.'

'You mean young women are abducted?' Kamakshi could not suppress her rage.

'Not when they are escorted by any male relative or even a female friend. All the women who have disappeared had visited him alone.'

Ranbeer thought for a while and said, 'We shall help you lodge the complaint. But haven't you already done it?'

'I have, but the cops never take it seriously whenever a complaint is lodged against any of these bastards...I mean the tantrics.'

'The cops won't take us seriously either. We need to present them evidence. I suggest you take us to Tukaram's house secretly. Let's hope we manage to shoot him while he is trying to dupe some young woman...even better while he is in the process of abducting her...and only then when we show our footage to the cops shall they take action.'

'Tonight then?' the man asked eagerly.

Ranbeer nodded. 'What time?'

'We meet here at 8.30 pm. And let me give you some addresses. These are people that I met while sleuthing for information on Tukaram. They have suffered and should be helpful for your documentary.' The man jotted a dozen names and numbers on a piece of paper and took their leave.

By evening, at least eight people had shared their experiences. 'It feels like I have witnessed a live encyclopaedia on the atrocities committed on hapless people under the guise of tantra,' Kamakshi announced.

'The most bizarre incident is of that teenage girl. Imagine she was actually fooled by a tantric into believing that the rituals would not be successful if she did not sleep with his disciple!' Meera remarked.

'I can't digest the fact that she believed the tantric when he told her that if she wanted her ex-boyfriend back within seven days, she would need to have intercourse with his disciple. And that if she only agreed to let him caress her private parts with his tongue he would be back within twenty-one days. Good for that dumb woman that she chose the second option.' The cameraman laughed sarcastically.

'Well, that tantric was one of the petty criminals that roam this town and this so called disciple was his accomplice. He was probably stalking her for some time and that is how he discovered her desperation and staged this ploy,' Meera said.

'Do you all not see why the dumb woman did what she did?' Maya startled everybody. Turning towards the cameraman she continued, 'Don't you understand that when men and women consummate their relationship, they rarely feel the same way? For most men, physical union is only pleasure and conquest. But for women apart from pleasure, it is so many more selfless things.'

'I know what you are talking about,' Kamakshi interrupted when she saw the confused expressions around them after Maya had paused speaking. 'For a woman, sexual union amounts to unconditional surrender of the soul. When a woman allows a man to enter her body she is actually telling him that he has the exclusive privilege of uniting with her soul. Is it so difficult then to understand why a woman who can soulfully love her man can also sacrifice her own body for his good?'

'Well, these people have willingly given a chance to their tormentors to exploit them,' Ranbeer scoffed.

Meera cast a glance at her girlfriends. They seemed unperturbed. 'Then why are you making this documentary at all, Mr Ahuja?' she retorted.

Ranbeer ignored her. He was jotting some notes. 'The only valuable thing that I have learnt from her experience is that the *Vama Marga* form of tantra often relies on a human channel. The sexual energy used by the tantric is often contained within his disciple who has to be physically present at the time of the rite. Our con tantric knows this and therefore he tricked the girl by telling her that her sexual energy transmitted through this man would be the force that would usher the miracle she needed...of softening her estranged lover's heart. And, of course I know that this is a tarnished version.'

'Why don't you consult Gauripradа before inferring anything?' Kamakshi struggled to camouflage her surprise.

'How could I forget that he is the gospel of dependability? Especially after he has conveniently forsaken us today? Remember, he was supposed to meet us today morning and educate us on the history of *shav* sadhana?'

'He has just messaged me. He was caught in some *griha pravesh* ritual in the morning. He is meeting us after an hour. He can accompany us to Tukaram's house,' Meera allayed.

Ranbeer reluctantly nodded and looked at his watch. 'Should we go and meet the last person on our list? His name is so unusual—Bheeksha Das—it almost feels that he is one among the tantrics.'

Bheeksha Das was an inconspicuous-looking man. Draped in a faded orange lungi and vest, he was sipping tea from a coconut shell in front of his hut.

'Bheeksha*ji*, we wanted to talk to you. We are researchers and gathering information on tantra,' Meera said after introducing themselves.

Bheeksha froze when he heard the last word of her sentence.

A shrill message alert belted on Meera's phone. 'It must be...,' she glanced at it and stopped. There was a simultaneous alert on Ranbeer's phone which he chose to ignore.

'Everybody who comes to Banaras comes searching for salvation or in connection to death. Few come searching for the chord that connects the two.' Bheeksha's statement intrigued the group.

'What can you tell us about tantra?' Maya asked.

Bheeksha burst out laughing. 'Do you even know who the real tantric of this town was? All the combined knowledge of the Aghors could not match his knowledge.' The man had knelt forward and was staring into Maya's eyes.

'If Gauriprada has just told you about Vaishnava and Shaiva tantra, ask him to be more humble than he is. For there is more to tantra *shastra*.' He flashed an eerie smile.

'So he already knows that Gauriprada is helping us; wonder how many more people know.' Ranbeer thought to himself.

'We know who the real tantric is. . .Limar Singh. . .' Ranbeer stopped as Bheeksha raised his palm.

'Limar Singh is just a mendicant; if he was so powerful, he would not be so helpless in whatever his mission is.'

'Then, who is it?' Ranbeer and Meera almost pleaded.

To their dismay Bheeksha turned his back to them and fell silent.

The concluding gongs of the Ganga *aarti* were now subsiding.

'I agree this strange town has so many things that nobody cares to know about. If only people cared to know and understand more, a lot many things would have got better.' Bheeksha continued.

Kamakshi took hold of Bheeksha's palm and gazed softly into his soulless eyes. 'I can imagine how unjust it is to be burning dead bodies all your life, to be the custodian of the sacred eternal fire that brings salvation and yet be treated as a social outcast. It is against God's will that people like you have always been barred entry from temples. But trust me, we understand and care to know everything that you have to say.'

Bheeksha's eyes moistened a little. He started speaking only after the priests had finished blowing into the conches marking the end of the evening *aarti*.

'For at least seven centuries now we have been lighting the pyres of the dead and freeing them from the cycle of rebirths. And, we are the only ones who know all the secrets of the dead!'

Bheeksha abruptly went into his hut and reappeared with a small cardboard box. It contained a piece of rusted metal. His eyes were gleaming as he pressed the metal into Kamakshi's palm.

'This is a broken part of a locket maybe,' said Kamakshi.

Bheeksha nodded. He pointed excitedly to the symbol engraved on the metal. It was completely undecipherable with rust. 'One of my forefathers had found this from the ashes of a king that he had cremated.' Seeing the astonished expressions around him, he continued, 'In the olden days, several Maharajas used to visit Kashi on pilgrimage and live in their forts for weeks and months. Some of them died and had to be cremated here. My forefather preserved this metal all his life and passed it to his son before his death. This son handed it down the generations and now it is with me.'

'We don't understand the connection of this metal to our question,' Meera reminded. 'Who is the real tantric of this town?'

Bheeksha flashed his eerie smile again. 'For several years, I used to wear this locket around a thread on my neck. I would have never known its significance had I not met that pilgrim from South India. One day, I noticed that a man was following me to Harishchandra Ghat from Godowlia Chowk. Suddenly, without introducing himself he had asked me where I had got this locket from. When I questioned him why, he told me something that…that I have never told anyone until this day.

This locket is special because of its symbol. The open book placed half over flames and half over Mahadev's meditative forehead symbolises a powerful tantric cult that was secretly spreading its roots in the eleventh century.' Bheeksha again pointed to the rusted image.

'But why secretly?' Meera asked.

'Because it did not want to attract attention from the Shaiva and Vaishnava tantrics.'

'Why?' Everybody was now very curious.

'Around the tenth and eleventh centuries, there was a lot of conflict between the mainstream cults. Some people even believe that the Shaivas wanted to destroy all the texts of Vaishnava tantra that were spread across various religious centres. The Vaishnavas too retaliated in a similar way. Now, the founder of this new tantric cult knew that his cult would not be able to withstand the avalanche of attacks from the mainstream cults. So, he was spreading his teachings secretly among a small but dedicated following.'

'This man thought it unwise to publicise his teachings, more specifically his writings, so he did not keep anything in the archives of any religious establishment. Therefore, this cult remained largely undiscovered.'

Meera remembered what Baccha had told her about the Aghori tantric who had authored the sacred text. He too had been spreading his cult secretly.

'This man had never written anything.' Bheeksha's statement startled Meera.

'I did read somewhere that the tenth and eleventh centuries were periods of conflict for various sects and cults of Hinduism. Did not know that applied to tantra too,' said Ranbeer.

'I guess many texts on Vaishnava tantra, actually even Shaiva tantra were destroyed during these centuries,' Kamakshi reasoned.

'Only a few though, as the libraries of the religious establishments that housed these texts were very heavily guarded. And, in any case, most tantric texts are actually hidden in caves and *Shakti Peeths*.' Bheeksha's gaze returned to the locket. 'Am assuming you just want to know about the religious feuds and not about what the pilgrim who identified this locket told me,' he said, clutching it with a sense of exaggerated self-importance.

'Of course we want to know and you have to tell us,' Meera placed an arm over his bony shoulder and cast a glance at Ranbeer.

'The tantric that pioneered this new sect belonged to Karnataka. All his followers were from the south and east. In fact, this sect was completely unknown to people living in the north and west of India. But around the sixteenth century, a man from Banaras had embraced this sect. He trained for many years under a guru in Mangalore. Like the other followers he had a locket with this symbol. And the strange thing is he had lost it; he had reported the loss to his guru who had urged him to find it anyhow, especially because the locket had some extraordinary powers. But he did not manage to find it during his lifetime.'

'And your grandfather found it while cremating a king, so obviously the king had stolen it from this man... err disciple...but is your pilgrim friend sure that the disciple was not this very king?' Ranbeer finally found his voice.

'Absolutely sure. He was a rich man but not a king.'

'Intriguing, but it's hard to understand why the king had stolen it...if at all he did...and from which state did this king hail from?' Maya quizzed.

'He was the king of Magadha. Well...wait a minute...' For the first time in the evening Bheeksha looked confused. 'My father just said that it was a corpse of the royal family of Magadha. It could very well be the corpse of a queen or princess too.'

'And, how did that man who told you this story know about it in the first place?' One of the crew was curious.

'Because his family is among the very few surviving followers of this sect. His forefather too had trained under the same guru that our anonymous man from Banaras had trained under,' Bheeksha informed.

Just at that moment there was a commotion in the adjoining lane. An ascetic with matted locks was being trailed by a crowd. 'Limar Singh, right?' Maya asked.

'So, this very disciple who had lost the locket was the greatest tantric of Banaras…how careless of him though,' Meera spoke half to herself.

Bheeksha merely stared at her.

'Which of course also means that this form of tantra was…or is more powerful than the rituals of the Shaivas and Vaishnavas, or even the Shaiva Aghors,' Maya remarked.

'Yes, because it assimilated the strengths of both the traditions,' was the simple reply.

'Then how do you say that Limar Singh is just a mendicant? Can't you see the connection? He came to Banaras questing for a powerful, undiscovered tantric text; obviously a text pertaining to this sect,' Ranbeer insisted.

'Like I said earlier, the tantric who pioneered this sect had never written anything. His tantra *shastra* was only transmitted orally.' Somehow nobody found Bheeksha's reply convincing.

'Well, we are late for our next assignment!' Ranbeer looked at his watch and exclaimed.

'Thank you for telling us all this, Bheeksha*ji*,' everybody chorused reverentially.

The *chandaal* nodded and contorted his eyes to a trance-like expression as they were leaving.

As they reached the ghats, Ranbeer said something that startled them. 'This mysterious tantric might not have written any text. But he might have inscribed his teachings on other things, like for instance in lockets...probably this was why his disciple was robbed off the locket.'

a mysterious disappearance

Gauriprada was waiting for them on the ghats with Upadhyay*ji*. His look told them that his companion had already briefed him about the mission.

'Tukaram does not receive any clients after nine,' Upadhyay*ji* said a tad admonishingly.

'We stumbled upon something very interesting,' Meera whispered to Gauriprada with a nudge. 'You won't believe this but the world's most powerful tantric order remains undiscovered…' Meera stopped when she saw Gauriprada's expression change. She could not decide whether the priest looked scared or menacing.

As they started walking towards the market area they suddenly came face to face with Limar Singh. Strangely, this time they could not sense any unusual energy. The ascetic had a chiselled face and fierce, red eyes. He seemed preoccupied in his thoughts and nonchalantly strode past them in the opposite direction. *'Is it possible that this crazy man is shadowing us?'* Maya wondered.

Right at that instant, Meera and Ranbeer's message alerts started beeping. Ranbeer looked at his phone and stopped. Meera looked at her inbox and understood why. They had received a threat to stop work on the documentary! These messages were now definitely demanding a discussion in private.

They entered a cluster of dilapidated semi-residential structures. 'This place smells familiar,' Maya whispered. She realised that the place had the same odour like Rustom's staircase.

'It also looks familiar,' Kamakshi pointed to blotches of bluish powder that littered a half-cobbled lane that meandered treacherously between poorly constructed buildings.

'This is the place,' Upadhyay*ji* pointed to the ground floor of an ugly building. A greenish halo was emanating from one part.

Stealthily, the group walked towards the side window. 'This almost looks like the opening of a prison cell,' Kamakshi whispered as they strained their eyes through the dense grill. Finally, there were sounds of footsteps and muffled conversation. Two men emerged from a door leading to the inside.

One of the men, as Upadhyay*ji* affirmed, was Tukaram. With his hair piled up in a tall vertical bun, steel earrings and armlets, he definitely looked the part. The other man's face was only partially visible. They seemed to be engrossed in a conversation that was not audible.

'It seems like they are arguing about some transaction,' Ranbeer whispered.

Soon the other man raised the shutter and stepped out. 'No drama happening,' Ranbeer concluded after Tukaram had switched off the bulbs and disappeared inside.

'We have to come back,' Upadhyay*ji* insisted as they walked back.

After the man took their leave, Gauriprada invited everybody to his house for dinner. 'Also, I will tell you about the history of *shav* sadhana.'

Ranbeer replied thoughtfully, 'I need to head back. My boys shall come with me. But if the girls want they can accompany you.' He turned to Meera, 'In fact, I shall be grateful if you hear everything from Pandit*ji* and brief me in the morning.'

Meera agreed readily as she had been hoping to talk to Gauriprada in Ranbeer's absence. She wanted to ask him about the *Naga* ascetic and Bheeksha's locket. Besides, she also wanted to tell him about Ranbeer's disappearance on the night that she had been attacked on Shivala Ghat. Fortunately, Kamakshi and Maya decided to head back to the guesthouse as well.

'*Shav* sadhana is regarded as one of tantra's most important and most secret rituals. The details of this ritual have largely been disseminated across the ages through oral tales on tantric feats,' Gauripada paused when he saw Meera's face light up.

'Really? How interesting. And, do you know any of these tales?' she inquired with hope.

The priest shook his head. 'However, a few texts also exist that are comprehensible to the exceptionally learned and discerning practitioners of tantra. This is because it is one of the most complex *sadhanas* which is part of the *Vamachara* (left-handed or *Nastik*) order of worship. To practise *shav* sadhana correctly one has to undergo years of initiation. Even minor aberrations of the prescribed procedures can be harmful for the *sadhaks*. Especially because, this form of tantric meditation involves a corpse.'

'You mean that ghosts can torment the *sadhak* if he falters on the rites?'

'Yes. Even the selection of an appropriate corpse is vital,' Gauripada paused as his wife entered the room to serve a meal of vegetable korma, dal and rice.

'*Shav* sadhana originated in Bengal. Vasudeva Bhattacharya was the first human being who was apprised about this esoteric ritual by a celestial voice. This happened while he was engrossed in worshipping the Mother Goddess at Kamakhya Temple. The voice also told him that he will attain moksha after he is reborn as his own grandson. At the time of his death, Vasudeva engraved the mantra on a copper plate and gave it to his servant Purvananda and instructed him to pass it on to his yet-to-be born grandson. Purvananda carried out his deceased master's instruction when the grandson Sarvananda attained an appropriate age. He even volunteered to be the corpse for the ritual. Despite several hurdles encountered in the course of his sadhana, Sarvananda successfully completed the ritual. Pleased by his unflinching dedication, the Goddess blessed him with a special gift—he could make something happen by merely pronouncing it. She also revived the servant.'

'Which year did all this happen?' Meera quizzed.

'I am not very sure about the year. But this is the truth of its origination though several people claim that it was actually the Aghoris of Kashi that established this practice.'

It took a while for Meera to assimilate the background of the macabre ritual. 'Pandit*ji,* did the corpse actually speak to the Aghor on the night that we were filming?'

Gauriprada shrugged his shoulders slightly and answered, 'Hard to say. It depends on the sheer prowess of the Aghor. The corpse might have actually come to life for those fleeting moments or it could well have been an optical illusion. The practitioners of *shav* sadhana can make a dead man talk, if they are truly accomplished in all the details of the rites. In the olden days this was the case with all the practitioners. Today, however, the possibility of illusions cannot be ruled out.'

The rest of the chat with Gauriprada turned out to be a disappointment. The priest was cagey after she told him about everything that Bheeksha had revealed. He had no answer to her questions. Sensing his indifference she decided against sharing her experience about the night of the attack and the threat messages.

'I am going to be in Haridwar for the next fifteen days. So we will resume shooting the other practices once I am back,' he informed while she was leaving.

'Strange that you did not tell us earlier about this,' she replied in a half sarcastic voice and left.

It was about 11.55 pm when she reached Shivala Ghat and she could see a halo of light at the far end. This time she decided to be cautious and instead of heading towards the halo she entered the guesthouse and climbed to the terrace.

Meera could see five hooded men disembarking from a steamer. It looked like they were tugging at some boxes with a rope. After some time another hooded man appeared, wheeling a hand cart. The men loaded the boxes into the cart and two among them took their positions beside the man wheeling it. As the loaded cart and men became a tiny speck, Meera's heart started pounding. Obviously, whatever was happening was illegal.

Without knowing why, she darted to Ranbeer's room. The light was on and the door was slightly ajar. She peeped in and couldn't believe her eyes. He was missing again!

The next two days had one uninterrupted pattern. Every night by around 11.30, Ranbeer would go somewhere. Finally, on the third night, Meera decided to trail him.

'*Where the hell is he going? Damn, this is leading nowhere.*' She had trailed him through half the residential stretch of the modern town. And then, she heard someone calling out to her in a decibel that qualified somewhere between a whisper and a low shriek. She froze and turned her head to find Kamakshi walking right behind her.

'I know I surprised you but don't be,' Kamakshi's tone exuded camaraderie. 'I too have been noticing that Ranbeer goes somewhere…I have noticed that you have been keeping an eye on him…I've also found a few things about him very odd….'

'So you too decided to trail him?'

Kamakshi nodded. 'I have known him for a few months. And I know that Ranbeer is sure that all occult practices are nothing but a sham. So, it baffles me that he has done so much research.'

'I know what you mean.' Meera held Kamakshi's hand and started walking. Ranbeer was now about fifty steps ahead of them.

'There are a few other things about him that are strange. Shall tell you later,' Kamakshi whispered and pressed Meera's palm.

'A few nights ago I had entered his room. I sensed someone was outside. Was it you?' A flash of light from a passing motorcycle lit Kamakshi's face at that instant as she nodded.

Finally, Ranbeer stopped. The girls, who were about twelve steps behind, froze. He looked around and silently opened the gate of a house that had a massive structure at the middle of its large compound and crept inside. For a while Meera and Kamakshi could not understand where they had come to. Then they heard a faint sound of a gong.

'He has come to the temple of the family that Limar Singh had blessed!' Meera whispered.

The girls decided to retrace their steps to the guesthouse. They did not want Ranbeer to know that they had trailed him. Something told them that his mission was not entirely harmless! Despite the exhaustion they were experiencing they reached Everest Café within twenty minutes and dispersed to their rooms. '*Gauripradа has to be told about this, no matter what,*' Meera told herself as she struggled to sleep. Suddenly, Gauriprada's return from Haridwar felt like a long wait.

April was drawing to a close. While Ranbeer was making considerable headway with his shooting, Maya had enrolled herself in a Veda class and Kamakshi, much to everyone's surprise, had started writing poetry. After hearing Gauripradа and accompanying the documentary crew, Maya had been very intrigued about tantra.

'I am almost beginning to think that an entire parallel world exists—a world that is steeped in mysticism. Therefore, I really want to learn our Vedas. I want to understand if the occult sciences contradict or complement their teachings,' she said and thought to herself, *'Even a few weeks ago I could have never imagined that tantra would lead me to a purpose.'*

'My poems are going to be published in a blog. I'm going to get paid on a monthly basis for this and other creative content,' Kamakshi informed Maya.

'I am glad you figured your expenses. After all we can't stretch our savings forever. I was withdrawing money from the joint account I share with Alok all this while, but he has closed the account recently… So I am going to teach pottery making in a local training centre here, just ten hours a week…enough money to sustain my monthly expenses,' Maya said. 'And Arvind has assured me of some financial help as well,' she bit her lip.

'Hmm…lucky Ranbeer and Meera…they don't have to worry about money. I believe Ranbeer has a lot of bank balance…apparently he has earned handsomely from his previous assignments…and Meera anyway is on a scholarship stipend,' Kamakshi remarked.

Before Gauripradaʼs arrival, two unexpected things happened. Professor Bharadwaj asked Meera to attend a conference on Sanskrit studies, which was happening in Delhi on 8th May.

'It is actually a conclave. It might be useful for your thesis. And you have to introduce yourself to Professor Nick Karmar. He is an Australian who teaches Sanskrit in the University of Rome. Get his coordinates and email them to me that very day,' Bharadwaj instructed.

The other surprising thing was an unusual theft. A thief had ransacked the library of the Centre for Vedic Studies where Maya also attended her classes.

'Why would a thief target a library?' Kamakshi voiced what everyone was thinking. 'None of the books were missing. Some pages were torn from a few ancient scriptures and strewn on the ground. And, the most baffling part is that this has been the third such incident in two weeks. Our guru said that the libraries of two other centres of Veda studies have also been ransacked,' informed Maya.

'Is this some uncanny serendipity?' Ranbeer exclaimed. 'Some months ago, an archaeological archive in London had also been ransacked. The newspaper report said that instead of stealing rare manuscripts and coins the thief had stolen the entire array of human bones and skulls.'

Meera, who had been hearing everything with a bewildered expression snapped her fingers, 'Maya, ever since you enrolled for Veda studies, I was trying to recall something that I had heard about this centre even before arriving in Banaras. Now I remember. My director had told me that this centre houses a book written by a scholar that mentions certain religious texts that cannot be classified within any existing religious order.'

'I heard it too. You won't believe what I found.' After rummaging in her purse Maya produced a meal voucher. 'I found this lying at a corner of the library after it was ransacked. Am sure you understand what it implies.' She was now pointing to the lettering on the voucher. The script was undecipherable. 'Well, this is Kannada,' she announced.

'So, the one who broke in is probably from Karnataka or has some connection with the state,' Kamakshi exclaimed.

'It must be only an inane piece of paper that was dropped by an innocent somebody,' Ranbeer scoffed.

'Why don't you hand it over to the administrators?' Meera suggested.

'I did...like Ranbeer, they were dismissive. I will keep it with myself...and maybe investigate on my own.' Maya started laughing when she saw the amused expressions.

In the meantime, Meera had made a mental note to learn more about the incident from Gopal Sarai, the head librarian. She instantly realised that a major security lapse must have occurred while he was away.

'I will be staying in Delhi for some more weeks as I have to source a few rare books for our library which is going to take time,' he had informed her during a recent telephone chat.

The evening of 8th May 2013 turned out to be an unforgettable one. The conference hall was packed. As Meera was beginning to get impatient for Professor Nick Karmar's speech, her cell phone started vibrating. She ignored it. After a few minutes it started vibrating again, this time for three consecutive times. Meera darted to the washroom to see who had been calling so frantically. The first vibration was actually a message. To her surprise it was from Gauripradа and it had just one letter—R. The second, third and fourth vibrations were calls—all from him. She called back and found that the number was out of reach.

The conference concluded in another hour and there was no sign of Karmar. Meera glanced at the itinerary and realised to her dismay that he had addressed the crowd for fifteen minutes in exactly the same time that she had darted out of the hall. What bad timing!

The participants and audience were now heading in the direction of the lawn for dinner. Meera requested a scholar to identify Karmar in the crowd. He pointed to a tall man with a receding hairline.

With a cocktail in hand, Meera ambled in his direction. She somehow felt it would not be wise to reveal her accurate identity. 'I am Meera. I am French and in India on a scholarship for some research work,' she smiled and extended her hand.

'Let's sit and talk,' was Karmar's friendly reply. 'So, this is your first trip to India?' he asked.

'Fourth trip. I have been here on holiday before and...'

'And you love this country, like me.' The professor finished her sentence with a smile. 'There is something about India, which makes you either love or hate her. And when you love her you keep coming back.' His description of India revealed his passion for the country.

'What could he be so passionate about?' she wondered.

'What exactly about India fascinates you? Her culture or the fascinating rituals of her temples?'

Instead of answering, Meera decided to be bold and pose a question, 'By any chance do you research on Hinduism?'

Karmar narrowed his eyes and looked at her before answering, 'I research on tantra.' His expression was still friendly as he continued, 'I have been visiting India twice annually in the last two years because I am working on a paper on occult practices and their scholarly practitioners. I have to submit it to a group of investors in London who are setting up a unique think tank that I am not at liberty to talk about.'

'So, I am assuming that this paper is going to be the selection criteria for the people who will be part of this prestigious think tank?' Meera thought it was best to shoot the questions that mattered.

'This paper will not just license entry into the think tank. The people who submit the best papers shall be part of the governing body. It is envisaged to be a three-member governing body and about twelve scholars have been nominated by the investors. Out of the three people who are selected for this powerful governing body, the one who submits the best research paper will be given a few additional responsibilities and some very special privileges,' Karmar explained.

'Which are the places that you have been visiting for your research work?' she asked.

'Tarapith in Bengal, Dhumavati Temple in Madhya Pradesh and Kamakhya Temple in Guwahati. I understand the esoteric practices by observing the lives of the people who are associated with these *Shakti Peeths* and by talking to a couple of occult practitioners. Also, I have managed to befriend a couple of powerful tantrics at Kamakhya who are in charge of the temple administration.'

Meera asked, 'Are there any real occult practitioners in modern India?'

'I know that for every genuine practitioner there are five hundred fakes but yes the genuine ones do exist, even today. And not all genuine tantrics are savage or dangerous. Many perform miracles for the good of mankind but are modest and unassuming in their appearance and mannerisms. My friend Kashinath Goswami in Kamakhya is one such man.' Karmar sipped the last dregs of his whisky before continuing, 'In fact, this time when I met

Kashinath, he looked very disturbed. He told me that an anonymous man is trying to create mayhem in the sacred realm of tantra.'

'What mayhem?' Meera asked excitedly. For the first time, Karmar looked reluctant to answer. There was a silence that broke when Meera dropped her spoon. The professor bent over to pick it up saying, 'Let me fetch you another,' and walked away in the direction of the buffet table.

When he returned, the conversation steered to generic observations about life in India. Before leaving, Meera quickly exchanged their contact details.

The next morning Meera woke up groggily. She cast a clumsy glance at her watch and was alarmed to see that it was already 11 am. She realised that her phone had been unusually silent and saw that it was on silent mode. Seven missed calls! Three from Ranbeer, two from Baccha and one each from Kamakshi and Maya. All made after 7 am. She decided to call Maya first.

'Did you hear the news?' her friend sounded nervous.

'What news?'

'Gauripradа arrived in Banaras the day before yesterday. And he was kidnapped yesterday. I mean, most probably he has been kidnapped as the police say that he is alive.'

'What!'

'He has been abducted from Vishalakshi Temple after he had conducted the evening *aarti*. His son told us that Gauriprada often stays back after everybody else departs.'

Meera was speechless. 'But why would anybody...what about his call records? What did the temple look like after he was abducted? Any clues?'

'There were signs of a scuffle and some drops of blood were found at one place. The police are sure that he was kidnapped and not killed. They have found an unusual number in the incoming records of his cell phone and are investigating it. The phone was lying somewhere outside the temple.'

'How are the police so sure that he was abducted and not killed?'

'Because had they been dragging a dead body out they wouldn't have managed to upturn so many things as they did.'

Somehow this logic did not reassure Meera. A simultaneous thought sent a chill down her spine—Gauripradа was obviously kidnapped because he was helping them. The threat messages were now the first things to be given to the police. She wondered if Ranbeer had already done it.

'Meera, I think you need to immediately return to Banaras. And, by the way, just the night before this happened, Baccha had spotted the *Naga* sanyasi outside Gauripradа's house. He assumes that Arshad had visited Gauripradа and therefore the sanyasi was standing outside. Baccha also feels that he saw someone fleeing from the opposite side of the house.'

'And where is Arshad now?'

'He has not been seen anywhere since yesterday afternoon.'

'I don't think Arshad is connected to this abduction. So, we shall worry about him later. And I will return soon,' Meera disconnected and dialled her travel agent.

She dialled Ranbeer after precisely an hour and a half after checking the messages on her phone. He answered the phone in a surprisingly nonchalant tone.

'I shall be in Delhi for the next few days. I am meeting someone who is going to tell me who abducted Gauripradа.' Meera informed him.

'Don't be ridiculous! You are just putting yourself in danger.' Ranbeer said in a clearly agitated voice.

'But I have received a message from an unknown number that I don't want to ignore. It said that I should meet him at the Connaught Place Barista at 7 pm on May 15. I called back but the number was switched off. It could be a hoax. But I can't risk not meeting this person. It might be useful, for your documentary and all of us.'

a strange discovery

It was the evening of May 15. Meera was sitting in Barista at Connaught Place. She glanced at her watch with a pounding heart. Five past seven. Still no sign of the informer! After the first SMS six days ago, she had been wondering how she would recognise the informer. But the person had allayed her apprehension a couple of days back by sending a second SMS, saying that Meera was known to the informer!

There was no suspicious character anywhere. *'Except one,'* Meera realised as she caught sight of a woman concealed in an abaya sitting alone in a table near the entrance. *'But the caller was a man. Or could it be a woman? Of course it could be!'* She half expected the abaya-clad woman, who now seemed to be reading a newspaper, to come up to her. It was about 7.45 pm. More people started crowding into the café, blocking her view of the woman. After about ten minutes when the table was visible again, she saw to her dismay that it was occupied by a young couple.

She went over to the counter and settled her cheque. She walked out of the café and ambled along the Outer Circle. After a few minutes, she beckoned an ice-cream seller and bought an iced lolly. It was then that she noticed a paper tacked to her purse. She straightened it and saw that it had six words—*Now you can return to Banaras.*

'I am returning by the afternoon train tomorrow,' she informed Ranbeer at night. As she recounted the events, his voice became tense.

'Do you realise that Gauripradaʼs abductors know all about his acquaintances, especially you? We should not be talking so much over the phone. Look after yourself and be safe in the train. I had called to tell you something strange that I came to know this evening, but it is better we speak in person,' Ranbeer said before disconnecting.

The next thirty-six hours seemed to be excruciatingly long for Meera. She was anxious and a little frightened throughout the journey. Two conflicting thoughts were crowding her mind. Ranbeer had sounded like the friend that she had always known him to be. So, could she trust him with everything, especially now when Gauripradaʼs had gone missing? After all, Gauripradaʼs abduction meant a blow to his documentary. Meera concluded that Ranbeer couldn't be on the abductor's side and therefore she should tell him everything that she would be telling the cops. But then, what about his disappearances at midnight and the fact that he had stolen her reference book? Also, what about that strange metal piece and the photograph that she had spotted on his desk?

The train wheeled into Mughal Sarai station before schedule. Ranbeer and Kamakshi had come to receive her.

'I am used to travelling alone,' she said blankly as Kamakshi embraced her.

'These are not normal times,' Ranbeer said.

After a shower, Meera joined her friends in the dining area for breakfast. 'What did you want to tell me?' she looked straight at Ranbeer.

'Well, this might just be a coincidence. Maybe it is not connected to the abduction but we found the weapon with which he was probably…err assaulted,' he replied with a confused expression.

'What is it and where did you find it?'

'Actually, Baccha found it in the spot where the motorboat used to be moored. Remember the mysterious motorboat that used to chug into Shivala Ghat around midnight? It has stopped coming since the last two days,' finished Maya.

Kamakshi simplified the account. 'Day before, around eight in the evening, while on a stroll near the ghats, Baccha found a knife that was partially stuck in the wet soil.'

'Oh, anybody could have dropped it,' Meera interrupted.

'The blade was stained with blood and right at the place where the blade meets the handle there is a small piece of cloth. Looks identical to the crimson kurta that Gauripradaoften wears,' Ranbeer said.

'Show me the knife.' Meera emphasised on every word as she spoke.

Ranbeer started wearing a hand glove and proceeded to open a transparent packet.

'This is indeed a piece of Gauriprada's...' Meera's jaw dropped. The handle of the knife was engraved with a mutilated owl. After she could find her voice she asked, 'I hope Baccha has not touched it. There will be fingerprints.'

'He picked it with his handkerchief,' Ranbeer assured.

'Should we not give it to the police for investigations?' Meera asked with a sense of urgency.

'Not before they find out about the unidentified number in Gauriprada's incoming records that evening,' was the surprising reply.

'But why are we procrastinating over the handover?' exclaimed Meera.

'Sometimes, it is important to have an edge over the official investigators. I mean, we have to find Gauriprada and also discover the reason for which he was kidnapped. Remember, he is connected to our documentary and this abduction has everything to do with it. The police will try their best but they might not go beyond their call of duty. Moreover, they will not be interested in unearthing anything about why he was abducted. So, we have to know a few things before them,' Ranbeer explained.

The Dashashwamedh police station was peaceful that evening. A constable ushered Ranbeer and Meera to Inspector Tiwari, who was in charge of Gauriprada's case. Tiwari came straight to the point. 'We have retrieved the call details for the entire month. There are no unknown numbers except on the evening of May 8,' he paused and attended to his landline.

'What is that number? And in whose name is it registered?' Ranbeer asked after Tiwari banged down the receiver.

The Inspector gave them a mobile number ending with 91. 'It is registered in the name of Gautam Sharma. But the strange thing is that the address in the records is 501, Railway Colony, Guwahati,' Tiwari replied with an exasperated expression.

'And who is Gautam Sharma? Sir, did you call back on this number?' Ranbeer asked as he jotted down the number and the accompanying details in his diary.

'It is out of service,' was the curt reply.

The two friends took the officer's leave and walked towards the ghats. Most people were sitting in close proximity of the holy river and relishing the breeze. Meera and Ranbeer climbed some steps for they wanted to be away from everybody's ear shot.

'I don't know,' Ranbeer was the first to speak.

'Me neither. We don't even have anybody in mind, like a suspect, that we can secretly trail to reach Gauripradа.' Meera was blankly looking at the black waters. 'Don't you think we should tell the police about the threat SMSes? That is really the preliminary step.'

'For a moment I thought that was our only way. But after you had that incident at Barista, I decided we shouldn't. Whoever is behind all this is obviously watching all our moves and...I don't know why but I feel that if we report the messages to the police things might just get more dangerous for Gauripradа. Our first challenge is to find the true identity of the caller of that number. Maybe we should go to Guwahati and check on that address.'

'That is indeed the first step in our investigations. And Guwahati will also be a useful place for your documentary. After all it is home to one of the oldest *Shakti Peeths* of this country.' Meera than narrated her conversation with Professor Karmar.

Ranbeer agreed. The two got up and headed in the direction of the guesthouse. There, they spotted Sakhat Bhopali, a local tout on Rana Mahal Ghat. He was infamous in Banaras for guiding unsuspecting tourists to the most expensive shops.

'The shop owners give him a commission on every purchase. He too owns a shop of imported leather goods and it is suspected that those are mostly smuggled items,' Baccha had apprised Meera last year during her maiden visit to Banaras. *'Sakhat's twin brother Suchit is infamous for his pranks and clandestine affairs. The Bhopali twins are a menace in Banaras and I hate both of them,' he had declared.*

In the days that followed, Meera got to know the Bhopali twins on her own as she would frequently bump into them in the alleys, ghats and market places. While Sakhat was always polite but formal in his greeting, Suchit was friendly and inquisitive. Gradually, Meera discovered that Suchit was actually quite harmless and that the rumours had trickled from his own exaggerated accounts of popularity with women tourists. Consequently, a friendly equation developed between her and the tout, which Baccha immensely disapproved of.

'Dont worry, I never talk about the things that really matter with him,' she had allayed his apprehensions.

Sakhat was reclining on one of the stairs and fanning himself with a handkerchief. 'Strange that he is not attending to his shop at this peak hour of business,' Meera mumbled.

'This is Suchit,' Ranbeer concluded.

Suchit walked down the stairs to greet them. 'So, where you headed to?' He shook Meera's hand, completely ignoring Ranbeer.

Ranbeer looked uncomfortable. They did not want anyone outside their circle of close friends to know anything about their connection to Gauriprada and the sleuthing mission. Besides, Suchit Bhopali was known to be a gossipmonger.

'We are going to Rustom's house now. Need his help with something.' The words escaped her as she desperately tried to divert his attention from her previous remark.

'Rustom left town exactly three nights ago. Sakhat was supposed to accompany him but could not because he had to attend to some urgent work concerning his shop,' Suchit informed. 'I last saw Rustom some evenings ago near Vishalakshi Temple.'

The two friends were now alert. Rustom's departure coincided with the time of the abduction. They wanted to know more but did not quite know how to ask questions without raising the man's suspicion.

'I remember him telling me something about going out of town, sometime back. But he left quite abruptly,' Ranbeer remarked in a disarming voice.

Suchit looked at him with a puzzled expression and said, 'Then he must be a good friend of yours. Because Rustom rarely discloses his travel plans. Nobody usually knows except Sakhat.' This was an unexpected revelation about the musician.

'And Sakhat tells you everything?' Meera asked.

There was a short sarcastic laugh. 'No, he does not. But Madam*ji,* I always come to know. I am smarter than they think.'

The two friends exchanged a quick glance after Suchit pronounced 'they' instead of 'he'. A few things were becoming clear—Suchit and Sakhat were not on the best of terms—something that Meera had always suspected because Suchit had invariably clammed up whenever she had inquired about his twin brother. Sakhat was closest to Rustom. The two friends concluded that while Rustom might be totally unconnected to Gauriprada's disappearance, they needed Suchit on their side. After all, a local ally to assist them in their sleuthing mission would translate to an edge. 'Do you also know anything about this trip?' Both the friends inquired.

'This is one of his monthly boat trips. He has gone to get a fresh batch of goods.' At the mention of boat trips, Meera had an uncanny feeling that perhaps Rustom was connected in some way to her assault at Shivala Ghat.

'I know. He departs on a motorboat from Shivala Ghat.' She could not bear the suspense any longer.

Suchit was startled. An awkward silence followed.

Ranbeer finally said, 'I know what you mean when you say that Rustom is secretive. He has never revealed the purpose of his trips. We have always wondered what he goes to bring every month.'

'I am not surprised,' Suchit answered a little hesitantly. 'I don't know what he brings but I do know one thing. It is illegal! Rustom does a lot of things that are not permissible by law.'

'Like?' Meera asked.

Suchit started spilling the beans. 'He has multiple prepaid phone numbers. I know a couple of shopkeepers in Godowlia market from whom he has purchased more than one SIM card. I think he uses these numbers when he is out of town, probably under a fictitious identity.'

Meera was about to ask something when Ranbeer nudged her. They could not trust Suchit entirely. It would be unwise to alert him, at least at this stage. 'How does it matter to us what Rustom does with multiple numbers.,' Ranbeer said casually and glanced at his watch.

He pretended to look worried and continued, 'I have to meet someone. Suchit, we shall meet again tomorrow, maybe at Everest Café for dinner?'

The tout instantly accepted the offer. 'I would love to spend an evening with my friend,' he looked at Meera and smiled with a slightly mischievous wink. And then, looking at Ranbeer, he said, 'For all we know, Rustom also has multiple identities! I once overhead Sakhat telling someone that he had gifted Rustom a leather folder in which he stashes his real identity and all other secrets.'

Ranbeer was too dazed to react. Just as they were about to walk away the tout said in a low voice, 'I know that you are making a documentary on tantrics. I can help you more than anyone else in Banaras.'

more about forbidden traditions of worship

Maya and Kamakshi who were briefed about the developments were equally baffled. 'I am excited to go to Guwahati now. For all you know, we might find out that the unknown number belongs to Rustom and he forged the address,' Kamakshi told her friends, who had gathered at the balcony outside Meera's room.

After a long silence Ranbeer turned to Kamakshi and said, 'Why would Rustom forge a Guwahati address in the registration records? It could be any other city closer to Banaras. If you ask me, the abductor is an unknown devil.'

'Your theory makes sense but I was thinking of something else also. Don't you think our first step should be finding all the numbers that are already in Rustam's possession? That way we will know if the one that Inspector gave us is his,' Maya suggested.

'It might not be that easy. The shopkeepers are likely to alert Rustom. We either have to involve the police or hire a private detective. And I don't know if there are any in Banaras,' Ranbeer reasoned. As an afterthought, he asked, 'Meera, what was that number from which you received those messages in Delhi?'

'How could I not think of that?' Meera went inside the room to fetch her mobile. She rushed out. 'It's not one number. Oh God, how silly of me to have not noticed! The two SMSes have been sent from two different numbers and the surprising thing is that both these numbers are identical in terms of the first nine digits! Only the last digit differs. The first number ends with 4 and the second ends with 5.'

'And my threat messages also came from a number that has exactly the same nine digits and ends with 7!' Ranbeer was clearly astonished.

Everybody was stunned.

'After hearing about Rustom's reputation with multiple numbers, are you still not convinced that he has a direct connection with the abduction?' Meera asked Ranbeer.

'But what on earth could be his motive?' Ranbeer replied.

'Are you sure Suchit will come? And do you think he can be of any help?' Meera asked as dinner time approached.

'Come he will. And help too,' Ranbeer scratched his head and continued, 'I only know that we have to take our chances.'

'I guess these chances need caution too,' Kamakshi remarked. 'I think Maya and me should keep out of today's meeting as Suchit might get intimidated,' she added.

It was nine when Suchit Bhopali arrived at Everest Café.

'Hello, *dost,*' he greeted Baccha with a cheeky smile before moving to a table. 'I am Meera*ji*'s guest,' he pompously announced.

Baccha ignored him and buzzed Meera's room on the intercom. 'Madam*ji*, your guest has arrived,' he blurted and disconnected.

The conversation with Suchit was nothing like what Ranbeer and Meera had imagined. 'Your documentary must include the skull worshippers,' he said, munching on a plate of chicken cutlets. Turning to Meera he added with a rehearsed smile, 'The ritual is very entertaining and happens every Saturday after midnight at a place under everybody's nose, secretly.'

Ranbeer nodded at Meera to take charge. 'But I must say that you are the smart one around. How foolish of the people of this town. They fail to notice such fascinating things that are happening right under their nose,' she remarked with a charming smile.

The tout gulped his *jal jeera* and started choking. Before he even regained his composure, he blurted, 'It is not strange that nobody knows about this place. It is right in the ghats. But underground. This place of tantric worship is in a chamber that is located underneath Chet Singh Ghat. And it can be reached through a passage that only some powerful tantrics of Banaras know.'

'And, how do you know this place?' Ranbeer could not conceal his bewilderment.

'I have secretly trailed Sakhat and his friends to it. They carry packets containing assorted powders which they hand over to the tantrics. Once they also carried a carton that had talons of birds,' was the stunning reply.

'Gauriprada never mentioned about a secret chamber underneath Chet Singh Ghat. Maybe he does not know about it or maybe he has deliberately not disclosed this information,' Ranbeer whispered to Meera while Suchit was asking the waiter for something else.

'What else do you know about the skull worshippers?' Meera asked Suchit.

'I know that they are Aghori tantrics. Their bodies and foreheads are smeared with ashes. The ritual is nothing like anything that you might have seen in your life. On the nights I witnessed it I didn't need my pinch of *ganja* before sleeping.'

'Will you lead us there this Saturday? I hope we shall all be safe?' Ranbeer realised that they could not afford to miss it.

'With pleasure,' Suchit obliged with a bow. 'And if I have been safe all four times, I can guarantee your safety. But we have to go very quietly without shoes. Even a cough can be fatal,' he assured and cautioned together.

Meera quickly scribbled one of the numbers from which she had received the messages in Delhi on a piece of paper and asked, 'Suchit, do you by any chance recognise this number?'

'This is my brother's roaming number. He has another number like this. From what I know, Sakhat often uses these roaming prepaid numbers to assist his friends in shady dealings.'

Ranbeer and Meera were now getting impatient for Suchit to leave. They had a lot of information to discuss and plan their strategy.

It was almost four in the morning. The two friends had discussed the details of the abduction and the somewhat incriminating evidence against Rustom and Sakhat throughout the night, sitting on the balcony of Meera's room.

Meera stretched herself and said, 'So, we have now concluded that Rustom and Sakhat are suspects.' The memory of Gauriprada's SMS containing just the letter 'R' troubled her and the breeze felt chilly.

As Ranbeer left her room, Meera thought to herself, *'But if Sakhat had messaged her, who was the woman in the abaya? Or was it a man? Of course, it was Sakhat in the abaya.'* Another confusing fact clouded her logic. Suchit had told them that his brother had probably not stepped out of town for a month now. She was too tired to figure a logical explanation just then. She undressed and snoozed off the moment her head hit the pillow.

She slept past lunchtime and woke up only when there was a shrill ring on her room intercom. 'Someone has come to meet you at the reception,' it was Baccha's manager.

'I shall be there soon,' she answered.

Dressed in a cotton shirt and baggy trousers, she went down to the reception. It was Gopal Sarai, the librarian of the Centre for Vedic Studies.

'What a pleasant surprise! You are back,' Meera greeted him with a smile. 'Since my friend is pursuing a course in your centre, we often discuss the strange ransacking that happened at the library. Maya tells us that the administration is somewhat cagey about disclosing the details of the investigation. Now, I can ask you. Have the culprits been nabbed?'

'No. And even the police are not investigating now, despite repeated requests. Some more strange things have happened after that. The police dismissed these fresh incidents as trivial and even refused to register an FIR,' Sarai settled himself beside Meera on a sofa and confided.

'I understand your concern over this incident as you are the head librarian,' Meera gently touched Sarai's stiff shoulder. She could clearly sense that the man was very perturbed. After a brief silence, she asked, 'What can I do to help you?' As she asked the question she realised that she had simply offered her help as a courteous gesture and would prefer to keep away. With a sleuthing mission and upcoming thesis submission, she had no bandwidth for additional responsibilities.

'Actually, given the subject of your thesis I thought you could probably be of help,' the man replied a little awkwardly.

'I don't quite understand how,' was the instant answer.

Sarai took a deep breath and said, 'I had approached your research guide for help. But…' he left his sentence unfinished and gazed blankly out of the window.

'So, Professor Bharadwaj has directed you to me. He is a very busy man and cannot accommodate your request. But for the life of me I cannot understand how either of us can help you!'

Sarai looked directly into Meera's eyes and said, 'Professor Bharadwaj wasn't pleased to see me at all. When I started broaching the reason for my visit he was vehemently dismissive and even discouraged me to approach you. So, to be honest, he doesn't know anything of what I am going to tell you. And, you have to promise me to keep this from him. Confidential!'

A little dazed, Meera slowly nodded. She remembered that Sarai had lent her a very valuable reference book and in the preceeding months had gone out of his way to answer her queries on Vedic literature. 'Tell me everything.'

The man took a deep breath and proceeded, 'After our library was ransacked, the authorities concluded that nothing had been stolen because none of the books were missing. Even the torn pages of the books and manuscripts had been left behind by the thief. But a few days later, we were shocked to discover that several important passages of a book detailing the influences of South Asian and African civilisations on ancient Hindu traditions of appeasing gods through animal sacrifice have been obliterated by the thief. The intruder had applied correction fluid over some crucial passages. The rituals detailed in those passages are controversial and have sparked debates and discussions in high profile academic bodies.'

Meera was wondering about Sarai's insistence now, *'He hasn't mentioned anything of significance and of what interest is all this to me?'* She started thinking of an excuse to cut short the conversation.

Sarai continued, 'Well, the book is the original unabridged book on the subject. And there is no second copy in the world. It was written by a Vedic scholar in the sixteenth century, it is the only book that explains both the cultural and mythological intricacies leading to the origin of some savage tantric practices.'

'But you just said the rituals that have been omitted from the book have sparked controversy. This means that even people who have not read this book have knowledge about the rituals. It means that they have read about them somewhere,' she interrupted.

'The scholars who are engaged in debates have done intensive research and reading on this subject. But they have all referred to fairly modern and abridged versions of this book and other contemporary research papers that have a bearing on the subject. So....'

'So this means that whoever ransacked your library and obliterated those valuable passages is a learned man! And obviously he has something to gain from this.' At the sound of footsteps, Meera turned towards the door and saw Maya walking in.

'I heard from the manager that you are here with our librarian,' she stated casually and seated herself beside Meera.

Gopal Sarai merely smiled at Maya and continued, 'Not just that. The existence of this book is a closely guarded secret. Most Sanskrit scholars and academicians across the world do not know of its existence. Only the administration in charge of our library knows that the original book exists even today. And, we have strict instructions to issue this book only to the Veda scholars who are connected to spiritual establishments and a couple of educational institutions.'

'I don't understand why the existence of this book is so confidential.'

'To protect it from being misinterpreted by vested interests. Being a research scholar yourself it is easy for you to understand how at times original knowledge is distorted by influential scholars to gain positions of authority. And we fear this is going to happen in this case too. The thief must have photographed the passages before obliterating them.'

The reply made sense.

'And he did not steal the book as he couldn't risk the chances of getting caught with it,' Meera said. The sheer complexity of the case was now beginning to dawn on her. 'Why are you telling me everything? What makes you trust me and how can I help you?'

'You are from the Oxford Centre of Hindu Studies which is one of the two academic institutions that we have permission to issue this book to. Incidentally, after the rampage, apart from the police we immediately alerted the spiritual establishments and academic institutions who are privy to the existence of this book. Later it struck me that this book falls under the scope of your research. I apprised the other stakeholders of our library about your thesis and we were all wondering whether you would be interested in including this book in your thesis,' Sarai explained.

Sarai's request was now making sense. 'Since you have guarded the existence of this book for so many centuries, I do consider it my privilege to include it in my thesis. I have been striving to gather breakthrough material and this definitely is one. I assume you are expecting something in the bargain,' she asked in a forthright manner.

'You can help us a lot. Actually, after Bharadwaj dismissed me, I called your director and he told me that a section of your thesis investigates how some important texts across centuries have been eradicated by vested interests.

Maybe, you can do some investigative research and throw some light on why this incident happened. That way we shall get closer to the truth and the culprit,' he finished.

Sarai's suggestion of investigative research seemed ridiculous and unfeasible. Meera concluded that at best she could mention the book in her thesis. Strangely against her will and reasoning she replied, 'Of course, I will be happy to help you. Will you please email me all the details and the synopsis of the book? Also, I will need details about the contents of the erased pages.'

Maya, who was hearing everything all this while, thoughtfully took out a piece of paper from her purse and looked at it intently. Meera knew she was scrutinising the meal voucher that she had retrieved from the library after it had been ransacked.

'I found it lying on the ground the day after the incident.' Maya handed it to Gopal Sarai. He looked at it with a blank face and returned it without a comment or question.

After Gopal Sarai left, Meera wondered why Professor Bharadwaj had behaved so strangely. Nevertheless, she diverted her mind to her pending research work for the day and after a quick lunch hurried in the direction of the university library.

It was 6 pm. Meera had just returned from the library, exhausted. She decided to go to the outdoor section of the restaurant.

The sky looked like an infinite canvas of gathering clouds. After exactly five hours, Meera, Maya, Kamakshi, Ranbeer and his production crew would be meeting Suchit at Chet Singh Ghat. '*I hope it does not rain. For it will be slippery in the dark passages*,' Meera worried silently and closed her eyes in prayer. The first raindrops trickled down!

At 11 pm, the group gathered at the reception area. Though the rain had stopped three hours ago, a light drizzle remained. The ground outside was soggy and everybody was dressed in dark windcheaters, jeans and floaters. 'We better carry a pair of socks along with our torches,' Ranbeer suggested. 'We can put them on for protection when we leave our floaters behind to go underground.'

Everyone nodded. They had to be prepared for all unforeseen exigencies.

A wind with a gushing sound greeted them on the ghats. As they walked to Chet Singh Ghat, everyone felt like they were part of a crime thriller. Suchit was already waiting for them. He was wearing a hooded jacket that looked heavy for the season.

'Aren't you feeling hot?' Ranbeer asked as he introduced Maya, Kamakshi, and his colleagues.

'It is at least five degrees cooler near the secret chamber.'

'I had always thought that it is hot underground,' the young boy holding the portable camera remarked.

'It is hot in the rest of the passage. But I think the ritual chamber is air-conditioned,' Suchit replied.

As they followed Suchit in a single line, everybody was beginning to doubt the authenticity of the skull worshippers. 'If they are genuine why would they have such a modern chamber?' Maya wondered aloud.

'But if they were imposters why would they perform such rites in secret every Saturday? After all imposters are only busy tricking people,' Kamakshi reminded.

Chet Singh Ghat was one of the least illuminated ghats. Today the moonless sky made it look darker. The ground was slippery and strewn with debris and rubble from the fort, which the rains had washed away. After what seemed like an arduous, three-minute walk that entailed a brief upward climb, the group reached the northern fringe of the fort. This part was an extension of the original construction and resembled a simple two-storeyed structure. There was a door marking the entry to this part. Suchit opened it without any effort.

After removing their floaters and stacking them in a hole on the exterior wall, they entered in a single file. Ranbeer flashed his torch in a circular motion across the ceiling, walls and floor. It seemed like the interiors of an abandoned heritage building. The scale of depreciation was immense and cobwebs hung from everywhere.

As the eight people proceeded, they trod on a variety of objects. Some made clanging sounds while others emitted soft thuds. Suchit had instructed them to switch off their torches as they could not afford to alert anybody.

'It is said that powerful ascetics who travel from Badrinath and Haridwar to various *Shakti Peeths* across the country stay at Chet Singh Fort while crossing Banaras. These ascetics are lost in their meditative trance for days or rummaging for ashes, bones and skulls in the cremation grounds. If their trance is undisturbed, they are harmless. Otherwise, their wrath can be fatal,' he informed in hushed tones.

'Why don't we see them?' Kamakshi asked in a whisper and immediately added, excitedly, 'Hey, I can see a couple of them.'

A few feet ahead, two silhouettes were visible in the glow of a motley swarm of fireflies that flew inside from the gaps in the walls. Suddenly, they could spot a bloodshot pair of unblinking human eyes. Limar Singh was sitting in one corner. He was motionless and seemed dazed. *'What on earth is he doing here? He indeed has inscrutable ways!'* everyone thought silently as they crossed him. The ceiling seemed higher. This was a sign that they were beginning to exit the periphery section of the fort. The main section felt eerie. Bats were nestling in crevices of the fort wall and silhouettes of bony tantrics with matted locks became a regular spectacle.

After a few minutes they crossed a deserted section. A halo of light was illuminating their path.

'From what I know, this fort has always been dilapidated and there is no electricity,' the cameraman remarked. They soon discovered that the light had escaped from the cracks of a narrow door built into one of the walls. Unable to contain his curiosity, the cameraman went to the door and tried opening it. It was locked. To everybody's surprise, there was a peeping hole. Ranbeer was the first to peep in. Piles of wires and fibres, switchboards, a variety of tools and even a stabiliser were mounted on a massive table. 'There must be bulbs on the walls,' Suchit said in an impatient tone that implied that they had to reach their destination fast.

They reached it after descending a narrow stairway comprising at least three dozen slippery granite steps. These steps were leading underground, and the group tiptoed clutching at the walls on either side that were but only a couple of inches away. The roof too was sloping precariously downwards and almost touching their heads. It was claustrophobic and completely dark. Ranbeer and one of his colleagues switched on their torch lights after carefully adjusting the brightness to low.

The steps directly ended at the secret chamber, which was gradually becoming visible after descending about twenty steps. At the twenty-sixth step, Suchit who was leading the way, turned to his left, lowered his head and squeezed into an opening in the sandstone wall. He signalled to the others.

They were now walking along a semi-circular space, which seemed better ventilated and like Suchit had said, much cooler. '*Probably the effect of sandstone*,' Ranbeer thought. From this space, through small circular holes inset on the right hand wall they could see the secret chamber below. Ranbeer and Meera silently fathomed its significance. Erected right below the turret, it was a place to keep battle ammunition or prisoners. Or maybe it was a chamber envisaged for secret meetings, even at the time of Raja Chet Singh. This narrow, semi-circular space above was probably the place from which the guards kept vigil over the prisoners.

About half a dozen ascetics were chanting mantras and getting ready for the rituals. The place was shrouded with smoke and nothing was clearly visible, for a while. '*Om Sri Maha Kalikayai Namaha,*' the decibel of their chorus was multiplying.

It was exactly 11.25 pm. A thud of footsteps was emanating from the stairway that they had passed, just a few minutes ago. Suchit wordlessly urged everybody to freeze movement. Soon, three men hooded in black scarves appeared. Their faces were visible. One was Sakhat.

They were not carrying anything and marched straight to the ritual chamber. At their sight, the ascetics stopped their chanting. Much to everybody's surprise the smoke was beginning to clear! '*This means that the roof of this chamber has a smoke outlet,*' Meera deduced and marvelled at the architectural acumen of Indian kings.

One of the ascetics had walked to the entrance of the chamber to greet the visitors. Much to their dismay, the group in hiding could see nothing of this man. He was clad in a black flowing robe, a red scarf concealed his hair and he had his back towards them.

'This is all we have,' Sakhat spoke first as he produced a big brown envelope from his jacket's pocket. The man hissed something under his breath and almost snatched it from Sakhat who now looked apologetic. 'They are arriving with fresh provisions. I promise you next time we shall compensate,' he allayed.

The ascetic said something with clenched teeth that nobody could decipher. Without further conversation, Sakhat and his accomplices departed.

The chamber was silent. The group strained their eyes through the circular holes. A cauldron with a concoction of scented herbs was simmering over a fire of logs in the centre of the room. Right next to it stood a *trishul* with a skull mounted over it. As the smoke cleared, they could see the most spectacular idol of Goddess Kali. It was about nine feet tall and placed against the focal wall of the black-stoned chamber. Adorned with a garland of skulls, the hands of the towering idol carried weapons and a severed head. Bracelets, anklets and earrings in pure gold gleamed in the darkness casting a halo over the dark, fierce yet mesmerising features of the goddess. Only a brocade cloth wrapped her private parts. On the other end of the room, six skulls were placed on a red cloth. Across the floor of the chamber two dozen geometrical patterns were drawn. Urns smeared with dabs of vermillion and mounted with coconut shells were placed over each of these drawings.

Dressed in black robes and red cloth head gear, the ascetics were sitting in a circle around the cauldron. An assortment of powders and grains marked each of their territories in a semi circle. The ascetic who had received Sakhat was sitting with his back towards them. He was reciting some hymns from a red book in front of him. The rest were repeating after him. At intervals they threw handfuls of grain into the flames that were lapping the cauldron. It was clear that he was leading the ritual and training the others.

The two hands on Ranbeer's watch came together. There was complete silence below. Only the flames were crackling. The ascetics had all stood up on one leg with closed eyes. This was the first time that the faces of the three who had sat facing them became clearly visible. *'They look rather young,'* Maya thought as she saw their ash- and sandalwood-smeared faces.

'They definitely do not look like regular Aghors or even regular tantrics,' Kamakshi excitedly whispered.

Their lips and bodies now started trembling. An eerie sound started reverberating around the space. Without warning, the ascetic who had been leading the proceedings, stretched his hands upwards and started swaying. The others instantly followed. They were constantly chanting—*Om Sri Maha Kalikayai Namaha.*

Ranbeer signalled his cameramen to start capturing the spectacle on film. Before the silent onlookers could understand what was happening, the chamber got shrouded in smoke again. Despite the nearly impenetrable covering of ash and smoke, they could see frenzied movement below. The fire below the cauldron had leapt to a dangerous height and to everyone's amazement, faces, forms, symbols and even numerical formulas erupted in the flames. As each image spurted, the preceding disappeared. For almost fifteen minutes, an array of bewildering images left the silent onlookers transfixed.

Intermittent puffs of smoke now started escaping to the circular passage above the chamber. Suchit and a few others started rubbing their eyes while Meera struggled hard not to choke. Finally, the flames receded. The ascetics had disrobed themselves and smeared their bodies and faces with a thick layer of ash. They were all looking alike. '*Cremation ash that was contained in the urns,*' the eight surmised. The empty urns were now strewn across the floor while the coconut shells remained on the drawings.

Sitting precariously close to the flames, the head ascetic was bending his upper torso over the now disciplined flames. The others looked on in reverence. In the next moment, he held his finger over the flames and injured it with a sharp object. Blood started trickling to the flames! Chanting *Om Sri Maha Kalikayai Namaha,* he walked up to the diety and offered his blood at her feet.

'These tantrics are definitely invoking the power of the evil forces,' Maya whispered.

The cameraman nudged Ranbeer and whispered, 'We are running out of battery.' It was around 12.40 am and the group had a feeling that the ritual was drawing to a close. The final moments were equally captivating. Each of the ascetics fetched a skull from the red cloth and filled it with the liquid that was brewing in the cauldron. They stretched themselves into a more relaxed position to enjoy the drink.

Right then, Suchit let out a loud sneeze. None of them stopped to think and instead fled at the quickest possible pace. They did not stop till they were outside of the fort. 'I don't think any of them heard us fleeing or even the sneeze,' Ranbeer said, panting.

'But good we did not take a chance,' Meera added.

After Suchit took their leave, the seven walked on wordlessly towards their guesthouse.

Meera was tossing on her bed. When she finally fell asleep, she had a nightmare. To her surprise, the next morning Ranbeer greeted her with an excited expression. 'I could not sleep at all. I have only been thinking of one thing. Gauripradа had apprised us of almost all the important traditions of tantric worship. The ritual that we witnessed yesterday did not fall under any description. Not even broadly.'

'I don't quite understand.'

'Well, one thing is clear, the ascetics were not fakes. So it is possible that the head ascetic was teaching a new way of practicing tantra. A more savage form perhaps that borrows from several existing traditions. In that case my documentary will have to address many more layers of complexities than I am prepared for.' His eyes gleamed with excitement.

more about karmar and ranbeer

It was nearing the end of May. The cops had made no headway in finding Gauripradа. 'We have combed every inch of Banaras and its outskirts. Pandit*ji* seems to have vanished from the face of this land,' Inspector Tiwari informed.

There were fewer tourists in Banaras and Baccha had ample time to help the crew identify locations for anchor shots. After Gauripradа's disappearance, apart from the skull worshippers, they had managed to shoot only one ritual, with Baccha's assistance.

'I know of a place where this tantric practices *Kulachudamani* tantra,' he had proudly informed. It turned out to be a gruesome form of tantra that entailed invoking the dark powers by using the bones of a dead black cat, crushed into powder.

Ranbeer utilised this light phase to write everything that Gauripradа had told him about the history of tantra *shastra* and its influences.

In the meantime, Meera had buried herself into her work. 'I have managed to archive information about quite a few forgotten and missing texts but have not been able to propose any convincing analogy to explain their disappearance,' she shared with Maya and Kamakshi.

'So, when are you planning to wrap up your thesis?' Maya inquired.

'I don't know. Actually, I have a few other challenges too,' Meera replied with a lost look. She was referring to the request of Gopal Sarai and the thought that Rustom had some connection with Gauripradа's abduction.

One day, after Meera returned to the guesthouse from a gruelling morning at the Bharat Kala Bhavan Museum, she found Baccha sitting at the reception with an unusually excited expression. 'I was waiting for you, Madam*ji*. Do you remember that I had told you that someone had told me that the tantric who had authored the text…the text that Limar Singh has come here for…had lived a secret life?'

'So, who is it?' Meera asked immediately.

'Ranbeer.'

The answer at once unsettled the trust that Meera had regained for Ranbeer in the course of the last few weeks.

'And, when did he tell you this?'

'Sometime in November, Madam*ji*, please don't tell him that I told you this but Ranbeer*ji* had come to Banaras in November to immerse his father's ashes and had asked me a lot of questions about Limar Singh and the other tantrics of Kashi.'

'And, why should I not tell him?'

'Because he had sworn me to secrecy… He had said that if I don't speak about this trip to anyone he will reward me… I mean, he will share a small portion of the prize money that his documentary is sure to get,' Baccha finished, sheepishly.

That afternoon, Meera decided to go and meet Professor Bharadwaj in BHU. There were several challenges that had accumulated in the course of her research on which she needed his help. She had also been wondering why he had been so dismissive of Gopal Sarai's request.

Bharadwaj was addressing his PhD students when Meera reached the Sanskrit department. As she waited in his chamber, she reminded herself that her guide was one of the finest professors of Sanskrit in the whole of Asia. 'He is an authority on every subject that comes within the ambit of the language,' the Director of the Oxford Centre for Hindu Studies had apprised her before she left for India a couple of months ago. A sharp voice interrupted her thoughts.

'You should have come with an appointment. I told you I am very busy till the end of June,' the professor said, brusquely.

'But you have not been receiving my calls and without your assistance my thesis is facing a deadlock. So I just had to meet you, Sir,' Meera replied in a courteous but assertive tone.

Professor Bharadwaj was now standing in front of his table and facing the young woman. There was something about his gaze that told her that he wanted to evade her.

A brief silence followed, interrupted by a shrill bell. Bharadwaj scratched his temple and said rather unpleasantly, 'Well, despite my packed schedule I can give you an hour tomorrow. At 3 pm. But if you delay even by a few minutes, it shall be your loss.'

Meera nodded and headed back in the direction of the main town. *'Why has he become so uncooperative?'* she wondered. Her resolve to ask him questions, strengthened.

When she reached the guesthouse, she found Ranbeer sitting in the older section of the café, facing the Shivala Ghat. He was in a sombre mood. 'You are back earlier than I had expected. Where are the others?' she pulled a chair near him and asked in a strained voice.

'I was not in the right frame of mind to shoot. I wanted to make such a kickass documentary. I wanted to film every possible practice known and unknown to mankind. But after Gauripradа's disappearance I am crippled. I'm contending with generic shots of the town and relying on bytes of the local people. It seems like a documentary on Banaras and not on tantra!'

Ranbeer clasped her hand and said, 'Listen Meera, we just have to find Gauripradа fast. I have a very strong feeling that our visit to Guwahati and identifying the mysterious Gautam Sharma is our first step towards ascertaining the motive for this abduction.'

'Let me call up Professor Karmar tonight. Since he is researching on tantric practices with the cooperation of the trustees of Kamakhya Temple, he might be willing to give us some leads in terms of shooting. If this happens, at least your documentary will benefit from this trip,' Meera said.

Little did she suspect that the call would be a turning point for their investigations!

She dialled Karmar's India number later that night.

'Hello, young lady,' his voice was friendlier than she had expected it to be.

'Hello, Sir,' she returned his greeting in a charming voice and realised that she had not quite prepared for the conversation. Much to her relief, like the previous time, Karmar took the lead.

'I was planning to call you.' There was a long pause. Sensing the surprise at the other end, Karmar explained, 'I spoke to Professor Bharadwaj a couple of days back and he told me that he had asked you to meet me at the conference and exchange numbers.'

'Well, I have called you to request for some help.'

'Is it related to your work?' The reply came almost instantly.

'A friend of mine is making a documentary on tantric practices. Perhaps, you can educate him about the practice in *Shakti Peeths* and suggest some locations in and around the hills on which Kamakhya Temple is built that can be incorporated.'

'You seem to be surrounded with people who have an interest in the same subject!' Karmar remarked in a surprised voice.

'Yes, Ranbeer and you are currently engaging in the same subject. It is. . . .'

'I am not referring to your friend,' Karmar interrupted. His next sentence stunned and silenced Meera. 'Your research guide, Bharadwaj is also doing incisive research on the subject. I am surprised you didn't know but he is researching on the significance of symbolism in the tantric traditions of worship.'

'Well, he knows that my friend is working on this documentary. I am surprised why he never mentioned that he has a similar academic interest,' Meera finally answered.

There was a short laugh at the other end. 'Maybe because it is not just an academic interest; the interest is laced with ambition and from what I heard of Bharadwaj, he has a reputation for being suspicious. Guess he is far more stealthy and cautious than the rest of us could care to be.' Karmar's tone was a little sarcastic.

'What ambition? And how is he a part of the rest of you? I mean who and what are you referring to?'

'It is nothing as dramatic as you are thinking. The fact is, Bharadwaj is one of the twelve candidates nominated for the think tank,' Karmar sounded more casual now. 'Coming back to your request, I promise to talk to your friend and understand what his requirements are. If they do not threaten the interests of the temple administrators, I shall gladly help. By the way, I am in Guwahati for a fortnight starting June 10. Give me your friend's number. I shall talk to him and if I find his requirements suitable I shall solicit Gautam Sharma's support. Gautam will have to grant the clearances and permissions for the shooting. Frankly, he might not have the time as he is fairly occupied and disturbed with the menace of Laal Singh,' Karmar added. The fact that a Gautam Sharma existed in Kamakhya *Peeth* was so explosive that Meera did not register the mention of a menace.

Before she could say anything, Karmar cut short the call saying, 'I have some important paper work to finish. But if we need to continue our conversation, you can call me tomorrow by 1 pm.'

In a daze, Meera walked towards the restaurant to join her friends for dinner. 'Where is Ranbeer? I need to talk to him right now.' She scanned the room and was puzzled to find him missing.

'He went to meet Gauriprada's son an hour back,' Maya replied.

Meera briefed her friends about her conversation with Karmar. As she finished, Ranbeer entered the dining area.

'I have to tell you something urgent. It is something that we could have never imagined,' Meera walked over to Ranbeer and nudged him.

'Well, I have had an overdose of information today.'

The reply was startling. Meera walked back slowly towards the buffet table wondering why Ranbeer was being evasive.

Laal Singh and the Pelvic Bone Menace

Meera and Ranbeer were the only two people awake before sunrise at Everest Café, the following morning. The fiery hues of the first sun rays were struggling to break through the clouds.

'So there is more to Gautam Sharma, maybe much more than we even suspect now,' Ranbeer sighed as he strolled on the terrace.

'I shall try to find out more about him today when I speak to Karmar,' Meera replied. Notwithstanding her growing suspicions about Ranbeer's motives, she was experiencing a surging excitement for their sleuthing mission after speaking to Karmar.

'How was your meeting with Gauriprada's son yesterday? Why did he summon you?'

'I don't know. Whatever he shared has no bearing on my work. Or I might be wrong. I might be in the line of danger,' Ranbeer replied.

Seeing the perplexed look on Meera's face, he explained, 'See, I am shooting a very controversial documentary. So it is not easy to trust even people like Gauripráda who were readily volunteering information.'

'Did his son warn you about something?' There was a long pause as Ranbeer lit a cigarette. Kamakshi had just arrived for her morning exercise.

'Rishiprada said that I can continue to shoot at my own risk. Apparently in the last few months some events have happened in the realm of tantra that caused quite a stir.

Several tantrics who perform their rituals near riversides have discovered remnants of the female pelvic bone. In all the instances, the pelvic bone has been partially embedded in the sand and encircled with a blood-soaked cotton cloth. And after every discovery the dead body of a woman mutilated at the hips has been found floating in the river.' Ranbeer stopped and shut his eyes.

Finally, Meera said, 'I still don't understand the connection or the danger to you.'

'Rishiprada says that the occult fraternity is largely in agreement that some man is intruding into their territory to defame them. They feel that this man is deliberately mutilating the bodies of already dead women. The theory is that he is unearthing skeletons from burial grounds and after dissecting the pelvic section, planting the pelvic bones in their secret places of practice to mislead people.'

'So, this anonymous man is using pelvic bones to frame these tantrics as sexual exploiters and killers of women?' Kamakshi was starting to see some sense.

Ranbeer nodded. 'After discovering the remnants, some people have informed the police. And the police have organised night vigils at some sites.'

'And obviously the tantrics are not being able to perform their rituals. Of course, none of these rituals are connected to pelvic bones. But then, I always thought there is no law that can convict them,' said Meera.

'Well, Rishiprada tells me that the occult fraternity knows that if these incidents continue, public outrage against them will multiply.'

'Apparently the occult fraternity across the country is coming together to nail this intruder and punish him. They will not spare anybody who encroaches on their territory and does anything against their interests and...'

'And obviously you are in serious danger if they discover you filming their practices. They might even think that you are the evil man,' Kamakshi interrupted.

'But the man can be another tantric following his own savage rituals?' Meera's tone conveyed that she was beginning to feel that the theory was ridiculous.

'I had the same question for Rishiprada. He negated this saying, 'no text prescribes this barbaric ritual'. Some tantrics worship the female anatomy and indulge in pleasures of the flesh but this is blasphemy.' After a brief pause, he added, 'I have doubts about Gauripada's integrity and intent now. His son might be saying this to fend me away.'

Meera's antenna was alert. Was Ranbeer trying to say that Gauripada had staged his disappearance? If whatever he was trying to imply was correct then they were probably up against a deep plot. But, what if Ranbeer was trying to divert attention to Gauripada to conceal his own intentions?

The day ahead turned out to be exceptionally hot. '*The ghats have never seemed as secluded as today,*' Meera thought as she hurried in the direction of Vishwanath Gali. As she entered the market area, she spotted Kamakshi and Maya. They were carrying an additional *jhola* and seemed to be in a tearing hurry. Since Meera had to reach the university in time to meet Bharadwaj, she ignored them.

The telephone conversation that she had with Karmar an hour back was reverberating in her mind. 'I can commit my assistance to your friend only after speaking to Gautam. And he is mighty busy.'

'Who is Gautam Sharma?' Meera had interrupted.

'He heads the body that looks after the administration of Kamakhya Temple. A priest and scholar, he is an acknowledged authority on tantra. Gautam is in charge of the organisation of the upcoming *Ambubachi Mela*.'

Despite her apprehensions for Ranbeer, Meera had thought it unwise to reveal the reason for her interest in Laal Singh; without consulting Ranbeer.

'Is there any way that I can help you with your thesis?' Karmar had offered.

'Well, I can't think of anything right away. By the way, I am just a little curious about the Laal Singh menace. Hope it is nothing very serious,' she had replied as calmly as she could.

Karmar had laughed loudly and finally said, 'You are a very smart lady and know so much about everything that is happening.'

'I don't quite understand, Sir,' Meera had been sure that Karmar had been offended.

'Neither do I clearly understand how you know about Laal Singh. But am assuming your research network is very deep. Or maybe your good friend is doing incisive research on his documentary. But I am impressed.'

His final sentence had allayed her worries. 'I know nothing about Laal Singh. I was only curious because you mentioned him last night,' she had stated simply.

'Oh, did I?' the man had genuinely sounded surprised. 'Well, all that we know is that a mysterious man is venturing into the occult world. He has committed a spate of blasphemous acts and each act bears his signature in some form. At one of the sites of sacrilege, he has inscribed his name—Laal Singh. And now, if you don't mind, I will have to rush to a meeting.'

The professor had tried to disconnect the call when Meera almost shouted, 'Is Laal Singh behind the menace of the pelvic skeletons?'

After a lengthy pause, Karmar said, 'Now, I am very eager to talk to your friend.'

On her way to the university, Meera crossed the Centre for Vedic Studies. Without knowing why, she halted her auto to take a close look at the building. The courtyard was deserted. Suddenly, she spotted a man. He was lurking around one of the walls of a part that looked like the extension of the main building. Something about his appearance struck her. She soon realised that it was his hair. It was white. *'Could it possibly be Ranbeer? No, of course not!'* Meera thought to herself. She decided to assure herself and edged closer to the opposite side from which she could get a clearer view. Her heart skipped a few beats—it was indeed Ranbeer.

'What on earth could he be doing here, sneaking around?' she wondered all along her way to BHU.

The university clock showed the time as 2.50 pm. As Meera opened the door of Bharadwaj's chamber she was surprised to hear his voice. She had not expected him to be already there.

Without disconnecting the call, he gestured to her to sit on the leather couch adjacent to his table.

The professor was talking in a language that Meera could not comprehend yet strangely found familiar. After ten minutes, he disconnected.

'What did you want to ask me?' he asked rather abruptly. Meera did not know where to begin. Far too much had transpired in the past week for her to experience the ease that she had earlier felt in Bharadwaj's presence.

'I need your help in framing a couple of arguments explaining why certain Vedic texts are missing from the libraries,' she felt that it was best to come straight to the point.

'I have already told you that you need to correct the approach of your thesis. You need to explain the challenges that the academic world is facing after losing certain texts. The reasons for their disappearance are of no consequence,' the professor said, condescendingly.

'The challenges are already known. I have examined some important similarities between all the missing texts. There is interesting literature to suggest that the reasons for destroying or stealing these texts are linked to considerations beyond the purview of religion and academics. I think I have a terrific opportunity by way of this thesis to explore these causes, especially because I am privileged to have you as my guide.' Meera persisted.

'In my thirty-five-year-old teaching career I have not come across any such provocative literature!' Bharadwaj was unrelenting.

Meera decided to engage him in more casual conversation and ask some of her questions indirectly.

'Did you hear that the Centre of Vedic Studies has been ransacked?' she asked.

'These are the usual publicity stunts that foggy, forgotten archives and libraries often undertake...obviously to be in the news and limelight.' The answer was completely unexpected.

Bharadwaj was scribbling something on a notepad. Without raising his head he said, 'You can mail me all the names of the texts that you have enlisted in your thesis under two categories—missing and forgotten. I shall go through and suggest you another approach.'

'There is a third category—undiscovered. And I know about this fascinating ascetic who is in Banaras to discover one of the greatest texts of the Aghors,' she blurted without thinking.

Bharadwaj's pen fell on the ground. He picked it up and facing her, smiled for the first time. 'I must say that you are doing beyond your purview of research. What else have you heard in the past few days? I mean, if you tell me, I can probably guide you to write a fairly interdisciplinary thesis.' His tone was flat and did not convey either interest or sarcasm.

'Well, since my friend is making a documentary on occult practices, I happen to know about Laal Singh. After hearing of his barbaric acts, I have been very disturbed.'

'And why is that so?' A startled Bharadwaj prodded. 'Is it of any significance to you that some savage man is probably trying to revive a dangerous tradition in some foreign land?'

'Why are you surprised?' Meera tried to force a smile. 'I have enough friends in this country to be affected.'

'And how do you think I can help you find Laal Singh or discover the secret text?' he quizzed.

'Because you are researching on the significance of symbolism in the tantric traditions of worship,' the words poured out almost instantly.

Suddenly, the generously ventilated room became claustrophobic.

'I might be researching on the subject. That is an insufficient premise to assume any connection with crime and criminals.' Bharadwaj's voice was steely and sarcastic in equal measures.

Meera sensed that further conversation would lead to an unpleasant altercation. She glanced at her watch and politely took the Professor's leave.

the mystery deepens

In the days that followed, Ranbeer did not mention anything about his visit to the Centre of Vedic Studies. The documentary had been stalled because the heat wave had made it impossible for the crew to squeeze into closed spaces. Gauriprada's son had apprised Ranbeer that the menace of Laal Singh was getting more serious. Sensing that the situation would continue for some time, Ranbeer had sent his production crew to Delhi.

One evening, Ranbeer flipped through the pages of his diary. It was already June. 'By now we would have been editing the complete footage,' he muttered.

'I have almost given up on my thesis too. I have sent an email to Bharadwaj citing the names of all the texts that were part of this thesis and requested him for fresh direction. But he has not replied. He has gone out of town without even caring to inform me of his destination or return!' Meera remarked.

She started mulling about another incident connected to the professor. About ten days back she had been browsing through a reference book that Bharadwaj had lent her. She had found a loose page that had a visibly different texture from the other pages. When she read the contents she discovered that it was indeed the page of another book—maybe a book on ancient Shamanic traditions as this particular page elaborated on a rite of some ancient jungle tribe.

When she had casually asked him later if he had an interest in shamans, he gave her an admonishing lecture about why she should not be wasting his time inquiring about unearthly things like shamans.

On the other hand, they had made no headway in solving the mystery of Gauripradaʼs abduction and ironically, all this while Rustom had been absconding. Curiously, neither was Arshad Singh to be seen anywhere.

'But I have spotted the *Naga* sanyasi a couple of times,' Maya informed her friends.

Ranbeer had finally apprised the police about the knife that they had retrieved from Shivala Ghat. He had even told the cops about the threat messages and the message that had stalled Meera in Delhi after the abduction.

'Even after Suchit Bhopali's account of his presence near Vishalakshi Temple and the multiple numbers in his possession…it is just not enough to even qualify as circumstantial evidence against Rustom,' Inspector Tiwari had dismissed.

'But how can you overrule the fact that Suchit has revealed that both the numbers that had been used to stall Meera in Delhi belong to his brother and that Sakhat is Rustom's aide?' Ranbeer had argued.

Tiwari had just shrugged his shoulders.

'The fact that Rustom is our only suspect in the abduction and Sakhat is his ally says everything. I mean, now it is obvious that the number from which your threat messages came also belongs to Sakhat. After all, we can never undermine the fact that he owns the numbers through which Meera was stalled in Delhi,' Maya observed one morning at breakfast.

'Can we talk about what we can do right away?' Meera sounded a little agitated.

Ranbeer nodded. 'I am going to ask my agent to figure out the earliest tickets to Guwahati. We can't be waiting for Karmar. We have to get there and grill Gautam Sharma and possibly find out about Laal Singh. Are all four of us going?'

Everybody nodded.

'But I have been worried about Arvind.' Ranbeer added.

'What happened to him? I thought he was coming back from the jungles of Madhya Pradesh by the end of June.' Maya's voice revealed her concern for the ornithologist.

'Arvind has been receiving some grave threats over email…from a poacher.'

'What?' the three women exclaimed.

'And he never mentioned anything to me,' Maya added.

'All he said is that he has received three emails over a period of three weeks from an unknown ID threatening him to stop his work. And he also said that though he had twice ignored the threats, he is now unable to ignore some very perplexing events. He is coming to Delhi day after and says that it is crucial that I meet him.'

'I am coming with you. I have to help him in every way I can.' Maya could not camouflage the affection she was beginning to feel for Arvind.

Ranbeer looked at her. 'He doesn't need our help with anything. He needs to meet me to tell me a few things that are critical to *our* safety.'

For a long time nobody knew what to say.

Finally, Kamakshi spoke, 'But what connection can there be between the emails that he has been receiving and us?'

'I am clueless. But Arvind will not take anything seriously unless it is actually serious. He is very unlikely to tell me that there is something that I need to know for my safety unless he is dead sure.' Something in Ranbeer's voice worried everyone.

Maya and Ranbeer were packing their bags for a three-day visit to Delhi when Meera called him on the intercom. 'Karmar had called an hour back. He is in Delhi for five days. And he feels that it is important that he meets you and me before he speaks to Gautam Sharma.'

On the evening of June 4, Meera, Ranbeer and Maya boarded the train to Delhi. Kamakshi decided to stay back. 'I am in the midst of writing some intense poetry and don't want a change of place,' she had stated matter of factly to Ranbeer.

The night before, she had confided the real reason to Meera and Maya. 'In Ranbeer's house, you might come across something that proves our suspicion that he is hiding something...and if I am around he might be more cautious.'

As she finished, Maya had a confused expression. Meera quickly told her about all the things that Kamakshi and she had observed about Ranbeer in the preceding weeks.

'I cant believe this...sneaking and borrowing a book without permission, retracing Limar Singh's steps stealthily, prior unmentioned visits to Banaras, knowledge about the ascetic who authored the hidden text!' Maya was astounded.

Turning to Kamakshi, Meera asked, 'Why do you feel he will be more cautious in your presence? Did something happen in the past that makes you feel this way?'

'Actually, there has been an incident. Once I was sitting in his living room while he had gone to the kitchen. I noticed a worn-out photo album on one of the tables and started flipping through it. It had black-and-white photographs of Ranbeer's childhood. There were some photographs from his days in Italy too. However, what struck me as slightly odd was that the captions of his childhood photos were not written in English.'

'Hindi, of course, how is that odd?' Maya quizzed.

'They were written in a script I could not decipher. Somehow it seemed like a South Indian script.'

Meera instantly remembered the photograph that she had stumbled upon on Ranbeer's desk the night she had sneaked into his room. His father somehow resembled a man from South India. 'And you, like me, are sure that Ranbeer does not have any connections from South India...I mean family or close friends?' she asked Kamakshi.

'No. And from what I know he doesn't even remotely know any South Indian language. That's not all...when Ranbeer entered the room and saw me flipping through the photos, he was livid! He reprimanded me strongly for looking at his album without his permission. I was too shocked and offended to even react. But....'

'I know what you mean. In light of his behaviour lately that reaction can well imply that he has some secrets that might be even connected to Gauripradа's disappearance... secrets that are probably not in our interests,' Meera said.

Kamakshi smiled. 'We need to know those secrets. And no better place to search for clues than his own house.'

The other girls nodded.

Delhi was experiencing its first pre-monsoon shower as the train halted at the station. A chauffeur-driven, black Chevrolet Spark was waiting to take them to their destination—Ranbeer's house at Tagore Garden.

'We simply cannot dismiss this,' Arvind reiterated with earnestness.

A clammy breeze was making dinner on the terrace uncomfortable.

'But how are you so sure that Ranbeer is involved?' Meera demanded.

'I am surprised you still don't see the connection. How I wish you are right and I am wrong, but alas!' Arvind closed his eyes and let out a deep sigh.

'How does it not make sense? Why else will the poachers refer to his connections in all the emails?' Maya was quick to counter Meera.

Arvind opened his eyes and said with a baffled expression, 'I have received threats from poachers before, but never anything so cryptic.'

Ranbeer took the email printout from his friend's hand and read it carefully for the second time.

> Stay away from what is not your business. If you don't stick to your boundaries, we shall define them for you. Be careful about who and what you are working against. Be very careful about your connections. You are not just irking us but the higher powers too. They are not willing to spare you and your evil connections. It was our duty to warn you. Choose to ignore at your own peril.

Ranbeer shook his head and said, 'While I do understand that this includes people beyond you, it is unclear that there is a connection to me.'

Arvind repeated what he had said a few minutes back, this time with greater emphasis. 'I would have rubbished this email, the feathers and blood of owls littered around my tent too. But how could I overlook the newspaper clipping that was deliberately folded beneath the boulder all three times? It could have been sheer coincidence only once, but definitely not thrice or even twice.'

He was alluding to a feature article carried in *The Times of India* that elucidated the achievements of Ranbeer. The article had been published on January 29 of the current year across multiple editions. Much to his amazement, after receiving each threat email, the ornithologist had woken up in the morning to find his tent encircled with the blood, nails, feathers and talons of some of the most endangered species of owls. And each time, a clipping of this article had been placed very conspicuously beneath a boulder that lay on the ground close to one of the ropes that was anchoring the tent.

'The third time was scary,' Arvind took out one clipping from a plastic folder. Blood was spattered over it.

Ranbeer examined each of the three clips and noticed something for the first time. 'The editions are different. Interestingly, none of them are the Delhi edition,' he murmured.

'Hmm, one Bangalore edition, one Lucknow and one…' Arvind strained to decipher the edition of the blood-splattered clip. It was definitely not New Delhi as the only two letters visible in the middle of the word that connoted the city were 'a' and 'h'.

Maya cast an inquiring glance towards Meera. The younger woman slowly nodded her head to convey her agreement.

'So, what now?' Meera looked at Arvind.

'Do you think I have any clue about what is going on? I just know that the poachers who are threatening me this time are also threatening Ranbeer. They seem to be unhappy about something that we are doing and I have no clue what it is.'

'You are ignoring the bigger puzzle.' Ranbeer came out of the kitchen with a tray of glasses. 'You and I can count the people who know that we are friends, on the fingers of one hand.'

'The poachers are unhappy with you and me because we are doing something that is meddling with their interest. And that something is obviously connected to the owl.' Arvind closed his eyes and let out a sigh.

The very next moment Arvind sat straight, 'Wait, with your documentary, aren't you going to also expose how occult practitioners are endangering rare birds by using them in savage rituals?'

'Finally, a light at the end of the tunnel,' Meera exclaimed.

Ranbeer was slower to react. 'But we still don't know the way out from this tunnel,' he said and proceeded to light a cigarette.

'Meaning?' the two women chorused together.

With a blank look, Ranbeer reiterated his concern, 'How on earth did the poachers know of my friendship with Arvind? Does this mean that someone was watching us closely at Mashobra?' The memory of the shadow at Rosewood Cottage sent chills down their spines. *'Was it just a regular intruder or did he trespass with the intent of eavesdropping?' they silently wondered.*

'What if this someone is still watching us? We don't know what or who exactly we are up against but...' Maya felt dizzy.

'But we definitely know that we are in danger,' Ranbeer finished for her in his characteristic nonchalance.

It was time to retire for the night.

'Maya, can you come to my room please? Alok had contacted me yesterday. There are some urgent things you need to know.' Arvind's tone told the others that he wanted to talk to Maya in private.

The next morning, Arvind was packing his knapsack. He would be taking the evening train to Lucknow, his hometown. 'I am disappearing for sometime in the interest of my work and your safety,' he informed Ranbeer who entered the bedroom.

'Explain, please.' Ranbeer settled himself on the couch.

'If threats and associated bird killings continue, it is against my work interest. You see, I am responsible for ensuring secrecy for my assignments. Obviously, this time I have failed and it looks like the poachers are monitoring all my activities. Therefore, I am disappearing so that the leadership does not get the opportunity to dismiss me. I will remain undercover till we solve this puzzle and book the offenders.' Arvind's tone was now a lot more emphatic.

'And I presume the "we" here is you and me?' Ranbeer wanted to know.

Arvind nodded and added with a smile, 'I know a senior who can help me unearth the story behind these threats. He commands a lot of clout in the world of conservation. And you, my friend, have to cooperate.'

'How?' Meera had walked into the room and had heard the last part of the conversation.

Arvind looked at Maya as she trailed in. Her fair skin was glistening with sweat and her yellow cotton sari clung to her curves. A love mark on her slender neck narrated what had transpired between the two last night.

'By stalling the documentary work till the puzzle is solved. Ranbeer, you need to apprise me of anything suspicious that you come across from now on.' Arvind insisted.

Ranbeer and Meera realised that they needed to tell Arvind about all the uncanny developments at Banaras.

After hearing everything, Arvind grew thoughtful and then he slowly began, 'So, we are up against a deep, dark plot. I can clearly see a connection between the skull worshippers and Gauriprada's abductors. After all, Sakhat is connected to the skull worshippers and Rustom is the most likely suspect in the abduction. I also feel that there is a deep connection between the poachers and the abductors.'

'How?' The three friends quizzed.

'You have all ignored the fact that the razor knife with Gauriprada's blood stains is etched with the symbol of a mutilated owl.'

'Yes, of course,' Meera shrieked. 'This just settles everything…or maybe unsettles everything,' she almost stammered. 'And how could I forget that my assailant at Shivala Ghat had a knife engraved with a mutilated owl!' Seeing the blank look on Ranbeer's face, she finally recounted the details of that night.

'Arvind, did you, by any chance, overlook anything that could be a vital clue that was left outside your tent?' Ranbeer asked.

Arvind thought hard and shook his head.

Minutes after Arvind's departure, Meera dialled Nick Karmar's number. He picked up at the first ring and said, 'Today at 6 pm. Claridges. Room number 308.' Before Meera could reply, he disconnected.

'I hope our meeting with him does not deepen the puzzle,' Ranbeer said as he revved up the engine of his Chevrolet to head in the direction of the Claridges.

a revelation and some more discoveries

As they walked into his room, Karmar greeted them with a handshake and gestured them to sit on the sofa. 'I guess, you wanted to know about my documentary.' Ranbeer got to the point as soon as he settled himself.

The professor nodded but did not appear sufficiently interested. Ranbeer picked the cue and gave him a brief account of his work.

'So, you know nothing about tantra. You are just capturing some dark rituals to reiterate your message. I must tell you that the practice in the *Shakti Peeths* is very different. I have a responsibility towards the trustees of Kamakhya Temple, who are letting me research on their premises, to maintain secrecy.'

Sensing that Karmar was not particularly inclined to help them, Meera and Ranbeer decided to leave. Just at that moment the intercom buzzed. Karmar answered it and ordered dinner.

'Well, we need to meet someone at CP,' Ranbeer tried to initiate an exit.

'Everything can wait except what I am going to tell you now.' The professor's voice was commanding. Before his guests could react, Karmar added, 'And, would you like some dessert?'

'Caramel custard,' the two replied in unison, wondering at this sudden change.

'Did I tell you about the think tank that is considering me to be a part of its governing body?' Karmar narrowed his eyes and gazed at Meera.

'Yes, and it is fascinating....'

'It is getting too fascinating for my comfort,' the professor interrupted in an angry voice. 'Unknowingly, we were all going to be part of a conspiracy.'

'I am sorry but we don't understand...,' Meera could not contain her curiosity.

'The investors of the think tank made us believe that they are instituting a unique knowledge repository that will facilitate international organisations like the International Cultural Exchange Organisation in policy making and conflict resolution.' Karmar shook his head vigorously.

'Is it not so?' Meera's voice revealed her impatience.

'Hell no!' The professor was agitated now. 'Can you believe that this think tank is being set up with an ulterior motive? The investors instead want access to secret texts that contain rare tantric rituals in a bid to establish their supremacy among the existing tantric cults. I also suspect their motive is to sell these texts to vested interests for a colossal amount. And they had the audacity to trick us all into it.'

Karmar stopped to pat his sweaty brow with a handkerchief. Seeing the flabbergasted expressions of his guests, he took a deep sigh and resumed, 'I guess I have to tell you about the investors before anything else. Otherwise you will never understand the scale of treachery.'

The two visitors were now sitting upright.

'There are three people, the investors, behind this so-called think tank. But only one among them, Venkatesh, interfaces with us.

'Venkatesh is very popular in London's elite circuit and has many flourishing businesses. He is exceptionally knowledgeable and can converse on matters pertaining to culture, politics and history of every existing and extinct civilisation. Well-networked, he is associated with several prestigious cultural organisations and has presented interesting papers at several forums.'

'How did you meet him?' Ranbeer asked.

'I met Venkatesh a couple of years ago when he was delivering a lecture at a seminar organised by the University of Rome. He called me in December to apprise me of this think tank that he wanted to start along with two other investor friends.'

Karmar started fidgeting with his cell phone. 'All of us who have been nominated as potential candidates of this think tank had been approached by Venkatesh. This was not difficult for him since he has a good clout even in academic circles. And we had no reason to doubt the objective and vision of the think tank because Venkatesh is fairly credible and does not have any past history of crime or shady associations. At least, no known records,' he explained.

'Didn't you find it strange that the other two investors never interacted with any of you? That you never saw them nor know their names?' Meera was beginning to feel that despite his lofty academic stature, Karmar was a rather silly man.

'True, we haven't spoken to the other two nor seen their faces. But, at least, we know their names,' Karmar said, sounding offended. 'They are Alex Powell and Vijaylakshmi Iyer.'

'The third investor is a woman? And what do they do, apart from investing in this mysterious think tank? Also, who is this Powell?' Meera shot a volley of questions.

'Powell is from South Africa. And Vijaylakshmi, like Venkatesh, is Indian. All we know about them is that they have British citizenship, and are rich and influential. Well, since we knew Venkatesh, we did not feel the necessity to know anything more about either of them.' Karmar stammered while blurting the last sentence.

The doorbell broke the silence that followed. Karmar opened it to usher in a waiter who was wheeling in a trolley.

Ranbeer cast a glance at his wrist watch. It was nearing 7.45 pm.

'So, how did they trick you?' Ranbeer opened the discussion after the waiter left.

'Well, don't you get it? Obviously, it was not envisaged to be a knowledge repository!' Karmar cupped his forehead.

Meera started shifting impatiently at her end of the couch. 'Yes, we get it. It is meant to be some underworld network and you were all going to be used as mere pawns.' As the last two words escaped her mouth she realised that she might have offended Karmar.

'What she means is...,' Ranbeer struggled to repair the damage.

To his relief, Karmar cracked a smile and said, 'Well, that is precisely the truth... It is actually an underworld network. A secret and ominous one and we were indeed going to be used as pawns.'

After a brief silence, Karmar proceeded, 'The think tank is going to be a secret organisation that will wield control over the world through the might of the occult forces. The investors are interested in our research papers only. These papers will provide greater insight about the occult world. I mean, things that they do not already know and are not available in any public domain.'

'Each research paper will also mention the reference sources. Many powerful practitioners of tantra, voodoo and black magic lead very secret lives. Your papers will reveal the identity of such people. And obviously this will be valuable information for your fake investors.' Meera surmised.

'I am wondering what exactly they will tell you after getting your papers. I mean how on earth will they explain that they are no longer interested in setting up any repository or governing council? I presume, they are obviously not foolish enough to raise suspicion.' Ranbeer's voice resonated sheer excitement.

'You are right, my friend. I guess the tank and its council will be formed nonetheless to camouflage the real intentions.' The next moment, Karmar's eyes lit up and he almost shouted, 'Now, I understand why they promised special powers and privileges to the one who submits the best paper. They are basically going to use him as the biggest pawn. A key responsibility of this member is to ensure that researchers across cultural exchange organisations get easy access to places that are restricted to certain religious bodies. However, the only people who will benefit are Venkatesh, Vijaylakshmi and Alex.'

'Because in this way, they will become privy to many close-guarded secrets of various cult groups,' Ranbeer concluded.

'I guess you are dangerously close,' Karmar replied.

None of them really knew what to say.

After a while, Meera sat upright with a jerk and said, 'Professor Karmar, how on earth did you discover all this?'

'Venkatesh is already busy forging alliances in the occult world. He is approaching some of the most powerful bastions of occult practices and asking them to unite in his mission. . . .'

'He spoke to the tantrics at Kamakhya Temple?' Meera interrupted Karmar.

'He actually did. Spoke while facing them in flesh and blood... Hold on! I am telling you why he did not feel the necessity to disguise himself or communicate through letters or email. He simply took advantage of the anonymity that the occult world maintains from the outside world. Venkatesh understands that the guardians of *Shakti Peeths* and other realms of occult worship are never going to alert the outside world about his nefarious intentions. And, in any case, he did not disclose his real name or identity. It is also a fact that nobody recognises him outside the UK. By communicating through letters or email he could not have concealed his real identity so completely. I mean, he was wise enough to understand that his fictitious account or address might not have been foolproof.'

When Karmar noticed Meera and Ranbeer's confused looks, he added, 'And I am sure that this person is Venkatesh, my investor, because no other man in the world has a right arm that is fully covered by tattoos of the female genitals.'

The reaction was unexpected. Ranbeer started laughing heartily. Meera had not heard this laughter in the last two months. It was contagious and within seconds the other two people in the room joined in.

'Oh God! This man is hilarious. He wants to rule over the world but can't rise above his obsession for sex.' Tears were now streaming down Ranbeer's cheeks.

It took almost twenty minutes for the laughter to subside. 'And he showed the tattoos to Gautam Sharma?' Meera inquired.

'He didn't actually exhibit them if that is what you mean.' Karmar's tone was friendlier. 'Actually, while he was in Kamakhya Temple to meet Gautam, his right shirt sleeve caught on a nail and tore. Venkatesh always wears full-sleeved shirts to hide the tattoos. And now, young lady,

I too have a question for you,' Karmar abruptly paused. 'You seem to be very good with names. How do you always remember Gautam Sharma?'

Meera opened her mouth to answer when Ranbeer nudged her and said almost instantly, 'We will tell you everything, after you tell us one simple thing. Why have you chosen to tell us everything? I see absolutely no reason why we should know all this.'

Beads of sweat were erupting on Karmar's forehead. 'This is going to be the last revelation of the evening. Both Gautam and I feel that Venkatesh is, in fact, Laal Singh.'

'What? Why?' Both the friends almost shouted.

'There is a pattern to prove this. See, there are congregations of occult worship. And Venkatesh has approached about a dozen of them. Congregations that have rejected his offer have found pelvic bones planted at or near their sites of worship,' Karmar said.

'This is farfetched yet convincing. I just don't know what to say. And even if Venkatesh is Laal Singh, what bearing does it have on us?' Ranbeer said, wearily.

'Because Gautam tells me that Laal Singh is now not just spreading the menace of the pelvic bones. He is doing a few more things that are telling the occult fraternity that he can be dangerous if he faces dissent. Since you are filming the dark realm, you like all of us will do good to exercise some caution.'

'Well, now we really need to take your leave,' was Ranbeer's abrupt reaction.

'Not without you telling me why this young lady always remembers Gautam's name,' Karmar chuckled.

Ranbeer and Meera exchanged a long glance. It would be wise to tell Karmar about Gauripradа's abduction.

Karmar heard them intently and looked surprised when they mentioned that the name of the mysterious caller in Gauripradа's call records was Gautam Sharma.

'So, I was right. We somehow need to collaborate,' he remarked after Ranbeer had finished his narration.

Ranbeer nodded in agreement and after a firm handshake, said, 'It was nice of you to share so much. I hope that you have understood that the nature of my requirements while shooting in the hills of Kamakhya Temple is purely creative.'

Through a side glance, Meera tried to gauge his expression as he uttered the last sentence.

'Yes, I have. And I suggest you aim to reach there by 20th June. I will be there in time for the *Ambubachi Mela*, if not earlier. For all you know, we may have a very exciting time. Laal Singh might be there...in disguise.'

Meera received a message from Maya on her way back after meeting Karmar. '*I managed to find the photo album. It was under the mattress on his bed! You won't believe this but I COULD decipher the script—it is Kannada.*' A second message from her read: '*And you need to know something that Kamakshi has just discovered in Banaras.*'

'There is some mystery about our friend...but for the life of me I can't figure out what exactly it is,' Meera whispered to Maya that night while they were sitting together on the terrace.

'Me neither. I have spoken to Kamakshi and asked her if we can take a chance and casually ask Ranbeer about his childhood and early life. She was vehemently dismissive.'

'Going by her experience with the album, I won't counter her. And what did she discover?'

'That Vividha Devi of Erotic Salvation is none other than Vasanthi *Amma*!'

'Really?' Meera looked amused.

'Well, a few days back, Kamakshi and I were having lunch at a restaurant in Godowlia Chowk. We had been noticing a blonde woman who was eating alone. She was was constantly fidgeting with her *jhola.* After finishing her meal she cleared her bill and moved to the washing area. Since she did not reappear for a long time we presumed that she was in the toilet. We remembered her only when we had cleared our bill for it was then that we spotted her green *jhola* on her empty chair. The woman was nowhere in sight and the manager confirmed that she had just left,' Maya said.

'Then?' Meera prodded.

'We rushed out in the hope of spotting her so that we could hand over her bag. And....'

'I think this happened the very day when I was going to meet Bharadwaj. I saw you but did not stop as I was in a hurry.'

Maya nodded. 'We saw her walking in the direction of the road that leads to Lahori Tola and trailed her...initially she was close enough to hear us if we shouted out to her, which we did, but the strange thing is that although she even looked back a couple of times and saw us with her bag, she did not stop. In fact, she hastened her pace. We understood something was not right and kept trailing her out of sheer curiosity. And guess where she finally stopped?'

'Where?'

'She entered the compound of the dilapidated temple... the same temple where we filmed Vividha Devi.'

'And, obviously, you didn't trail her anymore.' Meera's eyes were wide with amazement.

'Exactly. And after we got home we scanned the contents of her *jhola*. There was only a wallet with a few currency notes, a scarf and some tiny bottles of scented liquid.'

'This woman was obviously a disciple of Vividha Devi, which, of course, is not a spectacular discovery. But why didn't you tell me this before?' Meera asked.

'Simply because it was not a spectacular discovery... But now Kamakshi has discovered that Vividha is none other than Vasanthi *Amma*. Also, the *jhola* had a hidden pocket where we found two photographs—one of brass idols of the various incarnations of the Mother Goddess mounted on a shrine before a red curtain....'

'The very same place where Kamakshi had gone to meet Vasanthi...but this picture could be of some other exactly similar place too,' Meera excitedly interrupted her friend.

'Well, the second photograph confirmed it as the very same place because that was a photograph of the room in which she was molested. She says that all the details of the room have been captured clearly—the deep blue statue of Goddess Tara and all the paraphernalia, besides Kamakshi says she cannot mistake that room for the rest of her life,' Maya explained.

For a long while only the buzz of mosquitoes was audible.

'Oh my God! That meal voucher you retrieved from the ransacked library....'

Maya let out a low whistle and clutched Meera's arm. 'It skipped my mind totally...the lettering on that meal voucher is Kannada!'

Both the girls started trembling.

'Does it mean Ranbeer ransacked the library?' Both the girls asked aloud at the same time.

The next morning, they would be returning to Banaras and decided to plan further when Kamakshi could join them.

'If Karmar has not exaggerated anything, we are intruding into dangerous territory with Ranbeer's documentary,' Kamakshi sighed after they narrated everything that they had heard from Arvind and Karmar.

Ranbeer was rolling a joint and looked unfazed.

Meera's phone started ringing loudly.

'Hello Suchit. We were about to...' She listened for a good two minutes without interrupting. 'Are you very sure this is connected to the abduction?' she quizzed in an excited pitch. 'I'll meet you in half an hour,' she said before disconnecting.

'Rustom is back. And he might have a hand in Gauripradas's abduction. Suchit has overhead Rustom's phone conversation with somebody day before yesterday. And he thinks that we should know about it immediately.' Meera said.

'We are coming with you,' Kamakshi said and Maya nodded.

Ranbeer let out a yawn and said, 'I prefer to catch up on some sleep.'

'So, you mean to say that they have not abducted Gauripradas to kill him?' Meera repeated for the fourth time.

Suchit had just told them everything that he had overheard while he was passing his twin brother's shop in the late evening hours.

'They will never kill him until they get to some text through him. I mean that was what Rustom was repeating.'

'Obviously this is some extraordinary text…maybe the text that Limar Singh has come to discover…then why was Gauripradа abducted and not Limar Singh?' Kamakshi wondered.

'Gauripradа probably has a clue to this text. Rustom was constantly arguing with the person at the other end that if they killed the man they would lose a valuable lead. The other person was probably furious with his insistence and I could hear him raising his voice. Strangely, it sounded female. Rustom finally pacified her by saying that they would grill the man and get the details,' Suchit said.

'And, you are also saying that our man had shifted the conversation to some Laal Singh?' This time it was Maya.

'Yes, he said that Laal Singh was their real worry. Apparently, Laal Singh was edging close to the text and it was very likely that he would be reaching it before them. I think this angered the woman even more. She must have hurled abuses at Rustom for the bugger did not speak for long. He finally replied in a meek voice that he was doing his best to find out who exactly Laal Singh was and what his intentions were.'

'And, you also said that he spoke about some knife that he had dropped?' Meera prodded.

Suchit nodded.

'This is obviously the knife that Rustom had dropped near the motorboat. He knows that it could be evidence against him…or all of them.' Meera thought to herself. She wasn't sure if she should share this thought with Suchit yet.

'I think before disconnecting the call, the woman must have given two instructions to Rustom—finding the knife and the clue to the text. Because he kept assuring her that he would update her on both the things,' Suchit finished.

'Are you sure there is nothing that you have missed?' Kamakshi asked.

Suchit strained his memory. 'Well, Rustom started referring to some girl. He was repeatedly saying that she had not found the knife as she had been stalled in Delhi when the investigations were fresh.'

'This explains why I got that message in Delhi,' Meera was beginning to feel that at least some pieces of the puzzle were starting to fall into place.

Maya and Kamakshi exchanged knowing glances.

'And Suchit has already confirmed that one of the two numbers that had delivered those anonymous messages in Delhi belonged to Sakhat. But Sakhat was right here in Banaras when I had that experience with the abaya-clad woman…or man. He obviously could not have been in two places at the same time,' Meera wondered with a pounding heart.

Before anyone could say anything, Suchit abruptly got up from the steps of Rana Mahal Ghat where they had been talking.

'I have to meet someone,' he announced with a sense of exaggerated self-importance.

Meera caught his hand and said, 'Suchit, you really have been a big help. I was just wondering if you would do us one last favour.'

'I can do everything for you, Madam*ji*,' Suchit looked straight into her eyes without blinking.

'Well then, Suchit, be a sweetheart and find out who owns these two numbers.' Meera quickly jotted the other number from which she had received the second message in Delhi along with the number from which she and Ranbeer had received threats on a piece of paper.

Without even looking at the numbers Suchit assured that he would find out the details within two days. 'The recharge shop owner is my friend.' He shouted as he ran up the stairs.

'Both these numbers belong to Sakhat,' Suchit informed over the phone the next afternoon.

'Are you absolutely sure?' Meera excitedly questioned. *'This means that Sakhat does have a major connection to that abaya-clad informer. And now it is clear that it was Sakhat who was threatening us while we were shooting the documentary. He must have assisted Rustom in the abduction too,' she silently concluded.*

'Yes. The shop owner has a graphic memory. Besides, he maintains a logbook for the SIM cards that he sells with all the details of the customers.' Suchit paused. Referring to the number that had delivered the threats, he continued, 'He says that he especially remembers this number because the balance had not got credited instantly. Apparently, after Sakhat had left his shop, he had called him at least six times to ask why.'

'Does he also remember when this happened?'

Suchit instantly dialled his friend to find out. He then called Meera to inform that this was in the first week of April, the *Amavasya* evening to be precise. And I did not have to inquire about the other number because I instantly recognised it. Remember, you had inquired about a number that I had identified as Sakhat's and told you he has another similar number. Well, this is the one.'

The mention of *Amavasya* instantly triggered memories of shooting *shav* sadhana rituals and Vividha Devi's insane rituals, and corroborated Meera's suspicions about Sakhat. There was a long silence at her end.

'Madam*ji*, are you there?' Suchit asked.

'Aah, yes. Actually, I was just remembering something. You had mentioned that Sakhat was supposed to accompany Rustom at the time he had departed on that motorboat. But....'

Sensing yet another silence, Suchit interrupted, 'Yes, but he could not accompany him. Actually, Sakhat too had to go out of town in connection with some work concerning his shop. He had travelled to some place by road but I don't know where.'

'Well, it was Delhi of course!' Meera's heart was pounding with glee.

'Suchit, you don't know how fabulously you have helped us. Thank you and I will see you soon,' with that Meera disconnected the call.

As she relayed the telephone conversation to her friends in the evening, Maya jested, 'Meera, Suchit surely has a crush on you. He is offering all this information with the singular intention of pleasing you, no questions asked. By now, he has understood that Gauriprada was helping us with the documentary and that his abduction has crippled us.'

'I guess, we are just lucky, especially because Suchit is not on good terms with Sakhat and Rustom,' Meera concluded.

on the trail of laal singh

Two weeks of June were over and the first monsoon showers had arrived in Banaras. Ranbeer closed his eyes to enjoy the sound of the torrential shower.

When Meera joined him, he said, 'We are going on Laal Singh's trail. And this shall lead us to everything—why Rustom abducted Gauriprada, who his accomplices are and why they are so keen about finding this mysterious text.'

'You feel that Laal Singh is the nexus between everything?' Meera asked.

'Laal Singh is linked to everything. See, we now know that Rustom and his accomplices are behind Gauriprada's disappearance. They abducted him not just because he was involved with this documentary but because he has a valuable clue to some text. And now they are in competition with this mysterious Laal Singh to discover this text. That is what Suchit told you, right?'

'Yes. But there are two big pieces of the puzzle that don't quite fit, two pieces that we are forgetting.'

'I think I know one of them. Karmar told us that he suspects that Venkatesh is posing as Laal Singh. So I guess you are wondering what exactly could be the connection between the think tank and petty goons like Sakhat and Rustom? I mean there can be no grounds for any competition or conflict!'

Meera took a while to answer. 'I am unable to understand why all these people are at loggerheads with Limar Singh.'

'Why do you think they are at loggerheads in the first place?'

'You do realise that Limar Singh too has come to Banaras in quest of some sacred text?'

'Well, our documentary can be connected to the secret text too. After all, we are filming occult practices. And Baccha told you that Limar Singh is looking for a text written by some powerful Aghori tantric.'

Meera nodded and wondered why Ranbeer was still being so secretive about the fact that he himself had told Baccha that the tantric who had authored this text had lived a mysterious life.

'And, what is that second part of the puzzle?' Ranbeer quizzed.

'Arvind is sure that there is some connection between the death threats that he has been receiving and the challenges that we are facing. I just don't see how. I really think he is just stretching an imaginary connection.'

'But that news clip? Couldn't have been so much of a coincidence, right? I fail to understand why you are so completely dismissive about a connection.'

'Tell me why a high profile secret network that wants to rule the world by dint of the dark occult forces will have anything to do with an ornithologist? And, what possible connection could Arvind have with Rustom or Sakhat?' Meera was emphatic.

Scratching his forehead, Ranbeer finally said, 'We cannot jump to any hasty conclusions. Things will start getting clearer once we embark on the trail of Laal Singh.'

'And what is our starting point?'

'*Ambubachi Mela* in Guwahati. We have to be there before the 20th.'

It was 18th June 2013 and the Guwahati railway station was buzzing with people. They hailed a cab outside the station and headed in the direction of the guesthouse near Nilachal Hills.

'Can we request for an extension of our bookings, if the need arises?' Ranbeer had asked his travel agent a couple of days ago. Somehow he had a feeling that they would have to. The agent had replied in the positive.

The receptionist, a mild-looking man in his early thirties, greeted them and ushered them to their respective rooms. 'I presume you are the guests of the esteemed Temple Trust. Gautam Sharma has asked me to tell you that he will come only at 8 pm to take you to the temple,' he informed in broken Hindi.

At 7.45 pm, Gautam Sharma arrived. He was a dignified-looking man—fair, tall and lean. 'Karmar told me about you, Sir.' He took Ranbeer's hand and shook it.

The four friends were surprised at his command over the English language. 'I have done my PhD in Sanskrit from Gauhati University. In my boyhood, I had the privilege of being tutored by a teacher who was fluent in English and was particularly impeccable in grammar, unlike most teachers these days.'

They drove to the temple premises in a black Scorpio that belonged to the Temple Trust. Within ten minutes, the car crossed the winding route that led to Kamakhya Temple. Despite the all-enveloping darkness interspersed partially by moon rays, the friends could spot human silhouettes throughout their ride. They instantly knew that these were ascetics who were crouching among thickets and bushes, smoking heady concoctions of opium and other psychoactive drugs.

The car finally screeched to a halt in the expansive parking area. After climbing a flight of steps, flanked by small shops, they reached the actual temple grounds. From here they could also see the bottom of the Nilachal Hills. Lights illuminating the city of Guwahati formed a spectacular canopy. A black expanse was visible in the distance that they recognised as the mighty Brahmaputra.

None of them had exchanged a word ever since they had started their car journey.

Kamakshi broke the silence. 'Gautam*ji*, where are we going?'

The man smiled and said, 'Madam, we are going to Kashinath Goswami*ji*'s house. His wife has cooked dinner for all of us. She cooks excellent mutton curry. And you will love her preparation of rice in sweetened milk.'

'I didn't know Brahmins of Assam ate non-vegetarian.' Ranbeer blurted in surprise.

'Actually, we have a history and origin that is quite unique. We shall talk about it one of these days if time permits, although I doubt it very much. We have so many things to discuss and sort right now. Laal Singh for one...' He uttered the last sentence almost in a whisper.

'Has Karmar already arrived? He was unsure about his exact travel plans.' Meera asked.

'He reaches tomorrow morning. Actually, he had to rush to Kuvempu University in Shimoga urgently. The Vice Chancellor is an old friend of Karmar's and is apparently facing some grave trouble.'

They had now moved away from the main temple grounds and were heading towards the section of the complex that had the residences of all the priests. Kashinath Goswami's house stood out for it was bigger and freshly painted.

A rather harsh sounding voice greeted Gautam as he started climbing the half dozen steps that led to the verandah. Since the man had spoken in Assamese, none of the others could comprehend anything.

After what seemed like a good two minutes, a pot-bellied priest, presumably in his late-sixties appeared. He was wearing a crisp, white cotton lungi and only a sacred thread hung across his bare, hairy chest. He gestured them to follow him inside the house.

Unlike the younger priest, Kashinath was not as fluent in English but he managed to come straight to the point.

'So, you are making a documentary on tantra and tantrics? And you are exposing the fraud ones?' He looked at Ranbeer and inquired.

'That's right. And I shall be indebted to you if I can get your permission to film in the vicinity of the temple and Nilachal Hills. Your good friend, Karmar, tells me that you know everything, the truth behind all the mythological legends.'

Kashinath closed his eyes and thought for a while before answering, 'And you are not interested in offering your homage to the diety? After *Ambubachi*? It is supposed to be a very auspicious time.'

'Yes, we would love to. But we are in a bit of a hurry to return to Banaras. Karmar must have told you that our friend has been abducted. While we do know who the kidnapper is, we do not have any evidence. So we are hoping that we gather evidence here and return.'

Kashinath looked distracted and then he said, 'Laal Singh is a criminal. In fact, he is a murderer; a murderer and a thief. And we have to stop him. I can help you if you agree to help me.' It seemed like he had not understood anything.

Seeing the confused looks, Gautam took charge. 'What he means is that we are willing to help you with the filming of your documentary, and if that helps you find your abducted friend, all the better. However, we also expect you to do something that will benefit us as well. Laal Singh is on a dangerous mission. What exactly, we do not know. But he is determined and even ready to kill people who are getting in his way. So it is critical that we nab him. Since your work will expose the nefarious ways of the impostors in the occult realm. . .we are just thinking that probably he is starting to see you as a massive threat. We were hoping to orchestrate a situation to lure him using you as bait.'

'So that Laal Singh kills me and my friends?' Ranbeer was agitated.

Kashinath's wife appeared at that instant to usher the guests to the dining area.

'Not at all, let me explain properly and then, of course, it is entirely your decision,' Gautam urged.

Ranbeer agreed and listened to Gautam's plans with much apprehension.

'So you are suggesting that I should be filming at Bhootnath Muktidham after midnight where a couple of *chandaals* from the cemetery will pose as tantrics while you and several others from the Temple Trust will remain undercover nearby to keep vigil.' Ranbeer was working out Gautam and Kashinath's plot to trap Laal Singh.

Gautam smiled. 'In fact, we have already spread rumours among the *Ambubachi* pilgrims that a filmmaker has come to Guwahati to make a documentary on tantrics. And our plan is working.'

'You mean people believe the rumour?' Maya asked.

The three girls had been listening to everything intently.

'The priests are telling me that people and ascetics are inquiring about this man who has been funded by the International Documentary Association to shoot undercover and produce a documentary on how tantra is practiced at the sacred *Shakti Peeths*. To make it more convincing, our priests are telling them that the documentary will exert pressure on the Indian judicial system to formulate laws that will ban tantra. They are also telling people that the Temple Trust is livid at this man's audacity as his work will threaten the sanctity of the *Shakti Peeths*.'

'I must say I never felt so important all my life,' Ranbeer said, almost sarcastically. 'But how are you so sure that this Laal Singh will reach Bhootnath cremation ground right at the stroke of midnight, when we are enacting our crazy plot?'

'Because rumours are also floating that the first leg of the documentary will be shot in the cemetery on the night of June 20,' Kashinath said.

'And how on earth are you so sure that Laal Singh is in Kamakhya now?'

'I am very sure he is here, hiding among the throngs of ascetics.' Gautam's tone turned more serious.

'Why do you say that?' Meera and Kamakshi demanded.

Gautam and Kashinath exchanged a long glance. 'Well, because this is the only time in the year when he has a chance to access our sacred scriptures, although these are very closely guarded, without getting caught or raising suspicion. Among the thousands of ascetics who visit during this time, it will be impossible for us to keep a tab on the activities and movements of each ascetic among the thousands who visit during this time. As you must have guessed, many ancient scriptures of tantric rituals are right here at Kamakhya Dham,' the head priest explained.

'But I don't understand why you feel he would want to steal your texts?' Maya asked.

Ranbeer noticed that Kashinath had arched his bushy eyebrows and was looking straight at him. 'You obviously know that Laal Singh has been mutilating bodies of already dead women and floating them on rivers? Rivers close to secret sites of tantric worship?'

'We only knew of pelvic bones…' Meera was aghast.

'Well, he stole them from the cremation sites inhabited by Aghori tantrics who eat human flesh. He has also been rummaging these sites for the female pelvic skeletons. He was at a cremation site in Rajrappa during one of his adventures. The *chandaals* had probably caught and questioned him. And since he could not give any explanation without revealing his secret motives he actually killed them in cold blood.' There was stoic silence in the room as Kashinath finished.

'So?' Ranbeer, like Maya, was unable to see the connection that Kashinath insisted upon.

Kashinath took a deep sigh. 'You might know that during the British rule there was outrage against tantra. It is rumoured that the most powerful tantrics had then buried their ritual texts in two cremation grounds to save them from getting confiscated and destroyed by the imperial rulers. There are eleven such texts. This secret locations are known to only the head priests of three *Shakti Peeths*—Kamakhya, Dhumavati and Chhinnamasta. The strange thing is that Laal Singh is rummaging around in those very grounds.'

Kamakshi let out a whistle. 'So Laal Singh meant business and was not just having fun with the pelvic bones.' She regretted her mirth that very moment when she saw the disapproving faces of the priests.

'He has also broken into the house of the head priest at the Dhumavati Temple and searched his place for books and scriptures. At the Chhinnamasta Temple complex, he tried to break the door that leads to a tunnel. Some people say that this tunnel leads to a cremation ground and that an ascetic who devoted his life to Chhinnamasta Devi hid a scripture there that he had written in his own blood,' Gautam said.

'And obviously he is going to be targeting Kamakhya this time,' Maya said.

Ranbeer scratched his head thoughtfully and said, 'I still don't understand two things. First, how have we assumed that Laal Singh has not already found those scriptures? And second, you just said that the names of the two cremation grounds are known to only the head priests of these three *Shakti Peeths*. So how did Laal Singh come to know about them?'

'Well, the occult world already knew that the most sacred and ancient ritual texts were buried in two cremation grounds. Of course, except the three head priests, none knew which two grounds. However, there was a fear that some semi-literate or evil practitioner of tantra might eventually unearth the texts and misuse the knowledge. Today what they had feared has happened. Laal Singh is scouting for them desperately. Fortunately, the scriptures were secretly relocated to Kamakhya Temple from the cremation grounds near the Chhinnamasta Temple. They were brought here by Kashinath's father thirty years ago with the knowledge and consent of the other two head priests,' Gautam explained.

'Where are they hidden?' Kamakshi asked.

Gautam and Kashinath exchanged another long glance.

Finally, Kashinath said, 'Only the two of us know about this place. Of course, we cannot divulge this information to anyone—not even to people we wholeheartedly trust. We can only tell you that they have been hidden very carefully in a place where the thief is least likely to rummage in.'

'And coming to your second question, just like you, we are equally clueless about how Laal Singh came to know this secret. We are eager to ask him when we meet him.'

'Did Karmar know about the names of these cremation grounds?' Maya asked.

There was an awkward silence, the longest in the entire evening.

'Yes, he does know but only after we told him everything, after the menace of Laal Singh started,' Gautam replied.

'Well, I think we should now take your leave. We are honoured that you have trusted us so much,' Ranbeer smiled and prepared to leave.

'So, will you help us now?' Both the priests inquired at the same time.

'Yes, not because we suspect or rather know that Laal Singh somehow holds the answer to our friend's abduction, but because your mission of unmasking Laal Singh is noble. I am beginning to understand that tantra is not what I thought it to be when I started my documentary. It has a profound sanctity when practiced by people who have dedicated their lives to it,' Ranbeer's tone somehow clashed with his words.

'May Maa Kamakhya resolve all your obstacles and always keep you in her infinite grace,' Kashinath said in a relieved tone. 'Before you depart from Kamakhya Dham, we shall take you to a cave where *Chakra* sadhana, one of the most sacred rites of tantra is performed by yogis and yoginis where they seek liberation through physical union.'

'Wonderful! So I will meet you here tomorrow at 10 pm to plan our exact strategy and then proceed to Bhootnath Muktidham?' Ranbeer asked with a twinkle in his eyes.

Both the priests nodded in the affirmative.

After relishing a traditional Assamese breakfast, the three women decided to unearth the truth behind House 501 in the Railway Colony. Ranbeer had decided to stay back as he had to meet Gautam to take notes on *Chakra* sadhana.

However, the girls' mission was thoroughly disappointing as the lone old woman in that address was uncommunative and there were no further clues.

'There is nothing that we can conclude about House 501. It continues to be a mystery,' sighed Meera after coming back.

'Hmm... It is best to focus on our drama tonight at Bhootnath crematorium. Now I am desperately hoping that we nab this Laal Singh. This is just getting endless,' Ranbeer finished with an exasperated sigh.

Just then his phone rang and he answered, 'Yes, Gautam we are going to be there on time. And you need not send the car. We will...what?'

Ranbeer promptly put the call on speaker, so that everyone could hear Gautam, 'We are cancelling our plans. It's absolutely certain that our friend Laal Singh is in Shimoga now. Come over. We will discuss everything over dinner.'

'I don't think that we are on the right track. I mean, if he is not here, there is absolutely no guarantee that we find the man at Shimoga. It could be another false alarm.' Ranbeer said in an exhausted voice.

'I completely understand how frustrating this has been for you. But I promise Shimoga will be worth it. Please come by 6.30 pm. You have much to hear and plan ahead. With *Ambubachi* almost here, neither I nor Kashinath can leave the temple premises. So, we are depending on you and your friends for a lot of things. I am sending the car as the clouds are portending heavy rain.' Gautam had left no scope for debate or deliberation.

about earth energies

Raindrops lashed on the black Scorpio as it reached the foot of the Nilachal Hills. Everybody had been confident that at least a few answers would surface at the Bhootnath crematorium. But the conversation with Gautam Sharma a couple of hours back had dashed all hopes.

'You look tired, my friend. Have some strong Assam tea, you will need it to keep awake,' Gautam put a comforting arm around Ranbeer's shoulder, after he had settled himself on an armchair in Kashinath's house.

Ranbeer managed a nod while Gautam gestured to the older priest to start speaking. 'Karmar was supposed to reach Kamakhya Dham today, but he got stuck at Shimoga as his friend, the Vice Chancellor of Kuvempu University, is facing some trouble. Turns out, it is no ordinary trouble. Now, Professor Panicker is an acknowledged authority on various matters pertaining to our ancient culture and traditions.' Kashinath paused as a woman clad in a *mekhala chador* entered with a tray of mugs.

'Professor Panicker is also a geomancer,' the priest resumed.

'Didn't know there were any geomancers in India,' Meera observed.

'There aren't too many people in the world who know this subject. But India too has a few geomancers and Panicker is an authority on it.'

'Anyone care to enlighten me?' Ranbeer said in an irritated voice.

'Geomancers are also called dowsers. They study the energy fields of the earth. I mean, they ascertain whether a particular area has positive or negative energy. Geomancers also heal through earth energies,' Gautam explained.

'And how is Panicker's ability to study energy fields got anything to do with Laal Singh?' Kamakshi quipped.

Gautam let out a loud sigh. 'I now understand why our mission of unmasking him is getting so complicated... because this man loves riddles. His actions are misleading and do not reveal his real intentions. It no longer seems that he is after the ritual texts hidden here. Else why will he be in Shimoga instead of Kamakhya?'

Kashinath explained, 'About five years ago, Panicker was commissioned for a research assignment by the Ministry of Culture. He had to identify spots of exceptionally strong energy fields in the Indian subcontinent. This was intended to discover sites of worship of the Harappan, Mohenjo-Daro and Indus Valley civilisations. His findings were compiled in a 150-page book. Because the findings were highly confidential, this book had only two prints. One is in the custody of the government and the other was in the custody of Panicker. And now Panicker has lost his copy. It was stolen a week back.'

'Did that book mention anything about ancient *Shakti Peeths*, places of occult worship?' Meera asked, excitedly.

'You need to be a detective,' Gautam was genuinely impressed.

'Too bad we are still unable to unmask Laal Singh despite an Interpol agent in our team!' Ranbeer jested for the first time in the evening.

'This book also reveals the sites and caves in which some important symbols associated with our mythological beliefs could be buried,' Gautam enlightened.

'I guess Laal Singh is the only suspect. He might have thought that this book will help him trace the missing ritual texts,' Maya said.

'Well...he is not the only suspect. There is another man who can be guilty.' Gautam's answer was unexpected.

'Who?' Kamakshi prodded immediately.

'A couple of years ago, Sankalp Nair, a person of Indian origin from Nigeria had done an extensive study on geopathic stress under the guidance of Panicker. In fact, he had been referred to Panicker by Karmar himself.'

'And Panicker had told him about his book?' Meera asked.

'Not really. But he was aware of the fact that Panicker had authored something on energy fields. And the surprising thing is that this book was stolen from his personal locker in the university that can be opened through a specific number combination only.'

'Don't you think it would have been impossible for Nair to know this combination?'

'Karmar says that it is possible that Nair came to know about this number combination as he was constantly with Panicker for nearly three weeks. And Panicker is not a very careful man.'

'So, the thief could be either Laal Singh or Sankalp Nair? Which means we are going on yet another wild goose chase! And the worst part is that we don't even have a clue where to start the chase at Shimoga.' Kamakshi's voice was crestfallen.

'This time, it is not so hopeless. Panicker's book has a section that outlines the high power spots where these ancient mystic symbols are probably buried. Incidentally, he found that three spots emitted an exceptionally high frequency of energy. When he investigated further he found something interesting. Unlike the other spots that are radiating energy from metals, these spots are radiating energy from paper. This means that some incredibly valuable papers are hidden here. And our Laal Singh probably is searching for one of these papers. Incidentally, he has already rummaged at one of the three sites.' And all these sites are near Shimoga.' Gautam looked almost exhausted after the explanation.

'What could he be searching? Maybe ancient India's most powerful ritual text on tantra or something like a route map outlining its exact location.' Meera spoke almost to herself and startled the two priests.

She narrated all that she had heard about Limar Singh. The priests looked more solemn as she finished.

'So, there is more to this Laal Singh other than his disguise as Venkatesh and he is probably not operating alone. He is indeed orchestrating his designs very stealthily and strategically,' Gautam said.

'You think Limar Singh is probably helping Venkatesh or Laal Singh in his mission? Or maybe Venkatesh is not Laal Singh. Maybe Laal Singh is Limar Singh after all. Actually, when I heard Baccha's account it did kind of strike me as strange that despite his psychic powers Limar Singh was still searching for the text,' said Meera.

'Every time we draw a conclusion things get murkier. I have spoken to Karmar at length. Ranbeer, he will call you tonight. You will reach Shimoga in a couple of days and along with Karmar and Panicker keep a close vigil at the other two sites where the route map to the text can be hidden.' Gautam was assertive.

'How are you so sure that Laal Singh has not found what he was looking for in the place that he had rummaged in?' Ranbeer asked.

'He had rummaged in a dilapidated Kali Temple in the heart of Shimoga. This temple is five hundred years old. On the rock wall behind the statue of the Goddess is a door. Nobody knows about this door except the priest and his forefathers. I mean nobody knew about it until Laal Singh broke into it. It opens into a hollow space that contains the ritual texts. And none of these were stolen. This morning when the priest entered the temple he found that the position of the idol had shifted and the door was ajar. The thief had thoroughly searched the space and strewn the texts across the floor.'

'How did Karmar and Panicker come to know about this incident?' Maya asked.

'Shimoga is a small town. Everybody comes to know such things,' Gautam replied. The look on his face conveyed that he was beginning to get anxious and impatient in their mission of nabbing Laal Singh.

the twelfth ritual text

The rain had stopped and the group prepared to leave anticipating their onward travel to Shimoga soon.

As they were leaving, Meera turned and asked, 'Wait, I remembered that you had said that there are eleven ritual texts hidden here. Usually things like these are twelve or some even number. Eleven is kind of odd, I felt.'

'Not that we did not find it strange too. But there were always eleven of these texts. I mean from the time that we knew that our forefathers had buried them,' Kashinath replied with a confused expression.

'Okay,' Meera smiled and the four friends stepped out of the front door.

Just as they were beginning to climb down the verandah steps, Gautam shouted, 'It was originally twelve and I think, I am sure about it now.'

'What? What makes you say that?' Maya asked.

'Your story of Limar Singh. He might be a fraud but there is definitely some truth about his quest for the sacred text. It makes complete sense…that a twelfth ritual text exists…the most sacred and powerful one that was hidden separately and remained undiscovered…that even the guardians of the *Shakti Peeths* did not know about. Well, maybe one of them just knew.' Gautam sounded like an excited boy.

Meera retraced her steps and said, 'I am not going back until you tell me why you feel that somebody just knew about this.'

'I just remembered that Sharath Hegde, the head priest of Dhumavati Temple, had hinted that there are twelve texts.

This was some years ago and I was not too interested in speculating on his hint at that time. But I do remember that he had also said something else that had left me confused. One night, when he was barely twelve years old, Sharath Hegde had overheard a conversation between his father and uncle in a closed room. He heard his uncle mention "the twelve most sacred texts of *Agama shastra*". He stepped closer to the door in the hope of hearing more but couldn't hear much except his uncle saying that if the tragedy had not happened he would have become an accomplished tantric.'

'Your friend never cared to find out from his uncle later about what the tragedy was?' Maya asked.

'Well, he hadn't till the time he had told me about this incident.'

'All I can say is that it won't hurt to learn more about the tragedy that his uncle was alluding to,' Meera remarked.

Ranbeer, who had been listening to everything exclaimed, 'You think we shall discover anything of consequence from that tragedy? Ridiculous!'

Everybody was taken aback by Ranbeer's reaction. He looked very agitated and his fingers were trembling slightly. He ignored the quizzical expressions and started walking towards the car.

'Why is he acting so strangely? He is almost being defensive,' Meera started mulling. All her suspicions about Ranbeer started racing through her mind again.

Meanwhile, Gautam was alternating his gaze between Meera and Ranbeer. Finally, he nodded in Meera's direction with an expression that conveyed how he was equally surprised at Ranbeer's reaction.

Nobody could say anything for the next few minutes.

After a while Ranbeer walked back towards them, franatically swatting at mosquitoes with raised arms.

He lifted a portion of his half-sleeved shirt on his left arm to scratch himself. 'These insects are a menace,' he blurted.

Ranbeer's exposed arm revealed an armlet, an elaborately carved one that everyone noticed.

'Hey, that is a beauty... What exactly...' Maya was silenced by Meera's admonishing glance.

'The night is beautiful, Maya, but we need to leave now,' she blurted with an awkward smile at Ranbeer.

He had straightened his sleeve and was now looking at everyone with an inscrutable expression.

The humid air was beginning to feel heavy.

As they were exiting from the main door, Meera and Gautam exchanged a final, meaningful glance.

'Kamakhya Devi has been very kind in giving us insights. At least, one thing is clear as these raindrops that are falling from the heavens,' Ranbeer told the three women as they stood in their guesthouse balcony with outstretched palms the next morning. 'Laal Singh is scouting for a missing sacred text. Maybe, the very text that Limar Singh has come to Banaras for. And now we have to only find Laal Singh.'

'You mean to say that he is not interested in the other eleven texts? And that he was rummaging in the burial grounds just to find the twelfth text?' Maya raised her voice.

Ranbeer nodded vigorously.

'While we are helping Kashinath and Gautam to unmask Laal Singh, I also do hope that we fulfill our own mission. Finding Gauripada and completing our documentary. Wonder where he is...dead or alive...' Kamakshi was thoughtful.

'Remember what Kashinath said...by helping the Temple Trust we are appeasing the Goddess herself. She will bless us in our mission. And remember what Suchit told you, that Gauriprada's abductors will not kill him till they get to the sacred text.' Ranbeer sounded confident.

When he saw Meera's eyes twinkle despite the rain, he added, 'Now let me talk to Karmar and figure out our tickets. Maya, you know much more about the terrain of Shimoga than any of us. You will be a big help.'

the dhumavati connection

The rain was unrelenting the following day and night. A flash of lightning illuminated the temple premises. The three girls were sitting in Kashinath's sheltered verandah. Accompanied by Gautam Sharma, Ranbeer and his crew had gone to shoot the *Chakra* sadhana.

'The girls can give my family company for dinner,' Kashinath had said when they arrived a couple of hours ago with the documentary crew, who had just come from Delhi that day. '*Chakra* sadhana is not deemed fit to be viewed by women who are not participating in the ritual.'

Without asking questions, the women had complied. They were in fact relieved as they wanted to preserve their energies for Shimoga.

Meera's mind was constantly relaying the telephone conversation that she and Gautam had the previous night. An uncanny hunch had gripped her mind ever since Ranbeer's armlet had been revealed and she had finally decided to confide in Gautam Sharma who seemed equally intrigued about it.

'Hello, Meera. Was that the first time you saw his armlet? And why such a shocked reaction?'

Without thinking much, Meera narrated all their suspicions about Ranbeer.

The priest heard her out without any interruption. When she had finished, he let out a deep sigh and said, 'It might be nothing of consequence...but do you want me to investigate a little on the armlet? Of course, I will be very careful and engage him in conversations that will give me hints.

'Yes, please,' Meera had eagerly consented. 'And please keep this between you and me.'

In the meantime, Maya's phone had been constantly ringing. 'Why don't you answer it?' Kamakshi asked and disappeared into the living room.

'It is Alok, right? You had told us a few days back that Arvind had told you something about Alok. What is it?' Meera asked.

'Nothing that can change my mind.'

'Change your mind about what?'

'About not wanting to go back to him. He has even threatened to file a case against Arvind for abducting me from the asylum! Arvind has spoken to him over the phone and Alok has said a lot of things about me which I never imagined he ever would,' Maya finished her last sentence with a shift in tone.

'Are you sure Arvind has not exaggerated this bit?'

'If he had to lie about anything, he would not have saved me from the fraud like he did.'

'So, what are you going to do now?'

'File for divorce, maybe,' Maya replied.

'Why don't you both come inside? These are such fascinating pictures and stories,' Kamakshi hollered from inside.

Maya and Meera found Kamakshi in an animated conversation with Kashinath. They were flipping through a book of pictures.

'It's an amazing collection of all the sacred *Shakti Peeths* of India. There are even some rare pictures of rituals.'

Maya and Meera joined them. 'Which temple is this? I mean which goddess?' Meera almost shrieked. She was alluding to a picture of a dishevelled looking old woman with open hair sitting on a horseless chariot. She had a crow perched near her shoulder.

'This is Maa Dhumavati. She especially favours spinsters and widows.'

'I have never seen this form of the goddess. But I have seen something very familiar to this...,' Meera interrupted. 'I have seen a locket on Ranbeer's table once with this very image.'

'But Ranbeer does not belong to a clan that worships Goddess Dhumavati! Usually only her ardent worshippers wear lockets or talismans engraved with her image.' Kashinath looked surprised.

Meera's mind replayed the events of that night when she had sneaked into Ranbeer's room. Something told her that given this new discovery it was critical for Gautam Sharma to investigate on the armlet and the priests to have a chat with the custodian of the Dhumavati Temple.'

'Where is this temple located?' Kamakshi asked.

'There are a few of them. Dhumavati temples are in Udupi, Mangalore, Rajrappa and Datia. There is one right here, near Kamakhya Dham as well. In fact, there is one in Banaras too.'

Kashinath*ji* contorted his brows. 'Do you know that some weeks ago there was a theft in that temple? A copy of the *Saradatilakatantra,* which is a rare and valuable text pertaining to Goddess Dhumavati was stolen. We came to know this as we are connected to the entire temple fraternity of this country.'

'Really?' The three girls were aghast.

'How many more temples will these thieves break into?' Maya exclaimed.

Just at that moment, there was a call on Kashinath's mobile and he disappeared into the inner chambers to answer it.

'Well, now I remember,' Kamakshi excitedly snapped her fingers.

'What?' Meera and Maya chorused.

'Ranbeer does have some connection with Maa Dhumavati because I am sure he has gone to her temple in Banaras.

Once I overheard him asking someone about the directions in the guesthouse corridor.'

'Given all that we have seen about him, it can't be a coincidence,' Maya concluded.

'And now when I think of it he must have visited her temple in Udupi too. He had gone to Udupi in January for a holiday,' Kamakshi added.

The others had to conceal their surprise as Kashinath entered the room.

'Kashinath*ji,* that priest friend of yours...the one that Gautam was mentioning, where is he from?' Meera inquired.

'Mangalore. But why do you ask?'

'Well, we wanted to...' Maya began and stopped herself when Meera nudged her.

After a short pause, Kamakshi deftly changed the subject. 'Kashinath*ji,* will you enlighten us on *Chakra* sadhana?'

The priest nodded and explained not just the ritual but the sanctity of tantra. As he spoke about the selflessness and unworldliness of the *sadhaks* in the *Shakti Peeths,* the rigour of their rituals and the miracles that had manifested through their supernatural abilities, his audience was mesmerised.

'If we hadn't met you, we probably would have never understood that tantra actually has a pure essence.' Kamakshi stated.

'Yes. And I am so amazed by the philosophy of *Chakra* sadhana. Had you not told us that the yogis and yoginis participating in the ritual engage in sexual acts only to be united with the supreme power, I would have forever considered it to be a very blasphemous form of tantra. It is amazing how tantric sexual union differs from sex. The yogis and yoginis must be exceptionally adept at asanas if they are able to control their ejaculatory functions.'

Kashinath solemnly nodded and said, 'Yes, they are. It is imperative to be able to control ejaculatory functions during *Chakara* sadhana as the objective is never procreation but consecration. The yoginis are consecrated and elevated to the level of the supreme Mother Goddess. In other words, the Shiva Shakti union is achieved through the ritual.'

Ranbeer and his crew were filming what they later concluded to be the most surreal footage of their lifetime. They had travelled to an ashram at the end of the Nilachal Hills. There was a cottage on a slope that seemed unconnected with the rest of the ashram. Gautam Sharma had effortlessly convinced a moustached and muscular sadhu, who had been sitting silently on the verandah of this cottage, that the documentary crew should be allowed to shoot the ritual. Within twenty minutes of his consent, six men and seven women had appeared from inside and had granted their permission to every member of the crew by touching each of their foreheads with outstretched palms. While the well-toned and bare-chested men were clad in saffron lungis, the slim and shapely women were draped in lemon-coloured cotton saris. None of them sported blouses. The fragrance of tropical night flowers emanated from their open tresses while their skin smelt of wet earth and sandalwood. Coral anklets and armlets that adorned the women gleamed in the halo of the new moon. All seven women were sporting vermillion on their foreheads.

Wordlessly, Gautam, Ranbeer and his crew had trailed them inside. The moustached sadhu, who seemed older than the rest, started issuing directions to a couple of helpers to arrange the paraphernalia for the ritual while the six men and women sat over rugs that were spread in the corners of the large rectangular room.

'*Chakra* sadhana is one of the most sacred rites. It is a reiteration of the fact that our human body is a microscopic extension of this very cosmos. Actually, *Chakra* sadhana is all about seeking union with the divine consciousness.' The sadhu paused and surveyed the men with piercing eyes before adding, 'This is achieved through sexual union but in a way that is not comprehensible to ordinary mortals. While making love, our *sadhaks* guide their soul energy through the six critical *chakras* of the human body. The *kundalini* energy actually originates near the genitals and it needs to be guided near the third eye where the supreme powers of creation Shiva and Shakti reside. Doing this requires years of penance and practice of yogic postures and pranayams. Consider yourself to be exceptionally blessed to be able to witness this ritual as, according to our scriptures, witnessing it requires spiritual merit.'

Ranbeer had instantly felt that he was an exception as there was nothing remotely spiritual or academic about the impatient enthusiasm that was surging in him to see this non-private sexual act.

The sadhu squatted before a trident and drew a *yantra*. He recited some mantras in front of an urn embellished with auspicious symbols and encircled it with five human skulls. Offerings of cooked meat, fish, rice, fruits and betel leaves in brass bowls were arranged around the urn. For almost an hour the sadhu and the other participants of the *Chakra* sadhana recited mantras and touched the offerings at regular intervals.

'This is the mind purification rite,' Gautam whispered.

After it concluded, the sadhu filled another urn with wine and mounted a skull over it. Similar offerings and a different set of mantras followed. After it concluded, the participants feasted on the eatables.

A silence was fast enveloping the room as the women closed their eyes and started meditating. The men on the other hand started making gestures with their hands while reciting mantras. The earthen lamps started flickering.

As the glow steadied, the crew could see that each of the men had identified their female partner for the rite and was kneeling in front of her reverentially. What followed was an eye-popping spectacle. The men and women disrobed themselves. The men then started touching the women through different gestures from the navel to the pelvis and then down below. They smeared sandalwood paste on the women's face, breasts, navel and pubic parts. Reciting mantras, they then smeared the same paste onto their genitals. The men were now aroused. The yogis lifted the yoginis and settled themselves on the rugs in a cross-legged posture. The yoginis who were now sitting on their laps had blissful expressions. The men drew the women tightly to their chests and the union began. The air was filled with the frenzy of moans and groans. There were moments when the bodies became still that were invariably followed by the deep letting out of breath. This technique intensified the union.

'They are controlling their breath between the acts of union and guiding the *kundalini* energy upwards. This is no feat that ordinary mortals can...' Gautam's whispers were silenced by Ranbeer who was now aware of his own very hardened organ.

Within the act, there were stages in which the women would wrap their feet around the men's waists or simply straddle the men below their bodies. The men would then hold their breath and utter mantras often toying around their navel area with fingers.

'This is the zenith of erotic art...live and riveting,' a cameraman whispered as the concluding stages were filmed. The women had almost taken the shape of a circle as their hands and legs rested on the necks of the men. The participants started rolling on the ground and became totally lifeless and silent.

'This is the moment of total bliss. The *kundalini* energy has been guided to the highest *chakra*. The body becomes cold and lifeless and the head becomes warm at this stage,' Gautam whispered and unexpectedly knelt before the *sadhaks* and folded his hands in reverence.

It was 1 am when they returned to Kashinath's house. Ranbeer seemed to be in a bad mood. 'I don't know where I dropped it,' he kept repeating to himself.

'Will you please tell me what it is so that I can at least look for it tomorrow?' Gautam urged. He smiled to himself as luckily for him the armlet had slipped down from Ranbeer's arm that evening. Since the man was so engrossed in filming the ritual he had not even noticed that it was lying on the ground and Gautam had very surreptitiously pocketed it.

'Don't bother, please. It's my misfortune,' he almost hissed under his breath.

Turning to his three friends, he said, 'Come on girls, we all need to go and get a good night's sleep. We have exhausting work starting tomorrow.'

Shimoga again

After three days, the four friends were exiting the Bengaluru railway station. 'Can't we stay a night in Bangalore?' Kamakshi asked Ranbeer.

'Laal Singh will be targeting the next site very soon. I am just hoping it is not tonight. So, it is in our interest that we catch a bus to Shimoga at the earliest,' Ranbeer replied in his characteristic candour.

Throughout the bus ride, Maya had been silent. Shimoga brought back many painful memories. For a moment, she had decided that she would return to Banaras and not accompany her friends in the quest of the possible route map to the sacred text.

'You are welcome to go back. I know how tormenting it must be for you to revisit Shimoga,' Ranbeer had consoled.

But Maya had changed her mind after an hour. On the night when Ranbeer had gone to shoot the *Chakra* sadhana ritual, Kashinath Goswami had said something that had been reverberating in her ears. 'Sometimes personal misfortunes lead us to big missions. You are all very blessed and privileged to help in a divine mission.'

The bus halted at KSRTC terminal in Shimoga at 7 am. Karmar was waiting to receive them in the guesthouse reception area. Like their previous meeting, he did not exchange pleasantries.

'We have an arduous mission tonight. I suggest all of you have breakfast in your rooms and sleep for a few hours. We shall meet in the dining area for lunch at 1 pm,' he commanded before Ranbeer could introduce Maya and Kamakshi.

'Okay,' the four friends said flatly at the same instant.

'What is our itinerary for tonight?' Ranbeer asked at the lunch table.

'We have to split our group so that we can keep a vigil at both the sites simultaneously. Going by the account of the priest at the Kali Temple, Laal Singh has obviously not found what he was looking for. He is bound to strike at the other two sites very soon. We don't know which site is his next target but I do know one thing very clearly. It will be foolish on our part to make a guess and keep a vigil at only one.'

'Tell us everything in detail, please,' Ranbeer urged.

'Both the sites are out of Shimoga. One is in a small village called Yana in the Sahyadri mountain range. There is a massive rock called Bhairaveshwara Shikhara. There is a cave temple beneath that with a Shiva Linga and a bronze statue of Chandika, an incarnation of the Goddess Durga. And…'

'And the route map or the sacred text might be hidden in this cave. I am overwhelmed at my fortune to be part of this mystic adventure,' Kamakshi interrupted and startled everybody with her spontaneous outpouring of passion.

'The second site is in a jungle situated on the banks of the Tunga. It is a Kaal Bhairav Temple guarded by venom-spewing cobras.' Karmar stopped as the expressions on the faces changed dramatically. 'I am told that the cobras do not attack unless provoked,' he tried to assure them.

'If I recall correctly the idol of Kaal Bhairav is adorned by a serpent which uncoils from the idol only on full moon nights,' Ranbeer said.

It was now Karmar's turn to look amazed.

'Like I had mentioned to Meera earlier, I am genuinely impressed by the extent of your research,' he remarked.

'Tonight is a full moon night,' Meera contorted her eyebrows. 'I don't understand why we should all not be together. It is obvious that Laal Singh will strike at the Kaal Bhairav Temple tonight. After all, he won't get a safe chance to be there until the next full moon. So, doesn't it make more sense for our entire group to be waiting for him there? We will have to nab him with physical force.'

'I know that he will be dangerous and am not expecting us to nab him alone. What do you think I have been busy doing from the time you boarded the train to Bangalore?' Karmar sounded offended. 'Panicker and I have arranged for half a dozen armed security men. Two of them will accompany me and Panicker to Yana and the rest will accompany you to Kaal Bhairav.'

The four friends were beginning to realise that the implications of this mission were more serious than they had comprehended.

'Is it really important for you and Professor Panicker to start your journey to Yana today?' Ranbeer asked Karmar.

'I have a hunch that Laal Singh has accomplices and therefore will be striking simultaneously at both sites. So, it makes perfect sense for us to reach the Bhairaveshwara Shikhara Temple at the earliest.'

'If I remember correctly, Yana is less than 200 kilometres from Shimoga. Arvind had spoken of his adventures there,' Maya added.

'That is right. Panicker and I are leaving at 6 pm. The Bhairaveshwara Temple is sometimes crowded by pilgrims and mountain trekkers until eight in the evening. We are assuming that the thief will choose to rummage the site after that. And we are hoping against hope that he has not already rummaged and stolen what we are hoping to find.'

It was 9 pm. Ranbeer, Meera, Maya and Kamakshi, escorted by four security guards had travelled the forty-eight kilometres stretch from Shimoga town to Thirthahalli. They were now marching towards the river bank where two boats were waiting for them on the instructions of Panicker.

Maya felt a searing sensation in her heart. The memories of that fateful night nearly ten months ago started crowding her mind. '*But this time the situation is completely different. I am with the people who I trust the most and we are going on a sacred mission,*' she consoled herself.

Within twenty minutes, the two boatmen had steered the boat to the middle of the river's horizontal expanse. Maya realised that the terrain of the river changed more rapidly this time as within an hour and half they were coursing along the stretch that meandered between green banks.

Minutes after the two boats coursed into the stretch sheltered by branches of bountiful trees the boatmen started rowing more silently. All conversations froze. They were now very close to their destination and knew one thing—they could not afford to alert Laal Singh or his accomplices and foil their plans.

The boatmen moored the boats several yards ahead from the spot where Maya had disembarked the last time.

With pounding hearts, they proceeded towards the Kaal Bhairav Temple in a single file, with Maya in the lead. The ground was wet and insects of every perceivable variety crawled on it. The group froze as soon as they saw the temple a few yards ahead. Much to their surprise it was not empty. An ascetic clad in a black robe was inside. His movements were frenzied and he was loudly uttering some mantras.

The eight people quickly ducked behind massive bushes.

'It would be a pity if Laal Singh did not rummage the temple tonight because of this ascetic,' Meera whispered to Maya who was crouching beside her.

Much to everybody's relief the man finally came out of the temple. He stretched his body, face downwards on the ground, and lay still.

For some time, none of them could think of anything. The sight of reptiles crawling over the ascetic's body was both transfixing and horrifying.

Ranbeer glanced at his watch. It was 10.35 pm. 'Let's go,' he gestured to the others.

Without wasting time in thought, all of them dashed across to the temple and entered it in silence.

It was now shrouded in darkness and they had to tread cautiously on the granite stairs.

'Wait!' Maya suddenly exclaimed in a hushed voice. Her hand had touched the small patch on the temple wall that had a rough texture and iron handle. One of the security guards flashed his torch to reveal an unchiselled rectangular portion of granite, light pink in colour. An iron handle was attached to it. He tugged at the handle to reveal a hollow space.

'For all we know the map could be hidden here,' she whispered excitedly as the men started surveying the space in the light of their torches. It smelt putrid and the only things visible were a couple of human skulls, cobwebs and layers of dust. The men groped through the dust for something that felt like paper but did not find anything even remotely close.

They soon reached the hollow tunnel-like space that contained the shrine and silently took their positions behind the two massive granite pillars at the back of the shrine. Wordlessly, they continued their vigil till midnight. However, there was no trace of the man or his accomplices.

'I guess, we should wait until sunrise,' Ranbeer whispered as the others nodded their consent.

At around 5.15 am, the first light of daybreak filtered in through the many cracks of the temple walls. The group was now exhausted and very disappointed.

'Let's go,' Ranbeer gestured towards the exit.

The morning air was refreshing in contrast to the claustrophobic air inside the temple.

The boatmen were waiting for them. They informed that they too had not seen or heard anything suspicious.

'The action must have happened at Yana.' Ranbeer let out a deep sigh.

'Then we have nothing to despair. Let's call Karmar and hear the good news,' Kamakshi smiled cheerfully.

Sensing everybody's impatience, Ranbeer gestured to the boatmen to steer to the edge of the bank. He got out and after dialling Karmar's number paced up and down to find the best site that would offer an uninterrupted network.

'Hello, can you hear me? We. . .what? So have you nabbed him? I see. We will hurry up and join you soon,' he hung up and returned to the boat.

'They have nabbed him?' Everyone inquired excitedly.

'No. But they have found something that could be a big clue to unmasking Laal Singh. I didn't clearly hear what it is. But we have to reach Yana as soon as we can. Karmar said that they have observed something very strange at the site. And we all need to be together to make sense of it,' Ranbeer said.

the custodian of yana temple

Later in the day, Ranbeer and Meera were discussing an email that the former had received from the International Documentary Association that very morning.

'Is there no way that you can postpone your trip to Los Angeles?' Meera felt sorry for the crestfallen Ranbeer.

'I will have to go and file the nomination for the award in the Best Discovery category, which has just been introduced. This is the chance of a lifetime for me. I am confident of winning, given my findings on tantra *shastra*. This nomination cannot be filled online as it entails a lot of verification.'

'You always knew that this category would be introduced as you kept saying that your documentary has to make a discovery!' Meera thought to herself and instead said, 'It's unfortunate that they had to announce the category yesterday and deadline the nomination within a week. After all we are at a crucial juncture of our mission of finding the sacred text.'

Ranbeer smiled and said, 'So what? It's important that the text, if at all it exists, is found. I can then include it in my documentary and it will help me clinch the award.'

Meera was beginning to understand why Ranbeer had been behaving so oddly—the night excursions to the Shiva Temple that had been blessed by Limar Singh, his photocopying of her reference book, his secrecy at conducting research and even his presence in the compound of the Centre of Vedic Studies had been inspired by his singular ambition of winning the title in this prestigious category. *'But what about the locket of Goddess Dhumavati in his possession? Also, why did he tell Baccha that the tantric who authored the hidden text had led a secret life?'*

'By the way, there is good news for Maya,' Ranbeer interrupted her thoughts. 'Arvind will be arriving in a couple of hours. Actually, he had called me three days ago and said that he would join us and be part of this adventure while his senior from WWF unearths the mystery behind the threats. He had asked me to keep this a secret as he wanted to surprise you all...but we all know that this surprise will be especially delightful for Maya,' he added with a twinkle in his eye.

'Oh, really? And what did he have to say when he heard that we would be in Shimoga today?' Meera smiled.

'That he knows the terrain around quite well. He told me that he would take some decent photographs of the defining moments...that I could somehow insert within my documentary footage. I think that will be a help, especially because my crew too is not around.'

A white Tata Sumo and a grey Scorpio drove into the compound of the guesthouse at 4.30 pm.

The security guards who had accompanied them to the Kaal Bhairav Temple were waiting near the cars. As Ranbeer waved goodbye and opened the door of the Scorpio for his friends to get in, he couldn't help wondering at the dedication that these guards had demonstrated.

Within two hours of their drive, the cars entered a semi-forested area. The Sahyadri Mountain range was clearly visible at a distance. Suddenly, the driver of the Sumo that was leading the way brought his car to a halt. The Scorpio too halted.

Meera and Arvind lowered their tinted windows. The driver of the Sumo was talking to a group of men who were sitting on a cemented platform under a huge tree. From the gestures of the driver, it was clear that he was seeking directions.

'I think they have been helpful,' Arvind remarked as the driver gave a thumbs-up sign to the men and returned.

It was dark now and the moonlight could barely filter through the leaves of the massive trees. Only the headlights made it possible for the drivers to see the road ahead. From the jerks it was clear that this was just a motorable tract and not a road.

They reached a place that resembled a tribal hamlet. Skimpily dressed men, women and children were walking around the clusters of mud houses. Flags were swaying to the rhythm of the breeze in front of the houses. A closer scrutiny revealed that each flag had a symbol of the *trishul*.

The villagers stopped their activities as the cars screeched to a halt. A group of middle-aged men started in the direction of the cars. Their gestures were frenzied and they were speaking among themselves in the local dialect.

'It looks like they are not very pleased with our presence,' said Maya.

The drivers and the four guards got out to talk. It was evident that they were trying to tell the villagers that they were pilgrims and wanted to reach the Bhairaveshwara Shikhara Temple. The villagers looked unconvinced and started waving their arms and shaking their heads vigorously.

Sensing the escalating commotion, Meera stepped out and instantly drew their attention. Something about her attire—a simple white, cotton salwar kameez and saffron dupatta—seemed to extend that the group was indeed on a pilgrimage.The villagers started answering questions in a calmer tone thereafter.

'How far is it?' Maya asked the driver as he took his position behind the wheel.

'Not too far now. But the road might be more treacherous.'

He was right for soon the cars had to contain their speed within the second gear.

'Let me see if the network catches on now,' Meera took out her mobile and switched it on. 'Yes, in fact Karmar has been trying to reach me.' The phone started tinkling merrily as a string of messages got delivered. 'Once you reach Bhairaveshwara Temple keep coming straight for about half a kilometre. Keep looking to your right. We are camping in two red tents in a spot sheltered by pipal trees,' she read the message to the driver.

As they crossed the Yana Temple, the four friends folded their hands in reverence. 'There they are,' Kamakshi was the first to spot the four men who were standing before their tents, shining flashlights.

'Spill the beans fast.' Arvind smiled at Karmar and introduced himself as the large group settled themselves in front of the tents.

'Well, let's talk about the clue first. This beauty is trying to tell us something.' Karmar opened his fist to reveal an amulet.

Everyone stared at the wooden amulet that had a patch of red cloth in the centre.

'You actually thought this was a clue to Laal Singh? It doesn't say who he is and where he…' Meera stopped and let out a shriek. 'Of course, it does tell us where he is from! He definitely is an African or has some connection to Africa.'

'What?' at least half a dozen voices chorused.

'This is a west African talisman. If I remember my bedtime stories of witchcraft and sorcery, this looks like a *grigri*,' she announced.

'It is a *grigri* and we found it lying on the ground inside the temple,' said Panicker.

'I don't understand how this qualifies as a clue. I mean do we know any African that we can suspect?' Maya asked.

'Of course, we do,' Kamakshi exclaimed. 'Venkatesh's partner is African after all. That Alex character.'

'And you are also forgetting that Sankalp Nair is an NRI from Africa,' Karmar added.

'Your theory that Venkatesh is Laal Singh isn't wrong, it seems. I am impressed, my friend.' Meera's voice revealed her surging excitement.

'Now, we have to somehow get in touch with Sankalp. He might be completely innocent but we cannot rule out his involvement before talking to him. And after that we think of a way to expose Alex Powell, Venkatesh and Vijaylakshmi. I guess they are all partners in crime,' Karmar said.

'You feel that Sankalp Nair might be able to tell us something through which we can expose them? But he is not connected to them in the first place,' Kamakshi was now beginning to feel exhausted from the day's journey.

'There is nothing that says that Sankalp cannot be connected to them. I have a strong gut feeling that he is the key to the mystery. Trust me, we are now beginning to shoot in the light.' Something in Karmar's tone told them that he was right.

'If the thief has dropped his amulet here, one thing is clear—he has already come and stolen the paper.' All hearts sank as Arvind uttered this.

'But the old sanyasi who guards the temple must have seen him. We have to somehow gain his trust and talk to him,' Karmar said.

'Who is this man?' Arvind demanded.

'Well, last night while keeping a vigil, we all thought that we saw a shadow lurking near the Shiva Linga.'

'You mean Laal Singh or his accomplice? Why did you not grab him?' Maya was astounded.

'That is the strange thing. We crawled to the places where we thought we saw the shadow. And found nobody!'

'How is that possible?' Kamakshi sounded equally astounded.

Karmar scratched his forehead and replied, 'On scrutiny of the temple in the morning we realised it is not impossible. There are some shallow alcoves in the cave walls. It is possible that the man hid there. And in any case, he couldn't have been our man because he never came anywhere close to the shrine where we later found the *grigri*.'

'Now, what?' Arvind asked.

'I had the same reaction, but after we returned to the camp I saw something which might help us in this chase. I saw an old, wrinkled sanyasi who kept looking at us from a distance. He was standing behind this tree.' Karmar pointed to a tree with knotted barks that was a few yards away.

'Could he also be searching? I mean he might be entirely unconnected to Laal Singh but hunting for the text or map!' Meera almost whistled.

'I thought of something similar but then I realised he was probably guarding the shrine. I mean if he was after the map he would have fled from the site after rummaging for it. And the strange thing is that after staring at us for a long while, the ascetic raised his arms towards the sky and started muttering something under his breath. Finally, he departed in the direction of the temple.'

'There definitely is some reason,' Arvind said.

Maya dug out a water bottle from her handbag and some of the contents toppled out including the meal vouchers that she had retrieved from the ransacked library of the Centre for Vedic Studies.

'Where did you get these from?' Professor Panicker, who was silent all this while, almost shouted.

Maya recounted everything. 'These meal vouchers are for our staff, issued by our canteen. And no outsider can have them,' Panicker's voice was barely audible as he uttered the second sentence.

'I guess this means that the man who ransacked the library and the one who stole the book that you had authored are not two different people,' Maya observed.

Though the others were convinced by her logic they did not say anything as they were all mulling about the puzzle of the wrinkled sanyasi.

'Professor, you actually called us all the way from Shimoga to figure out the mystery behind this ascetic? But I...' Meera's voice trailed off and a set of lines contorted her forehead.

'I get it,' Maya interrupted. 'Obviously, because Professor Karmar feels that the sanyasi has seen the intruder...I mean Laal Singh...inside the shrine and that through his description we might have a good chance of knowing who it is,' she surmised.

'Exactly! I mean, if we have staked everything and come so far, we can't afford to dismiss anything,' Panicker replied.

'Well, maybe in the last two days we have run after yet another false alarm,' Kamakshi remarked, wearily.

'I shall be grateful if you give me the benefit of doubt until tomorrow morning. That man keeps lurking among the trees from 5 to 10 am. Maybe tomorrow he will follow a similar pattern.' Karmar abruptly got up and walked inside one of the red tents.

Too exhausted to think of anything, the others trailed into their tents as well.

At daybreak, the mountain peaks came alive in the growing orange halo of the sky. The group sat in a circle surrounding the camp fire. The twelve pairs of eyes were gazing in the direction of the knotted tree behind which the sanyasi had stood the previous day.

They took turns in going to a nearby spring to wash up. Just when Meera, Maya and Kamakshi were returning to the camp, they saw a human form in the adjoining thicket. It was indeed the mysterious sanyasi. Much to their delight, he was now scurrying towards the tents.

The girls quickened their pace and reached the tent.

'He is coming!' Maya said excitedly as the others looked away from the tree.

After a couple of minutes, the sanyasi came into view. He was vigorously counting his rosary beads and muttering something with closed eyes.

Just as they were all beginning to think of a non-intimidating way of approaching this mysterious man they saw him walking slowly in their direction.

'We never thought it will be this easy,' Maya whispered.

The ascetic stopped walking only when he was about five steps away. He was incredibly wrinkled and bald. Dressed in a faded cotton kurta and saffron dhoti, he looked well over a hundred years old. His eyes were however, unusually bright for his age and he was quite lean and tall.

Right at that instant, a sudden tide of clouds rushed in to cover the sun and large raindrops started dotting the ground. Panicker took the lead and addressing the ascetic in the local dialect asked him to come inside one of the red tents. To everybody's amazement and relief, he readily complied.

He surprised them yet again by taking the lead in the conversation.

'He is saying that he has remained alive till this day because he had to meet us,' Panicker translated for all of them.

Realising that he was not comprehensible to everybody, the sanyasi paused after every sentence.

'He is saying that we have all come together to assist him in his life's mission of guarding the route map to the sacred text and ensuring that it falls in the right hands.'

The sound of heartbeats became audible. Arvind opened his mouth to ask something but stopped as the man continued speaking.

'Almost ninety-five years ago when he was a young boy, a friend from his gurukul who was well versed in tantra *shastra* had given him an envelope. This friend had told our man, who was then studying to become a priest, that he should open the envelope only after sixty-five years. When our man doubted whether he would live that long, his friend told him that he would remain alive and that this fact had been revealed by one of his forefathers in a dream. This forefather had been a very powerful tantric. In fact, he had been the favourite disciple of one of India's most powerful and revered Aghori *babas*.

He is saying that his friend told him that on the night preceding his eightieth birthday he would get a dream in which Lord Shiva would appear. And that Mahadev himself would tell him the significance of the envelope and what he should do with the contents. As predicted, our old friend did have the dream on his eightieth birthday.'

'I don't believe that this is happening.' Arvind looked dazed and pinched himself to ensure that he was not dreaming.

Panicker, who was equally excited, proceeded to translate the next part of the old man's narration. 'He is saying Mahadev appeared in his dream and told him that he was pleased at the dedication with which he had studied various scriptures and served him all his life in the cave temple of Yana.'

It was now clear that this ascetic was once the priest of the cave temple.

'Shiv*ji* told him that the envelope had two maps—one etched in red ink on a piece of yellow cloth and the other drawn in black ink on a piece of red cloth. The map on the yellow cloth was extremely precious. It had the directions to the most powerful tantric text, written in the last thousand years. This text had the power to change the plight of mankind for good. But only one man on this planet had the authority and power to comprehend the mystic formulas in the text—an Aghor from Banaras. Mahadev told our friend that this man was now starting his thirty-year-long meditation in the Himalayas.'

Meera and Kamakshi exchanged a glance. So, Limar Singh was not a fraud after all. He was indeed chosen by Lord Shiva to find and guard the sacred text. They wondered why, despite all his special powers, he had not yet managed to find the text.

They found the answer as Panicker resumed his translation. 'Mahadev told our good friend that he could foresee that this Aghor from Banaras would succeed in eleven of the twelve penances he would perform in the course of the next thirty years. Unfortunately, he would falter on the twelfth penance. Therefore, though he would be bestowed special powers to apply the mystic formulas, he would not succeed in finding it on his own.

Mahadev revealed that the text would be rediscovered exactly thirty-one years later by people who would be questioning the sanctity of tantra. It would be rediscovered to usher a renaissance in terms of ancient and medieval India's mystic practises and this re-discovery would be particularly significant because mysticism in modern India would stand greatly tarnished by frauds.'

Maya and Kamakshi exchanged a knowing glance. *'So, Kashinathji was right when he told them that their personal misfortunes with tantra had led them on a divine mission. It was indeed the mission of rediscovering this sacred text in this era of mystic sinners.'*

There was complete silence as everyone tried assimilating what was just revealed. The wrinkled ascetic quietly sipped on a bottle of water.

'I have one last question for our old friend. How does he know we are the very people who are destined to make this discovery?'

Arvind's question echoed everyone's thoughts. They all waited with bated breath for the ascetic to reveal more.

the sacred text

Language could be a barrier but understanding human intentions was not dependant on it. The sanyasi revealed that their collective desire towards their quest bore the mark of divine sanction and he could easily see it in their aura.

The narration resumed again.

'By dint of his superhuman powers, the tantric who had authored the text could foresee that in the distant future, evil people would search for it to misuse it for vested interests. So he had sketched two route maps and before his death had handed the maps and sacred text to his favourite disciple in an iron box. The Aghor had instructed this disciple to hand the box down to his eldest son at the time of his own death. For seven generations, this disciple's family had to carry out the sacred duty of placing the box in the custody of the eldest son. And for eight generations of this family, only the eldest son would be entitled to know about the existence of this text. The eldest son born in the seventh generation would have to undertake the sacred mission of hiding the maps and the sacred text. The Aghor told his disciple that this great-great-grandson of his would be living in a time when the imperial powers ruling our country would be crusading against tantra. Hence, he would need to undertake the special mission of hiding the text and that it would be discovered nearly a hundred years later. And the route maps had to be placed in the custody of his friend, meaning our sanyasi here,' Panicker elaborated.

'Why did he draw two maps?' Maya and Arvind asked in unison.

The sanyasi smiled wisely before replying which Panicker duly translated to, 'As misdirection for the evil men who wanted it for their own vested interests.'

'And what exactly has our dear friend done with the two maps?' Karmar spoke for the first time in the last half an hour.

'He had placed the red map inside the Bhairaveshwara Shikhara Temple. In a crevice on the floor, close to the shrine for it to be stolen by the thief. And he did steal it,' Panicker finished with clear admiration at the sanyasi's wit.

'No wonder the man was not there at the Kaal Bhairav Temple, because he had already found the route map here... thankfully the wrong map!' Maya's eyes were wide open in astonishment.

'Where is the true map?' Meera asked with an unusual urgency.

The sanyasi did not require translation for this part and produced a square patch of coarse brown paper tied securely with a red string. He untied it to reveal a large rectangular piece of yellow cloth. It had neat drawings of concrete structures connected by a series of arrows. Lines in Devanagari were inscribed inside each of the structures in red ink.

Karmar and Panicker took the map and studied it intently.

Nodding at each other they announced, 'We have indeed been rewarded in our chase. We really have found the destination of the sacred text. It is not in any of the *Shakti Peeths* or inside any caves in the Sahyadri. It is indeed in Banaras!'

Unable to restrain their joy everybody in the tent started clapping. Kamakshi wiped away her tears of joy.

'Where exactly is it?' Everybody wanted to know.

'It is hidden inside a structure very close to the river bank. But the interesting thing is that the box inside which the text is contained cannot be seen if one enters the structure through the main door. It can be reached only through an underground tunnel, which starts from inside another building. And the entrance to this tunnel is marked by a symbol...looks like a yantra to me.'

Meanwhile, the weather outside had progressed to torrential rain and thundering clouds. So, they all sat discussing the various probable directions given in the map until the rains receded after half an hour.

The sanyasi was now lost in a meditative trance. His eyes were closed and he had a blissful expression on his face.

Panicker asked him something in a soft voice. The man nodded and said something that must have been purely fascinating as the professor and six guards were looking almost enchanted.

'Enlighten us,' Arvind urged.

'We are not just finding the sacred text, we are also finding Laal Singh!' Panicker replied.

'The incorrect map leads to an inconspicuous looking boulder in the grounds of Yash Kashi Temple. We could trap him there,' Panicker further explained.

'I don't see how...I mean he must have already got to it and on finding nothing, he must have moved on. So, how will we catch him now?' Meera asked.

'That my dear is the most fascinating part. The man who authored the text and these maps had not only wanted to safeguard the true hiding place but also wanted to trap the thief and obliterate his intentions. So, along with the duplicate map he included a binding tenet—that the sacred text should be found only on the first Monday of the month of *Shravan*. And that if it is found even a day earlier the power of its formula will be lost.'

'This is unbelievable! Now I know why people say that when we truly want something the universe conspires to make it happen.' Meera actually joined her hands in reverence to the Supreme Power.

The winds outside were now blowing at a more disciplined pace. The sanyasi got up and started uttering something that clearly sounded like blessings.

As he was about to leave, Kamakshi blurted without thinking, 'This tantric...his friend who has hidden the text... I mean his entire clan seems to be extraordinary. I was wondering if our dear old friend could tell us a little about them.'

Panicker smiled and translated her curiosity to the sanyasi. The old man nodded and gave an elaborate reply.

'This family was no ordinary family of tantrics. They could perform extraordinary feats that none of the powerful tantrics of the olden times could perform. They could perform rare miracles and even stop earthquakes. And they also had extraordinary lifespans. All the eldest sons, who knew about the existence of the text, died after a hundred and twenty!'

It was finally time for the old man to leave. Each of them got up and touched his feet. As they escorted him outside the tent, the sanyasi motioned to them to follow him no further. He had fulfilled his life's mission and now wanted to walk away alone...perhaps he wanted to retreat to another realm.

The Scorpio sped on in the direction of Shimoga. The six guards were following them in the white Sumo. They would depart at Shimoga but promised to escort them to Yash Kashi on the first Monday of *Shravan*—to nab Laal Singh and his accomplices.

'The building through which the tunnel can be accessed must be the gallery in Arshad Singh's compound,' said Meera.

'It definitely looks like it,' replied Kamakshi. She and Meera who were sitting on either side of the professor, scrutinised all the details of the map and with their familiarity of the river bank surroundings were finally able to pinpoint a lot of the structures drawn on the map.

'And the entrance to the tunnel indeed has a yantra. It is so familiar... This is the unusual painting in the gallery! The inverted pyramid inside the round flower is not just an adornment on the woman's forehead. It is actually a yantra that marks the entrance to the tunnel!' Kamakshi's voice was unsteady with excitement.

'Well, you girls along with Arvind need to unearth this sacred text. And we shall then have to hand it to its rightful guardian, Limar Singh. But not without unmasking Laal Singh,' Karmar smiled.

'Won't you be accompanying us to Banaras?' Maya asked.

'We shall join you before the first Monday of *Shravan* for the Yash Kashi venture. You are forgetting that though we have found the route map to the sacred text, the mysterious events that brought us to it continue to remain mysterious. I am going to get hold of Sankalp Nair and grill him. Moreover, I also have to reach Kamakhya Dham at the earliest. I have some pressing research notes to compile after talking to the ascetics that are travelling there for *Ambubachi*. As you know, I am already delayed,' Karmar replied.

Arvind had been looking unusually pensive. 'I am afraid I shall not be able to accompany the girls. I have to fly out tomorrow evening to Delhi. I need to attend to a couple of pressing issues,' he exchanged a knowing glance with Maya and held her hand.

'I wonder what could be more pressing,' Karmar smiled and added, 'But I am sure your reasons are convincing enough!'

Arvind quickly told him about the threats that he had received from poachers and how he was now absconding on the professional front. 'I suspect that the poachers know about my friendship with Ranbeer. They also have an inkling about our awareness of the tantric-poaching nexus. I mean they might be scouting for me and keeping a vigil on everything and everyone that I am connected to. I need to sort out the mess with my seniors and resume work too.'

Unknown to the others, another pressing issue demanded his presence that only Maya knew about. Alok wanted to meet him and understand why Maya had been evading him. His last text messages had been decisive but not entirely uncordial: *If you manage to convince me that you acted appropriately in taking her away from my reach, I shall perhaps start to understand her altered behaviour and set her free for any choice that she wishes to take.*

'We have hope in his last message. Please tell him I am a different Maya now and I belong to you,' Maya had pleaded in the morning when the messages got delivered.

'Have you informed Gautam and Kashinath about our success?' Meera's question cut through Arvind's thoughts.

'Their numbers are unreachable,' Karmar replied. 'We have to tell them soon though. Blessings of Kamakhya Devi have really worked miracles.'

'And we also have to ask them about the details of House number 501,' Kamakshi reminded.

Three days later the girls were sitting with Baccha Yadav.

'Like Ranbeer had said, going on the trail of Laal Singh was the right strategy. But I don't understand Arshad Singh's connection... I mean why is the sacred text hidden beneath his gallery? Also, won't it be difficult to enter that gallery? It is private property, after all, even if it has public access,' Meera wondered.

Baccha, who had been hearing everything, said, 'It is not strange that the route to this text starts from Arshad's gallery. The older people of this town say that his forefathers had great faith in tantra *shastra*. Some even say that many of them were endowed with occult powers. Once there was also a rumour among some temple priests that Arshad's grandfather, Brij Bhooshan Singh, had let a young tantric go down one of the two tunnels that start beneath his haveli. They suspect that the tantric went searching for something.'

'Haveli? You mean to say that the tunnel might actually start from the haveli and not the gallery?' Meera inquired.

'Of course. There are two tunnels that begin from Thakur*ji*'s haveli. Important tunnels that have long been forgotten. In fact, Gauriprada had mentioned about this,' Kamakshi said, excitedly.

'He did? And now I am almost sure that the kidnappers have kept him inside one of these two tunnels. This explains why the police have not found him even after combing every inch of Banaras!' Meera exclaimed.

'Some people say that Arshad Singh often brags about how a tantric had begged his grandfather to go down one of these very important tunnels, obviously to search for something incredibly valuable. In fact, he also knows the exact route of one of these two tunnels. And maybe it was Arshad who had... How stupid that all this has struck me only now!' Baccha stopped abruptly.

'I think I have guessed,' Meera's eyes were shining.

'Yes, the conversation between Gauripradа and Arshad that night…when the *Naga* sanyasi was standing guard… Gauriprada must have asked him about the route.'

'And you also saw someone fleeing?' Maya pressed.

'I am positive.'

'Rustom and his accomplices must have been keeping a watch over Arshad. They must have trailed him when he went to meet Gauriprada!' Meera thought aloud.

'Gauriprada probably got abducted because Arshad had suddenly disappeared from Banaras. Else Arshad and not Gauriprada would have been abducted,' Maya said.

'How are we so sure that Arshad has gone out of town and has not been abducted too?' Meera asked.

'Well, the *Naga* ascetic would have definitely alerted everyone if Arshad had been abducted.'

'Baccha, that painting in the gallery lobby that we assume to be the entrance of the tunnel… Didn't you mention that it was inspired by some sculpture inside the haveli?'

Baccha nodded. 'That was painted only seventy-five years ago from a famous sculpture that is inside the haveli. People say that it has been inside the haveli ever since it was constructed in the sixteenth century.'

'You will have to help us enter the haveli,' Meera insisted after partially recounting their experiences of the past few days to Suchit.

Suchit was only eager to be of help to Meera.

'Well, the housekeeper is especially close to me. I will go to meet her tonight and help you get inside without anyone knowing.' Suchit bragged.

It sounded like music to the girls.

At 11 pm, the three of them escorted by Suchit reached the gates of the haveli. Unfortunately, Baccha was held back due to important work, much to his chagrin. To their surprise, the guards were missing. They tiptoed in wordlessly.

After crossing the lawn, Suchit gestured them to hide behind a tree. He marched a few steps ahead and rapped on a side door. A young woman answered. At first, she couldn't recognise Suchit but when she did, she hugged him languidly and they went inside in animated conversation. The door was half open.

After fifteen minutes, Suchit reappeared and gestured the girls to enter. They scurried the distance of a few yards in silence and entered. Suchit walked away in another direction leaving them to proceed to the durbar hall.

'I just hope we manage this,' said Kamakshi.

She was flashing a torch as Meera and Maya scouted for the sculpture. They found it in the main hall. It was a five feet tall sculpture of a woman's face and torso placed against a panelled wall. And the forehead was adorned with a big round flower containing an inverted pyramid. The three symbols at each edge of the pyramid were clearly visible—a flame, an open book and the head of Lord Shiva lost in meditation. The three girls remembered what Bheeksha Das had told them about the symbol engraved on the rusted locket—the open book placed half over flames and half over Mahadev's forehead symbolises a powerful tantric cult that was secretly spreading its roots in the eleventh century.

'Probably this cult was pioneered by this very Aghor who authored the text. And only the family of the favourite disciple was privy to the existence of this text,' Kamakshi whispered.

The others nodded. 'Now, how do we enter the tunnel?' they wondered aloud.

The women pressed their palms against the chest and forehead of the woman by turns and in different combinations and sequences. After some tries, something clicked and the sculpture started moving forward. It halted a few inches away from the wall revealing a dark, open space. Meera quickly realised that this had happened because her palm had gently pressed against the middle of the inverted pyramid. She pressed the same point with similar pressure and it slid back to its original position.

'This is a lever-operated mechanism,' she whispered.

'Not all of us can go in together. We can't be trapped inside,' Kamakshi sensibly observed.

'I will stay back,' Maya said. 'In fact, I will go and join Suchit. I will pretend that I was just passing by and decided to venture into the haveli out of curiosity.'

'That will be perfect. You can come here at some pretext and open the door as soon as either of us gives you a missed call,' Meera added.

Cobweb-littered, musty-smelling stairs led the way underground. To their surprise, Meera and Kamakshi could experience sudden bursts of river breeze at regular intervals. After some distance, there was a sharp curve.

They were going right and then down again through a flight of steps that seemed broader. Soon, they reached a level space that seemed even darker than the rest of the tunnel. They walked on silently led by their flashllights and were soon greeted by the faint halo of electric light.

With pacing hearts and feet they reached something that seemed like a dead end. It was a rectangular granite structure about six feet high and six feet wide.

Neither of them knew what to do next.

'Where are we?' they kept asking each other as they flashed their torches over the almost foreboding structure.

The light seemed to be filtering from beneath!

Kamakshi caught Meera's shoulder and pointed at a symbol carved in one corner of the structure. There were three horizontal lines engraved on the granite with a red dot in between. They realised that they were underneath the Kashi Karvaat temple on Manikarnika Ghat. Without thinking Kamakshi pressed the red dot and to their surprise the entire patch of the granite on which the symbol was engraved slid open. At first, they did not see anything except an even brighter halo of light.

'There it is,' Kamakshi squealed in delight as she pointed at a folded piece of mustard yellow cloth lying inside the opening.

They bent down and stretched their hands to reach the cloth. Meera unfolded it to reveal a scroll which seemed about two metres wide and one metre long. To their relief and joy, it was indeed ancient India's most powerful tantric text inscribed with yantras and writings in black carbon ink.

a family secret

'It is already 12.30,' Meera flashed the torchlight over her wrist.

'This was well worth our time,' Kamakshi smiled. Her face radiated a glow like never before.

While retracing their steps, they heard a low moan. It came from the spot where the tunnel had curved to the left. It sounded like the feeble moan of an injured animal. Straining their ears, they could hear a muffled human cough.

Glancing at each other, the two moved their flashlights across the adjoining walls and ceiling in vertical and circular strokes. Nothing unusual came to light. They decided to keep walking and reach the tunnel entrance. As soon as they were standing behind the closed door, Meera texted Maya: *Found the sacred text. Come and open the door immediately but only if everything is perfectly under control.*

After a short wait, the door slid forwards. With faces flushed in excitement, Suchit and Maya were facing them.

Placing a finger on her lips, Meera urged them to walk towards the exit door.

'This has been possible only because of Lord Shiva's divine intervention,' Baccha was ecstatic as he held the sacred scroll close to his bosom.

It was 1.30 am and the three friends along with Baccha were sitting on the steps leading from Everest Café to Shivala Ghat.

'Where do we hide it? For all you know, the people who have been watching us might suspect something,' said Maya.

'We have to be very cautious and ensure that we do not talk about it in public,' Kamakshi agreed.

'I will lock it in my trunk. Nobody even suspects that I know so much about everything,' Baccha volunteered.

Something about the suggestion was convincing and they all nodded their heads in agreement. As they walked up the stairs they were all thinking the same thing—how would they hand it over to Limar Singh. He had been invisible for some weeks.

The next morning Meera walked to a secluded area of the river bank to dial the head priest. 'Kashinath*ji*, we have found the route map and also the sacred text.'

The other girls were patiently waiting for the call to end. Kashinath Goswami was obviously the one speaking as Meera was intently hearing him out. Her face turned pale.

'We shall remain eternally grateful to you and Kamakhya Devi. And yes, we hope to see you in Banaras at the start of *Shravan*,' she said before disconnecting.

'What is it?' the two girls prodded together.

Meera walked towards the steps of Shivala Ghat and sat down with a dazed expression. 'I could have never imagined this!' Beads of sweat started erupting on her forehead. 'It is about Ranbeer.'

Finally, Meera took a deep breath and said, 'I had told Gautam and Kashinath*ji* that probably we should find out more about the tragedy alluded to by the uncle of that priest from Dhumavati Temple.'

'And it was all the more important to find this after you said that you had spotted a locket in Ranbeer's room that had the image of the diety,' Kamakshi agreed.

Meera nodded. 'Well, Sharath Hegde's uncle is dead. So Kashinath*ji* and Gautam travelled all the way to Mangalore to meet his father who is now eighty-five years old. If you remember, Ranbeer had been complaining that he had dropped something while shooting the *Chakra* sadhana ritual.

Well, Gautam had surreptitiously taken it after it had slipped off Ranbeer's arm. You see, after seeing Ranbeer's strange reactions in Kashinath*ji*'s house I had confided in Gautam about all his mysterious actions. Gautam had offered to investigate on the armlet. But we never imagined that this armlet would explain so much and…' Meera clutched her forehead with a dazed expression.

'What was the armlet really like?' Maya asked. 'We have never seen it.'

'It is an armlet that has the symbol of an open book placed half over flames and half over Mahadev's meditative forehead.'

'Now I know why I thought that there was something familiar about the painting of that woman…I mean on that evening of musical performances,' said Kamakshi. 'I had spotted Ranbeer's armlet once while he was sunning himself on the terrace. Though I hadn't paid any attention to it, I guess the image had registered in my subconscious mind. He always hides it under his shirt sleeves.'

'Kashinath*ji* and Gautam were very surprised when they saw this symbol painted over the tin roof of a sprawling log house, exactly about a kilometre away from the Dhumavati Temple premises,' Meera continued.

'So they went inside?' Maya asked.

'Initially they did not think much about it and proceeded to Hegde's residential quarters. During the course of a casual conversation, Gautam asked Sharath's father about the tragedy that his younger brother had encountered. The old man was apprehensive about replying but when Gautam showed him Ranbeer's armlet, he calmly asked where he had found it. After Gautam told him everything, the old priest got up from his bed and without saying anything led them to the log house.'

'And then?'

'Inside the house was an old man. Sharath's father placed the armlet in his hands. After a while, tears trickled down his cheeks. Apparently, this armlet belonged to his younger brother who had run away from home about seventy years ago, when he was a young boy of fourteen.'

'You mean to say Ranbeer got this armlet from someone who had stolen it from this old man's brother?' Maya gasped.

Meera smiled. 'This long lost brother was Ranbeer's father!'

'How is that possible?'

'Even Gautam and Kashinath*ji* did not believe this till they heard the entire story. This old man is the eighth descendant of a disciple of medieval India's most powerful Aghori tantric. This tantric had pioneered a progressive cult of tantra by borrowing the best ritual traditions from Shaivas and Vaishnavas and was spreading his cult secretly in the eleventh century.'

'Oh man, so Ranbeer hails from it!' Kamakshi could not believe what she had just heard.

'Like the sanyasi at Yana had said, this Aghor had instructed his disciple that only the eldest son from eight subsequent generations would know about the existence of the sacred text. He had said that if anybody other than the eldest son learnt about the secret, the special *siddhis* and occult powers of the family would diminish. Unfortunately, this happened in the eighth generation.'

'This old man was the eldest son of the eldest born of the seventh generation, right?' Maya asked.

'Yes. And following the family code, one night his father, Devesh Acharya, had summoned him behind closed doors to tell him about how his own father had entrusted him the custody of the box containing the world's most powerful tantric text. A text that he had buried some years ago and which when discovered by the right person would change the fate of the world for much better.'

'This means that this old man's father, who is none other than Ranbeer's grandfather, had come to Banaras to hide the text during Brij Bhooshan Singh's days, more than nine decades ago. It also means that Devesh Acharya was none other than our wrinkled sanyasi's childhood friend!' Kamakshi exclaimed.

'Who could have imagined Ranbeer had such powerful connections.' Meera finished with a smirk.

'So, did our old man hear from his father where exactly the text was buried?' Kamakshi asked.

'Unfortunately, no! Just as he was about to reveal this there was a crashing sound from the verandah. Someone who had been eavesdropping on them had accidentally dropped a cane ladder. Both father and son rushed out and found no one. Nobody knows what exactly happened. The old man told Gautam and Kashinath*ji* that in those years, Devesh had a few disciples living in his home who were acquiring *siddhis*. Somehow Devesh had always been a little suspicious of a disciple called Shyam and felt that he had overheard the conversation. His instincts were proved right when there was a clanging sound of a trunk from the direction of Shyam's room at night, a sound that both father and son heard. Well, our man assumes that his father must have got up to investigate while he slept away. Devesh must have seen Shyam going out of the gates with his belongings and realised that the secret was out! And he must have followed him. Unfortunately, he did not succeed and was found dead in a meadow by some villagers at the brink of dawn. The poor man must have got a heart attack thinking that he had failed in his life's mission of guarding the secret.' Meera's voice was tinged with sadness.

'Shyam only knew that the text existed. He did not know where it was hidden. Which is why it remained undiscovered till yesterday.' Maya observed.

'And Ranbeer?' Kamakshi could not restrain her curiosity any longer.

'Well, Ranbeer's father was the younger son of Devesh. He disliked the fact that his father paid more attention to his elder brother as far as imparting *siddhis* were concerned and would often spy on their activities. Kripesh Acharya said that he is sure that his brother Nagesh, who was Ranbeer's father, was also listening to their conversation. And three days after his father's death, this brother had absconded never to be traced till this day,' Meera explained.

'But why did he abscond?' Maya asked.

'Because he was rash and impulsive and thought that he would discover the sacred text and...'

'And become the most revered mystic of modern India,' Kamakshi finished for Meera. 'And Ranbeer is not very different. His father must have told him everything before he died a few months ago and hence he has the singular ambition of finding the text and incorporating it in his documentary to win a very prestigious award.'

'Now I understand why Ranbeer is cagey about his family background. In fact, a neighbour had once told me that his father was adopted by his grandfather at the age of fifteen. But how are they so sure that Ranbeer's father is Kripesh's brother Nagesh?' Kamakshi asked.

'Because of the armlet. The followers of this cult wear a locket with this symbol. The armlet is a privilege of only the male members of this particular family who are privy to the existence of the text,' Meera explained. She also understood why Ranbeer had told Baccha that the tantric who had authored the text that Limar Singh has come searching for had led a very secret life.

There was pin-drop silence.

'Well, remember the tragedy that Sharath's uncle had alluded to was the unexplained death of Devesh*ji*. His uncle was one of his many disciples who lost out on their training and initiation because of this incident,' Meera explained.

'Are we assuming that Ranbeer is only scouting to get to the text because he wants to incorporate it in his documentary?' Maya inquired.

'What are you trying to say?' Kamakshi asked.

'I am just hoping he is not Laal Singh.'

For the next couple of hours they could talk about nothing else but their discovery about Ranbeer and the sacred text.

When lunch hour approached, Maya concluded, 'It will indeed be exciting to see how Limar Singh uses the formulas in this text to usher positive changes for mankind. Reversal of aging process is definitely something I am looking forward to!'

Kamakshi nodded and added, 'And I am now so convinced that genuine tantra, the way it was practised hundreds of years ago, was so noble. Now I understand why our mission of finding the sacred text was so important. This text will also dispel the myths surrounding tantra.'

Meera sighed, 'By the way, Gautam is also close to unearthing the truth behind House 501. He said he is meeting someone today and will call me after lunch.'

'Gautam had hired a detective to do a spot of sleuthing about House 501. His findings seem to corroborate that the number that Inspector Tiwari had retrieved from Gauriprada's incoming call records belongs to Rustom and he had forged this address,' Meera announced after lunch.

Seeing the nonchalant expressions of her friends, she continued, 'The house belongs to an employee of the Indian Railways, Abdul Siddiqui. The detective discovered that Siddiqui who lives in that house with his eccentric mother is actually a nexus between two poachers—Ashwaq Ali and Aahad R Khan. While Ashwaq Ali is notorious for poaching at the Kaziranga National Park, Aahad R Khan is one of the poachers in the most wanted list of the police. The police suspect that Aahad R Khan has changed his name to either Rashid or Rustom and that he is also part of a notorious gang that abducts young women for flesh trade.'

There was a chilling silence. Finally, Maya remarked, 'No wonder Rustom departs on a boat to fetch goods every month. These are smuggled goods. And now we know that Sakhat and Rustom are good friends because they share business interests.'

'Absolutely. After all, Sakhat runs a shop of smuggled leather goods.' Kamakshi inferred.

'Hmm...and we have also known them to deliver remnants of birds and animals to the tantrics, to be used as ritual ingredients regularly in Chet Singh Fort.' Meera wiped her sweaty forehead with a handkerchief.

'But why cite his name as Gautam Sharma in the subscriber records?' Kamakshi wondered aloud.

'Everybody around Kamakhya Dham has heard about Gautam Sharma. I guess Siddiqui did not stretch his imagination much while choosing the name,' Maya surmised. She then added, 'Had the name been different we probably would not have been so curious about it.'

Each of them was now beginning to understand that Ranbeer had indeed been implicated in the threats that Arvind had received because the poachers had feared that their nexus with tantrics would be exposed. After all, the documentary would have highlighted how owls and other animals were being exploited in occult rituals.

'While Rustom's involvement makes a lot of things clear, I am just hoping Ranbeer is not guilty of anything,' Meera solemnly remarked.

a murky nexus

The Everest Café was teeming with tourists. The girls too were sitting with their breakfast mulling on all the information that had resurfaced in the past days.

'Now that we have a lot of clarity about Rustom and his accomplices, I think we should make an effort to find Gauripradal,' Meera began. 'Also, Baccha tells me that Limar Singh too hasn't been seen in the last three weeks,' she added.

'Something tells me that Gauripradal is somewhere in the tunnels—Rustom and Sakhat are quite familiar with them, and remember the muffled cough we heard in the tunnel?' Kamakshi was enthusiastic.

'Well, it is clear that he is not in the tunnel leading to Manikarnika Ghat,' Meera reminded.

'Of course, neither did we bump into him nor did they get their hands on the secret text,' Maya remarked.

'That night before the abduction, Arshad must have apprised Gauripradal about the route of the other tunnel. And, the abductors made Gauripradal take them down hoping it would lead to the text.' Meera inferred.

'But I completely fail to understand one thing—how on earth did Rustom and his accomplices know that the sacred text is hidden in Banaras? And that it can be reached through some tunnel?' Maya wondered.

That evening while the three girls were sitting in the private section of the café, Maya stated that Alok and she would be divorcing on mutual consent.

'I am unable to forgive him for deserting me at a time when I needed him the most,' she stated, matter-of-factly.

'And Alok agreed that this is a good enough reason for you to dissolve the marriage?' the others wanted to know.

'Well, after going back from Yana, Arvind had met him and apprised him about all my misadventures. Alok was very reproachful of my actions and suggested the divorce himself. He added that he had had enough of me and that I had harassed him no end by absconding from the asylum.'

Sensing that Maya was slightly uncomfortable discussing this development any further, Kamakshi quickly turned the conversation around. 'Well, good riddance. Now, has Arvind's senior unearthed the mystery behind the email threats?'

'Not yet,' Maya shook her head.

'We have a call with Karmar and Panicker tonight via Skype at eight. Karmar has spoken to Sankalp Nair and has some information for us.' Meera apprised the two girls around early evening.

It was 7.50 pm. Meera's balcony was throbbing with anticipation as she adjusted the settings on her laptop. Maya, Kamakshi and Baccha were huddled around the small circular table on which it was placed.

'Hello, everybody,' Karmar and Panicker waved to them after the call connected.

Karmar came straight to the point. 'Well, Sankalp Nair does know Alex Powell. And from everything that I have gathered, it seems Powell is desperately scouting for the sacred text. The *grigri* we found at Yana Temple is probably his and I'm sure he has other accomplices.'

The four people at the other end of the connection were speechless.

Karmar continued, 'Actually, Powell has been using Nair as a pawn in the same way the three investors had tried to use me and the other nominees of the think tank. Powell, in fact, is well acknowledged as an authority on Archaeology in Africa. After deciding to embark on a study about the dynamics of earth energy, Nair had approached Powell for guidance. But Nair is completely unaware of the think tank or the existence of any text. I can vouch for his innocence as I know him since the time he was a student. Trust me when I say that I can read his expressions.

Now, I also asked him about his work under Panicker—his thesis on the construction industry. He had told me and Panicker that he would be submitting his findings to the Ministry of Housing and Urban Affairs, for them to understand how earth energies can impact construction activity.'

'And?' Kamakshi prodded.

'Well, it turns out that he did not submit his findings to the Ministry because Alex Powell bought the thesis from him. Apart from sharing interesting insights about earth energies, Powell had also partially funded Nair's expenses while he was in India doing his research. Hence, he could not refuse his benefactor's offer of buying his thesis,' Karmar said.

Panicker spoke for the first time, 'While he was at my university, Nair had told me that his benefactor had spent almost two decades camping at excavation sites across the world. If I remember clearly, Nair had also said that his benefactor has an academic interest about the origin of voodoo and witchcraft, and that during the course of his excavations he had even unearthed some forgotten symbols of African witchcraft.'

Panicker paused and added, 'I guess he had told me his benefactor's name. But I am bad at remembering names.

Karmar has been frequently talking about Alex Powell but even that did not trigger any recollection.'

'So Professor Karmar, we can now conclude that Powell is Laal Singh. It was he who had been rummaging in the Yana Temple and dropped that *grigri*. It is also clear where Laal Singh got those pelvic skeletons from—obviously these were preserved from his excavation expeditions.' Kamakshi surmised.

'I am sorry to disappoint you. While Powell is definitely involved in this riddle of Laal Singh and the sacred text, he is *not* Laal Singh. Laal Singh is most probably his accomplice.'

'*Saahabji,* how are you so sure?' Baccha asked.

'Because Powell has not visited India for over a year now. Nair said that Powell has been embroiled in some legal issues and the court has restricted his overseas travel,' Karmar replied.

'Are you sure Nair is just a pawn? For all you know, he might be the mysterious Laal Singh,' Meera remarked.

'You are forgetting that all this while that Laal Singh has been striking, Nair too has not been in India,' Karmar said.

Meera asked, 'Just two more questions. What was the exact focus of Nair's thesis?'

'It mapped specific spots in the Indian landmass that had unusually high energy,' Panicker replied.

'Did you share the details about your book with him?' Maya asked.

'Of course not! These details are highly confidential. But, yes, he was aware of my book.' The professor sounded annoyed.

'And he also knew where you kept it?' Maya prodded boldly.

'He knew it was in my chamber but did not know… wait…now when I come to think about it, in the last three months there were days when I had a feeling that someone was shadowing me.' As Panicker finished the Internet connection snapped.

Nobody could think or talk of anything else throughout the rest of the evening.

'If Alex Powell and Laal Singh are partners in crime, where does Venkatesh feature? Remember Karmar's suspicion that he is…' Meera stopped with a weird expression. 'Oh God, how could we forget! Of course Venkatesh is Laal Singh. He is operating in India while his partner is in Africa. How incredibly simple it is!'

'It is much more likely than not. But what could be the connection between Venkatesh and Powell and Rustom and his accomplices?' Baccha mumbled to himself as he dabbed some mosquito repellant on his feet.

For a little while, the others remained silent.

Finally, Meera said, 'I guess Baccha is confused about why Rustom and his accomplices are competing with them to get to the sacred text.'

Baccha nodded.

'I must have said this before. There is a fundamental piece of this puzzle that I fail to understand,' Kamakshi said.

'What?' the others chorused at the same instant.

'Well, think tank and all of that is understandable. But how on earth did any of these people know of the existence of the sacred text? I mean, the search obviously started after knowing that such a text exists.'

In the silence that ensued, the three girls realised that Ranbeer had been privy to the existence of the text all along. *'Is Ranbeer privy to some vital secret of the occult realm as well?*

Is the documentary an eyewash? Does he have any comrades in the occult world?' they wondered.

Meera got up from her chair and started rolling a joint. 'Somehow I am beginning to suspect Karmar too. We became part of this chase only after we heard him at the Claridges. What if there is nothing wrong about the think tank? For all we know it might not even exist. What if he is hiding something?'

'You mean to say he was actually manipulating us to get to the sacred text? That maybe he is Laal Singh?' Maya could feel the surge of anxiety in her heart.

It was Baccha who eased the tension. 'From whatever I have heard, I am very doubtful that Karmar is Laal Singh. If he was Laal Singh, he would have let us believe that the African man is Laal Singh. I mean that way we would not have suspected him. I somehow honestly think he could not have thought so far just to fool us and lead us on.'

'I agree. I mean this is just a little too farfetched,' Kamakshi said.

gauripradā at last

'There are numerous underground tunnels in this part,' Baccha apprised.

Baccha had taken the girls to stroll along alleys that coursed untidily between old houses and back entrances of various heritage hotels that dotted the riverfront.

Pointing to an archaic door of a palatial hotel, he added, 'In the olden days, these were the residences of royal families when they visited Kashi, mostly on pilgrimage. They have been converted into hotels after Independence.'

'I guess all the tunnels can be accessed from inside these buildings, so it will be impossible for us to reach Gauriprada,' Meera voiced their growing hoplelessness.

After a long silence, Baccha almost shrieked, 'How stupid of me! The tunnel leading to Darbhanga Fort can be accessed from outside. It can be accessed from the Shiva Temple in Scindia Ghat and it starts from Arshad Singh's haveli. I think this is the very tunnel that we have been hunting for.'

'What?' The three women were astounded.

'Well, Bhishan Singh Thakur, Arshad's forefather, had a secret love affair with the princess of Magadha. Because he was only a feudal lord, her father was against the match and he could not risk meeting her anywhere in town. So, Bhishan Singh Thakur got his men to tunnel a passage all the way to Darbhanga Fort, right upto the chamber of Princess Mahima. Apparently, this tunnel was a closely guarded secret and the people of Banaras heard about it only some decades ago when a Dutch historian who was researching the forts and palaces in the ghat area published his findings in the local newspaper,' Baccha explained in a jiffy.

Seeing the confused expressions, he added, 'Bhishan Thakur's secret affair with Princess Mahima is part of Kashi's folklore. I too have heard this story from my grandfather as a child. So, when the existence of this tunnel was revealed, people easily understood who built it and why. However, hardly anyone from the present generation knows about the tunnel and its background.'

'Well, Arshad must have known and apprised Gauripradа about everything. Let's go to Scindia Ghat then,' Kamakshi said in an excited pitch.

After a short, brisk walk, they reached their destination. In the interim, Baccha told them how he knew about it. He narrated that a couple of years ago he had come across Arshad Singh near an old Shiva temple of this ghat at around midnight. The sozzled man had been repeatedly saying that he wanted to enter the temple and open the red door. 'When I asked him what was inside the door, he said that his great-great-grandfather had found true love behind it and that he too wanted to go inside and find his soul mate.' Baccha finished.

'But how can you be so sure?' Kamakshi asked.

'Because Arshad had been insisting that one end of it leads to the oval room in Darbhanga Fort while the other end leads to the biggest bedroom of the haveli.'

They started surveying the area around. Adjoining Manikarnika Ghat, Scindia Ghat was one of the relatively serene ghats of Banaras.

'Some of the oldest temples are here,' Baccha said as they entered a cluster of temples.

The temple doors were shut and not a soul was around.

Finally, they came to a small Shiva temple created partially from the bark of a tree trunk and partially from stone.

To their surprise, the entrance door was latched from the outside.

'The priests latch the doors when they go for their afternoon nap to prevent monkeys from entering,' Baccha flashed a smile, as they trailed into the temple after him, clutching their floaters.

Vermillion-smeared statues of deities adorned the alcoves of the temple walls. A massive Shiva Linga in black limestone occupied the central portion. The three girls looked everywhere for the red door. It was nowhere in sight. Strangely, Baccha did not look worried. Instead, he knelt at the Shiva Linga and uttered some mantras.

'Where is it?' Maya asked almost in a whisper as soon as he opened his eyes. Without answering, he moved to the wall opposite him. As the friends edged closer, they could see a rusted door knob on a portion of the wall that had a black marble surface.

Baccha turned the knob in the anti clockwise direction. After the third attempt, the door started moving backwards. Inside it there was a hollow space, big enough for two people to stand together, and a door. Red paint was peeling from it.

Meera, who was the last to enter the hollow space, carefully shut the marble door and trailed inside the red door behind Maya.

After walking seven steps in utter darkness they reached a dead end. Flashing their torches, they could see a steep flight of stone steps leading downwards. The space reminded them of a tube for the steps were encircled by a stone wall. There was nothing to clutch at.

Baccha took the lead and started the precarious descent. Much to their horror, cobwebs littered the crevices of the wall. Occasionally, lizards and cockroaches scurried in and out of these crevices. After going down fifteen steps, they saw a rusted door on the wall to the left.

After descending what seemed like a hundred and fifty stairs, they were finally treading on flat ground. Here, the walls were fairly apart and it felt several notches cooler than the stairway. Soon, they stood facing a sandstone wall. A black hollow space was carved in the middle of the wall, it had three openings—one in the centre and two on either sides.

'I have a feeling that if we enter the middle one, we shall reach the tunnel that goes to Ramgarh Fort from Chet Singh Ghat. It is an underwater tunnel. We have to enter either of the spaces in the side walls to reach Gauripradа. I do know a little about the underground routes of Banaras,' Baccha said.

The opening on their left looked a little bright and airy. The other was foreboding. Stone steps led to both the openings.

'How do we know which is the correct route?' Kamakshi asked.

'Can you hear what I hear?' Meera grabbed Kamakshi by the shoulders.

Within half a minute, the rest of them could hear the thud of footsteps. Some people were coming towards them through the passage that they had just crossed.

Kamakshi darted to the steps in front of them. The others followed. Just as Meera crouched into the hollow behind the rest, they saw two men descending the tube stairway.

As the men walked on the flat surface they could see their faces. One was Rustom and the other was a middle-aged man that they had never seen.

Their voices were echoing. 'Why can't you give me my commission now? I have taken big risks for you,' Rustom sounded angry.

'How can you be so selfish?' The other man hissed between clenched teeth. 'And what risks are you talking about? You are going to gain from this secret as much as the rest of us.'

It is your and that woman's secret. None of us are going to benefit from it. We....'

'Well, high time you understand that we cannot exist without each other and can't afford to blackmail each other,' the older man interrupted.

The voices started trailing as the men turned to the left and entered the tunnel.

For a couple of minutes, none of them could move.

'After them,' Baccha whispered and darted into the hollow opening on the left.

The others followed. Fortunately, the tunnel arched at various angles.

'They can't look back and see us,' Meera whispered.

For a while they could only hear the voices ahead of them. It was difficult to decipher anything.

'If you are so sure that Laal Singh has already found the text then why on earth are we keeping this man alive?' Rustom's voice was audible.

'I don't disagree with you here. Trust me, I am sick and tired of walking these wretched tunnels. I know this priest is a complete nincompoop. He doesn't even know the routes, let alone be aware of any text. But what do I tell Vijaylakshmi? You know how dangerous she can get!'

By this time, it was clear that the elder of the two was connected to the woman investor of the think tank.

'But you have to tell her something at some point. And how are you so sure that Laal Singh has already found the text?'

'Any moron can figure that. He has stopped searching in the cremation grounds. He has vanished...obviously with the text!' The man let out a sarcastic laugh.

'You also suspect that your partner has a lot to do with Laal Singh? So instead of grilling this stupid man why don't we capture him and grill him instead?' Rustom sounded emphatic.

'I don't suspect his involvement. I *know* that he is involved. He is trying to double cross us just like we are trying to double cross him. But do you think he is some helpless man who can be kidnapped?' The man almost screamed.

'Oh yes. I have heard of the things he has done. Our entire poacher fraternity shudders at his name. I have also heard that no underworld dealing in South Africa happens without his approval,' Rustom said.

At the mention of South Africa, everybody's hearts started pounding. *'He is probably referring to Alex Powell. Now we are close to knowing the connection between Rustom, Alex and Venkatesh,'* they hoped.

Suddenly, the two men halted. Baccha retraced a few steps and motioned the girls to follow. They all crouched inside two massive holes in the sandstone walls.

'You have one more chance. Either you tell us about the passage to the text or we stop carrying food and water to you. You are smart enough to know that all we need to kill you is stop visiting you.' The older man started laughing ominously.

'Any last wish?' It was Rustom this time.

'You know my last wish, you freaking scoundrel! How I wish I could tell your truth to everyone in Banaras. That you are a bloody poacher! That you supply deer musk and owl claws to tantrics.'

'Had it not been for *Amma,* I would have killed you long back. But she insists on coming and seeing you one final time. You better get this straight. We are coming here exactly after three days. Either you give us the answer or prepare to die.' The older man threatened.

'I have no idea about what you want and what you are talking about. But I do know one thing. Even if I had the answer, you would have killed me.' Gauripráda sounded exhausted but fierce.

One of the two men must have kicked him at that instant for the poor priest started yelping in pain. 'Here is your last ration,' the older man announced in a pompous tone.

The men then started retracing their steps. Baccha and the three girls held their breath. As they crossed them, Kamakshi who had been the last to crawl into the hole saw something that made her eyes pop and jaw drop.

'What is it dear?' Meera whispered.

'His arm...' Kamakshi was unable to proceed.

'What about his arm?' Maya urged.

'It is completely tattooed with female genitals. I could see as Rustom's torchlight was right over it.'

about accomplices, aliases and encyclopaedias

'Are we all thinking the same thing?' Maya asked in an excited pitch.

'Yes, and this explains everything,' Meera moped her forehead with a handkerchief. 'Man, who could have thought that Rustom's accomplice is Venkatesh. And Laal Singh is very likely Powell's accomplice. The two investors of the fake think tank are in serious competition to reach the sacred text. This is incredible!' Meera exclaimed after she was sure that Rustom and Venkatesh were safely out of earshot.

Without replying, Baccha darted in the direction from which they had heard Gauriprada's voice.

The others followed. After a few steps, they saw a bamboo ladder standing against the right wall. It led to a large opening near the ceiling. Baccha climbed up into the opening as the girls stood below in silence.

'How could we have not come?' Baccha's voice was drowned by Gauriprada's sobs.

'I got all the ammunition. Will free you in two minutes,' Baccha said, cheerfully. Within a minute the girls could hear the sound of chains clanging on the ground and Gauriprada appeared in the opening.

'Are you sure they won't come back today?' Maya asked Gauriprada as they scurried along the passage.

Too overwhelmed to speak, Gauripradha had simply nodded.

They reached the flat ground surface sooner than they had expected.

It was clear that the abductors had brought Gauripradha through this route as he seemed to know the directions. He led the way to the tube staircase and climbed the first step.

He halted before the rusted door and started pushing. It did not budge. Without asking any questions, Baccha who was right behind him, tried his luck. With a screeching sound the door opened. The five were now standing inside what seemed like a narrow, straight corridor. Lush green moss carpeted the grey stone walls.

After walking in a single file for some time, they came to a dead end. Gauripradha pointed to a rickety ladder lying on one side. 'We need to climb up and push the circular shaft.'

The three girls and Gauripradha steadied the ladder against the wall. Baccha took the lead and started climbing. After ascending the final step, he found a handle of a shaft staring him in the face.

'Glory to Lord Hanuman,' he shouted as he started pushing the circular stone with his hands. To his surprise, without much effort he could dislodge the stone and throw it in the opposite direction. A flood of light and fresh air streamed in.

'So we are in the back lawn of Arshad Singh's haveli,' Meera who had been the last to climb out remarked as she and Baccha put the stone back in its place. It blended with the rest of the white marble enclosure encircling the fountain.

Barring Gauripradа, the others were in a daze. 'So they took you underground from here?' Maya finally found her voice.

Without answering, Gauripradа darted towards the elephant-shaped hedges. 'And now we will be foolish if we stand here,' he shouted over his shoulder. Crouching on the ground, he squeezed into a space between the legs of the elephant and wriggled out into the opposite side. The others followed suit. They were now standing in a secluded by-lane. Most of the streetlights were out of order and LED bulbs from a couple of ration stores provided the sole illumination.

The priest had covered his head and face with a black cloth. 'I shall walk separately and join you at the guesthouse.'

The others saw perfect sense in this precaution.

'Please, don't enter through the front entrance. Wait for us at the steps of Shivala. We will reach in half an hour,' Baccha cautioned.

Gauripradа narrated all the details of the conversations that had transpired between him and his abductors.

Meera solemnly remarked, 'If Rustom and his gang had abducted you only because you were threatening their work by helping us with the documentary….'

'I would have been dead by now,' the priest grimaced.

'Hail the sacred secret text, it surely must be a boon for mankind for it saved your life. You really didn't know where it was hidden?' quizzed Maya.

'I did, but I was too lazy to go and fetch it before anyone else did,' he replied, sarcastically.

Meera studied Gauripradа's expressions and wondered if like Ranbeer, he too had some ulterior motive.

'You knew the exact route of the tunnel that leads from Arshad's courtyard. But why on earth did you ever ask him about tunnel routes?'

Gauripradа took a long hard look at the ground. 'I confess it was my greed that got me into trouble. I wanted to find the text and give it to Limar Singh. I knew that if I was successful in doing this the whole of Banaras would acknowledge me as the most superior priest, worthy of taking charge of the management of the new temple complex.'

Meera remembered that Baccha had told her about this a month ago.

'How did you ever guess that the sacred text could be buried under Arshad's haveli?' This time it was Kamakshi.

'I had heard the rumour that some tantric had gone down one of the haveli tunnels in Brij Bhooshan Singh's days.'

'Arshad is still missing from town. His *Naga* sanyasi too is not around these days…wonder what is happening!' Maya said.

'Must be searching for the sacred locket which Arshad's forefather had lost.'

'What?' Everybody was startled.

Gauripradа started laughing. 'Well, I had asked Arshad why he had brought this *Naga* sanyasi to Banaras. He said because he wanted him to find a sacred locket. Arshad's family has been jinxed. Therefore, he had consulted the clairvoyant for a remedy. The clairvoyant said that this unending saga of misfortune had actually started about five centuries ago when his forefather, Bhishan Singh Thakur had lost a locket given by his guru.'

'Bhishan Singh Thakur—this is the same man who dug a tunnel to Darbhanga Fort to meet the princess of Magadha?'

As Kamakshi raised the question, Meera's eyes started twinkling.

'In which era did Bhishan Singh Thakur live?'

'Sixteenth century. In fact, he had constructed the haveli. But why are you asking?' Gaurіprada was puzzled.

'So this is the same locket that Bheeksha Das's ancestor retrieved from the dead body of the corpse! It was the corpse of Princess Mahima.'

As Meera finished Gauriprada looked dazed. The girls told him about everything that Bheeksha had nararted.

'I also remember that my grandfather had told me that among Arshad's ancestors, Bhishan Thakur was the most endowed in occult powers and that he had trained under a guru in South India. So, that locket which is in Bheeksha's possession should ideally be restored to the rightful owner when he is back,' Gauriprada said.

'It is true; losing either the locket or the armlet brings bad luck. See, how our Ranbeer is missing in action. I mean what bad luck to have been summoned by IDA at this time,' observed Kamakshi. 'I must say you have been mean to him. You haven't told him that we have found the text. I know you want to surprise him but I still think it's not fair.'

Meera smiled superficially. She knew that she had not told him anything because she was hoping that Laal Singh was not Ranbeer!

Everyone decided that Gauriprada should go back to his house and remain unseen for a while. They concluded that he should resume his duties only after Rustom and his accomplices were nabbed. They realised that they had no concrete evidence against him and given the complexity of the case they would need to involve cops beyond the local level.

They also decided to investigate the contents of Rustom's leather folder to ascertain his real identity—the folder that Suchit had apprised them about.

'If we come across any document that substantiates our claim that he is actually Aahad Rustom Khan, it will be very easy for us to lodge a police complaint,' Kamakshi reasoned.

'Indeed, and only Suchit can somehow get to the folder. Nobody will be suspicious if they see him lurking around Rustom's house,' Baccha agreed.

'Where are you going?' Kamakshi asked Meera.

'To the Centre of Vedic Studies. It's already the first week of July. And I am supposed to wrap up my thesis by this month end.'

'Then we shall see you later. I have spoken to Suchit. He said it should not be difficult to break into Rustom's house today.'

Gopal Sarai was manning the library of the Centre of Vedic Studies. Meera sat near a window and browsed through the notes in her diary. After forty minutes, she looked up in the direction of the librarian. He had noticed her and was waving at her.

Meera walked up to him. 'It's a surprise that you are here. I always thought you were involved in the administration and other important matters.'

'Well, little things are sometimes too important to be left in irresponsible hands,' Sarai replied with a serious expression.

'What happened?' Meera asked.

The man looked at her intently. 'Two encyclopaedias have also gone missing from our archives around the same time and these were critical reference material for research.'

'So the thief did steal. I did think it was incredibly weird that he did not take anything.'

'The thief did not take those encyclopaedias. These were stolen…I mean never returned by a scholar who borrowed them. Obviously he was not a scholar. He had faked his identity.'

'What?'

'Initially, we too could not believe that something like this had happened. After about four weeks, we smelt a rat and contacted the organisation. There was nobody by that name. Only recently we have managed to nab him but unfortunately, he had already handed over the encyclopaedias to someone. And despite stiff interrogation, he is adamant about not disclosing the name.'

'What were these encyclopaedias about?' Meera asked.

'They were related to archaeology—findings of important excavations in the Vedic Age.'

When Meera returned to the guesthouse she found Baccha putting chunks of ice along with buckets of water into the mega-sized cooler in the restaurant area.

'The others have gone to meet Suchit at Godowlia Chowk. I think he has been successful in his mission as he has invited them over for lunch,' Baccha told Meera the moment she appeared.

The Frenchwoman merely smiled and retired to her room. Her mind was reeling with a train of fresh thoughts. After a hurried shower, she dialled Maya's number.

'Meera, I can't tell you how happy I am. We are all winning! You got to hurry up and come here from wherever you are and hear everything. Arvind too had called an hour back. He is safe and will soon be joining work.' Every sentence was punctuated by sheer joy and unrestrained excitement.

'Okay! And you need to hear what I discovered today,' Meera replied.

'Hello*ji*,' Suchit greeted Meera jubilantly as she walked into the *dhaba* where Maya and Kamakshi were waiting for her.

'Hi,' she replied and dragged a chair from the adjoining table.

'You look serious. What is it?' Kamakshi asked.

Meera narrated the events of the morning.

'Archaeology encyclopaedias! There must be some uncanny connection between the man who rampaged the library and Alex Powell. It is possible that this man has some connection to our Laal Singh too,' Kamakshi said, excitedly.

'Well, we shall all see Laal Singh very soon now; the first Monday of *Shravan* is just four days away,' Suchit said.

Meera looked at her friends a little admonishingly. She wasn't entirely happy about the fact that they had told him everything.

Without even noticing her apprehension, Suchit merrily relayed how he had effortlessly broken into Rustom's house and got hold of his leather folder. 'I had the good sense to relock the house so Rustom won't suspect anything until he discovers what is missing,' he said proudly showing the A4-sized folder.

After carefully scanning through various bills, receipts and IDs—all in the name of Rustom Khan, Meera found a carefully folded piece of paper that was turning yellow. It was an affidavit made by a local court in 2008. Aahad Rustom Khan had become Rustom Khan in that year.

The chocolate brown passport belonging to Aahad R Khan had just one empty page left. It had been issued in 1993 and had not been renewed. All the travels, in the course of the last two decades had been to South Africa. 'And the funny thing is our man has travelled with this passport twice to Nigeria even after his official name change. Now check the contents of the last flap,' Maya urged.

Meera's eyes almost popped out as she saw there was another set of identity documents with the name Aahad R Khan. These papers were enough to put away Rustom behind the bars now.

'Do we give these to the cops right away?' Maya asked the others.

'We cannot hand it to just any cop. I have called up the police station. Tiwari and all the top cops have gone to Delhi on official work. They shall be back in a couple of days. And I guess by then Rustom and Sakhat will also be back,' Suchit replied.

Maya then updated Meera with news from Arvind's end. 'Arvind's senior who had taken charge of investigating the threats that he had been receiving, had apprised him that authorities would soon be cracking down on a mega nexus of Indian and African poachers. In fact, a couple of Indian poachers have already been nabbed and sent to police custody in Delhi. Astronomical amounts of deer musk, owl talons, rhino horns and elephant tusks have been retrieved from these poachers and apparently the police is now grilling them about their accomplices,' Maya relayed. 'This gang was also involved in threatening and even attacking conservationists in recent months,' she added.

'This means that Arvind can resume work...hopefully soon,' Kamakshi smiled.

The evening brought in more answers.

'Hi, Meera,' Karmar's voice had never been so carefree. 'Everything is clear now. We only have to nab Laal Singh... I called to tell you that I am reaching Banaras day after, with our six friends.' He was referring to the six security guards.

'We look forward to seeing you.'

Just as Meera was about to disconnect, Karmar shouted, 'I forgot to tell you the most important thing. Sankalp Nair has told me that Powell has been sent to judicial custody. Remember the case I was telling you about?'

'Is he embroiled with some poaching trades?' Meera asked.

'Indeed. I think all the pieces of the puzzle are now falling into place.' Karmar sounded ecstatic.

'And you will be delighted to know we have found Gauriprada.'

As she said the words, Meera was confident about one thing—they could trust Karmar completely. He had indeed always been on their side.

unmasking laal singh

The following day Rustom and Sakhat were still missing from town. Inspector Tiwari too was not back.

'Rustom, Powell and, I am assuming, even Venkatesh are honchos of that infamous nexus of Indian and African poachers,' Meera deduced. 'Little wonder that the investors of this think tank are super wealthy. This illegal trade sure swelled their coffers.'

'But nobody knows anything about their involvement with occult practitioners. After all, Rustom and Sakhat have been supplying remains of poached animals to tantrics,' Maya said.

'I wonder if this part shall be exposed. After all, there is zero likelihood of Powell and Venkatesh confessing about their plans of starting an occult network.' Kamakshi smiled sarcastically.

'Why on earth are you so pessimistic? We are finally nabbing Laal Singh, aren't we? It is common sense that once he is caught this part of the nexus will also come to light.' Meera had never felt so optimistic.

'How do we hand over Laal Singh to the cops? I mean, he is not a conventional criminal. Tiwari or any other cop will never take this hunt for the sacred text seriously!' Maya observed.

'Besides, we have no evidence to prove that he has killed the *chandaals* in the cremation ground,' Kamakshi added.

'Remember Panicker's book that was stolen? Sankalp Nair is obviously no longer a suspect. It is indeed in Laal Singh's custody! I somehow have this feeling that once we nab

Laal Singh, it will not be difficult for us to hand him over to the authorities,' Meera said.

'I am so excited to know who Laal Singh is. I am counting hours to Monday night,' said Baccha as he sat down beside them.

'The man has to have an unflinching purpose for reaching the text. After all, if he is an aide of Powell he must be aware that he is in police custody. I am beginning to wonder if Laal Singh will come to the spot at all,' Meera said.

'Well, our efforts can't go in vain.' Kamakshi closed her eyes.

'Are the rooms ready? Seven people are arriving this evening.' Meera inquired at the reception at about 11.30 am the following day.

Baccha was missing. There was no sign of him till lunchtime.

'It's strange that his phone is switched off too,' Meera observed to her friends.

As they were exiting the dining area after lunch, an excited Baccha ran towards them.

'Meera*ji,* there has been a raid at Sakhat Bhopali's house. The police have found packets of illegal drugs and a woman that he and Rustom had abducted. A notorious tantric called Tukaram Baba was involved in the abduction.'

'What?' Meera almost stammered.

'Where is Sakhat and who is this woman?' Maya asked.

'He is in Lucknow police's custody. Apparently, he and his aides have abducted several young women and handed them over to that notorious woman who runs Erotic Salvation. These women are secretly transported to Thailand and forced into prostitution. The police are now investigating all the link-ups. And apparently this particular woman was taken home from police custody by her father. A man called Upadhyay.'

The three girls exchanged a glance. None of the wrongdoers were going to go scot free.

Karmar looked very relaxed when he arrived that evening with the six guards.

'This is nothing but divine intervention, else we would have never found the answers to so many baffling incidents,' he said as he handed a brown packet to Meera who was waiting for him in the reception.

It contained a large piece of red cloth and an assortment of dried fruits. 'Blessings and *prasad* from Maa Kamakhya. Gautam and Kashinath send you their regards. They have asked me to tell you that after Laal Singh and his accomplices are in police custody you should go and pay homage to the Goddess and shoot the last leg of your documentary with their help.' The professor smiled.

There was a fierce and torrential downpour the next day. Golden and white streaks of lightning erupted through the charcoal grey clouds that were moving across the skyscape of the holy town at an unbridled pace.

'This is like a holy omen. Finally, the day of nabbing Laal Singh has arrived,' Kamakshi said.

Throughout the day, the three girls, Karmar and Baccha could think and talk of nothing but the events and discoveries of the case. The six guards went for a dip in the holy river followed by a visit to Kashi Vishwanath Temple.

'We could not have managed without these guards.' Karmar remarked as they were heading in the direction of Ramnagar Fort at 7 pm.

'How will they manage to convince the guards at the fort to let us in at this unearthly hour?' Meera wondered.

'They have their network,' Karmar replied.

After the four autos, which had ferried them to the gates of Ramnagar Fort departed, Karmar gestured to the guards to take charge. One of them confidently walked across to the entrance gates and spoke to the guard on duty for a few minutes. He looked back and flashing a broad smile gestured them to trail behind him, into the complex.

The rain had ceased and the crescent-shaped moon was struggling to peek through the mass of clouds. Ramnagar Fort looked foreboding and grand at the same time. In no time, the seven men and three women had crossed the paved stretch that connected the fort premises to Yash Kashi Temple.

The priest was there, chanting the evening hymns. Without much difficulty, they located the boulder described in the misleading clue by the erudite sanyasi at Yana. The ancient-looking granite boulder smeared with blotches of yellow and red paint was about seven yards away from the temple, close to the rear wall of the complex.

As they strategically hid themselves in dark, bushy corners of the area surrounding the boulder, they could only hear the sound of their pounding hearts.

The next three hours were a blur. At 10.50 pm, they heard the sound of footsteps.

A tempest was starting to brew.

'Damn! I hope the rain doesn't deter him,' Meera thought to herself and instantly realised that this was too important a mission for Laal Singh to skip.

Before she could think of anything, a man clad in a raincoat started walking in the direction of the boulder. His face was masked with a piece of cloth. As he reached the boulder and bent down, the six guards ran at lightning speed towards him. He must have had no time to react for they overpowered him with ease. The rest were now running towards them.

At that instant, a knife darted in their direction and rested on the shoulder of the man. He started bleeding profusely.

'After him,' Karmar shouted. While one guard supported the hurt assailant, the other guards ran after a man who was climbing down the steps of the verandah of the temple.

Meera and Maya unmasked the bleeding man while Karmar ran behind the guards. They could not recognise this man. He looked young, probably in his late twenties.

Within minutes the man who had thrown the knife was darting to the main gates with the security guards close on his heels. He turned and sprayed something that smelt of methane oil in their direction.

'Nobody gets me, you fools!' He chuckled between gritted teeth and started running.

Although they were spluttering, the guards lurched ahead. In that instant, something unexpected happened. The man froze on his tracks for a few fleeting seconds. This was sufficient time for the guards to nab him.

They were all now facing an ascetic. It was Limar Singh and his sudden appereance had astounded Laal Singh.

With bodies trembling in excitement, Karmar tore open his mask.

It was Professor Bharadwaj!

the triumph of survival

'Surviving nightmares are never easy. But after a nightmare, the first beams of the sun ushering daylight are all the more wonderful. Don't you agree?' Ranbeer asked Kamakshi as the two strolled on Shivala Ghat at dawn. Ranbeer had returned from the US the day before and after listening to everything that had occurred in his absence, he was quite pensive.

'Actually Ranbeer, after all that I have experienced at Kashi, especially after our chase for the sacred text, there is one realisation that has etched my soul. I suspect I shall carry it into all my future lives,' she finished with a twinkle in her eye.

'And what is that, darling?'

'Well, questions don't always end in answers. Sometimes questions and conflicts lead to more questions that are beyond the purview of human comprehension.'

'How right you are, Kamakshi!' Maya joined them. 'We are part of a dynamic universe beyond our comprehension. A universe created by the supreme force that is even beyond the universe and all existence.' She quoted a hymn from the *Rig Veda*.

'If the essence of every creation in this universe flows from one supreme force, then who are we mere mortals to judge what is good, bad, or ugly?' Kamakshi observed.

They strolled to the edge of the river quietly.

'So maybe this is what tantra is all about,' Maya bent down and cupped the holy water. 'Perhaps it is a surrender and celebration of our imperfections.'

The two women exchanged pensive glances.

Tantra for them was no longer a blasphemous practice. While they understood the sacred essence of real tantra, they were also beginning to experience its philosophical connotations.

A week had passed after their encounter with Laal Singh.

Ranbeer had returned to Banaras. While he had been jubilant at the discovery of the sacred text, he was very uncomfortable about the fact that his family lineage had been discovered.

A couple of evenings ago, Meera had candidly confessed to Ranbeer that she had suspected him to be Laal Singh!

'I mean, I was hoping against hope that you are not the man...but your actions invariably corroborated my suspicions,' she had said after relaying how she had discovered that he had photocopied her reference book and how she and Kamakshi had trailed him to the residential compound of the Shiv Temple at midnight.

'Actually, I was quite sure you are Laal Singh, after Gautam and Kashinath discovered your family lineage. The fact that you were so guarded about your locket and armlet countered all other logic,' she admitted.

Maya and Kamakshi too admitted that they had harboured the same suspicions.

Ranbeer had been silent for a while before explaining. 'Well, I was just driven by pure ambition. I was well aware of the fact that this year IDA would be giving an award in an unprecedented category—Best Discovery. I had gathered this from inside sources and I was determined to win the award. Though my works have received critical acclaim, I have never bagged an award and I understood this was my chance after I learnt about the existence of the missing text from my father,' he had awkwardly blurted.

'Hmm...,' Meera merely sighed. She remembered how after learning about the existence of this text, she too had felt that it would be a terrific addition to her thesis.

'And I... I did not want to reveal my true family identity. Actually, I wasn't very pleased myself that my own father, Nagesh Acharya, had absconded from his home just because he had this overwhelming desire to discover this text,' he added a little sheepishly.

The others now understood the actual reason behind his sly approach and smiled.

The six security guards had been of phenomenal help in nabbing Bharadwaj. His resistance had been savage and to everyone's surprise he had displayed the strength of an untamed bull.

Karmar and the three girls had rushed his bleeding accomplice to the emergency unit of the nearest hospital. The young man turned out to be an undergraduate student of Sanskrit at BHU and testified against Bharadwaj in the presence of the cops. He told them he had failed in two consecutive semesters and that Bharadwaj had promised to clear his papers, irrespective of his performance in the next semester, if he managed to fetch a particular piece of text from the premises of Yash Kashi Temple. Suspecting nothing, he complied.

Incidentally, the man who had forged a false identity and stolen the encyclopaedias from the Centre of Vedic Studies also came forward and confessed that he had done so at the behest of Bharadwaj. Apparently, he had remained silent on interrogation as Bharadwaj had threatened him of dire consequences.

'To be honest, I am not surprised that Laal Singh is Bharadwaj. I should have suspected it the day I went to his chamber to clarify the approach for my thesis. He was so cagey at my mention of the pelvic bone menace.' Meera told her friends.

'You had also mentioned that he was talking in a strange language to someone on the phone, a language that did not sound European or South East Asian but sounded strangely familiar. He must have been talking to Powell in African.' Kamakshi reminded her friend.

Meera now well understood why Bharadwaj had strongly discouraged Gopal Sarai from soliciting her help with the incident that had occurred in the library.

'Had they not known each other decades ago in Nigeria, Powell would have never chosen Bharadwaj as an accomplice and relied on him to get to the sacred text and double cross Venkatesh and Vijaylakshmi. Nobody knew that Bharadwaj is a qualified archaeologist and had worked in Nigeria for a year,' Karmar interrupted the silence. 'I mean none of us who had been nominated to the think tank were aware of this qualification.'

'Nobody knew this in India too, except the registrar and the vice-chancellor at BHU. I am sure that while submitting proofs of his qualifications at the time of his appointment, Bharadwaj never suspected that these would substantiate as evidence against him in a criminal case,' Meera remarked.

'It was wise of the cops to search his home when the encyclopaedia thief told them that Bharadwaj is secretly initiating a group of young men to Aghor tantra,' Ranbeer said. 'Now we know why the man who was leading the ritual in the underground chamber had his face masked in cloth. Because it was Bharadwaj and he knew Rustom and Sakhat but could not afford to let them know who he was. I guess he had some incredibly dangerous intent in initiating these youngsters.' Ranbeer observed.

The four friends and Karmar were sitting on the topmost steps of Shivala Ghat. The river was looking mesmerising at a distance.

'Bharadwaj was in London for a few days around the time that the archaeological archive had been ransacked. He and Powell had done it together. Powell, who too is now in police custody, has admitted this. No wonder that instead of stealing manuscripts and coins, they had stolen the entire array of human bones and skulls. They were collecting ammunition for their mission,' Karmar said.

'And who would have imagined that Vijaylakshmi is none other than the head sorceress of Erotic Salvation—Vividha Devi—and that she is also Vasanthi *Amma.* I am so glad this woman has been arrested,' Kamakshi said. 'Now I understand what Venkatesh meant when he was telling Rustom about commissions...I mean in the tunnel that day. Obviously these are the commissions that Rustom and his aides earn from Vividha, sorry Vijaylakshmi, by supplying women and intoxicating concoctions to Erotic Salvation.'

'Gauriprada had once told me that there was something more about Vividha Devi that he wanted to tell me. He probably suspected her involvement with poachers,' Meera remarked. 'Kamakshi, now I also know why you saw cartons of powder in Vasanthi *Amma*'s courtyard. And why you found the smell of the powder trail in Rustom's house familiar.'

Meera turned to Karmar. 'So you are convinced that Powell and Bharadwaj suspected that Venkatesh and Vijaylakshmi were trying to double cross them? That they knew that Venkatesh was approaching the *Shakti Peeths* for alliances? And therefore they planted these pelvic bones near all the *Peeths* that had declined support...to defame him?'

Karmar nodded. 'And now don't ask me how Powell came to know of Venkatesh's designs. Maybe he overhead some conversation between Venkatesh and Vijaylakshmi. Or...'

'Or maybe Powell had been monitoring his moves. If he had decided to oust Venkatesh and Vijaylakshmi from the think tank after getting hold of the sacred text, it is only natural that he was cautious,' Meera said.

'With a cunning aide like Bharadwaj, it would not have been difficult for Powell to keep tabs on everything that was happening in the occult realm of this country. After all, had it not been for him, Powell would have never even come to know about the secret text,' Ranbeer said. 'Treason and deceit is in his blood. Who could have imagined that he hails from a family of occult practitioners and that his father was none other than Shyam Bharadwaj?'

Meera sounded aghast. 'Now I know why he was so livid at me when I asked him about his interest on shamans. He was always reading and investigating on the occult realm but never wanted people to know about it.'

Baccha who had just joined them wanted to know more about this part.

'Bharadwaj's ancestors used to practice black magic. But they were ignorant about the *mahavidyas*. To acquire these *mahavidyas,* his father had sought the tutelage of Devesh Acharya in Mangalore. Initially the priest had declined but agreed when Shyam persisted. Besides, he never suspected his preoccupation with black magic. Apparently, Shyam was already in his late thirties when he had sought this tutelage,' Meera explained.

'By the way, Devesh*ji* was the man who had come to Banaras to hide the text during Brij Bhooshan Singh's days. He was the descendant of the favourite disciple of the Aghor who had authored this sacred text,' Kamakshi informed.

'Shyam Bharadwaj, like many others, had heard a rumour that the much revered Devesh*ji*'s ancestor had passed him some secrets about tantra *shastra* that nobody in the world knew about. So he was hoping to unearth these secrets and opportunity presented itself when one day he overheard a conversation between the priest and his son, behind locked doors.' Karmar narrated the rest of the story.

'How are we so sure that Bharadwaj is the son of Shyam Bharadwaj?' Baccha asked.

'Well, his father's name is stated in his academic records. The police with the help of the administration at BHU have investigated everything about Bharadwaj. They have scanned his research papers and academic submissions. In one paper, he has mentioned the cremation grounds where eleven of the most valuable tantric texts of the world were buried,' Meera elaborated.

'The same cremation grounds that we had disclosed to the police in connection to the pelvic bone menace.' Maya pointed out.

'You are forgetting that a *chandaal* was murdered in one of the grounds. So the cops grilled him about how he got to know about the connection of these grounds to the texts. He has denied any involvement with the murder but did say that he got to know about these texts from his father, Shyam Bharadwaj,' Karmar added.

'I guess we now well understand why Bharadwaj harboured a keen interest in the Dhumavati Temple of this town. He was probably fishing for some clues as the head priest of the Dhumavati Temple in Mangalore had hinted about the existence of the twelfth text. In fact, the police have established that Bharadwaj has stolen the copy of the *Saradatilakatantra*. Incidentally, this happened on the very day that he had sent me to Delhi to attend that conference,' Meera shrugged and continued, 'And I believe the cops have also retrieved the stolen copy of Panicker's book from his house. I still can't imagine how he shadowed Panicker to get to it. I always wondered about his unexplained trips. Now I know the destination. And yes, this also explains how lunch vouchers from the university canteen were lying on the ground of the ransacked library of the Centre for Vedic Studies.'

There was a long silence as everybody mulled over the sheer complexity of the mystery that they had successfully unravelled.

'My mother always told me that no matter how clever a criminal is in covering his tracks, he does leave a telltale sign somewhere. And in this case, the number that Rustom had forged with the Guwahati address really proved to be a massive Waterloo for all the culprits. It was so foolish of him to use a number registered in his accomplice's address to communicate with Gauripradа,' Kamakshi reasoned.

'I wonder what punishment will be meted to each of them,' Meera said.

'I had a chat with Tiwari. Powell, Venkatesh and all their poaching aides are likely to get fourteen-year jail sentences. So is Vijaylakshmi for running a prostitution racket. Venkatesh and Rustom are also facing additional charges for abducting Gauripradа,' Ranbeer informed. 'Apparently, Venkatesh and Alex have been spearheading all the poaching trades between India and Africa for decades now and Rustom has always been Venkatesh's most trusted henchman.'

'Hmm...given Venkatesh's Indian roots this is not surprising.' Maya remarked,.

'I'm sure Banaras will miss Sakhat for a long time to come. He was indeed the abaya-clad woman who had stalled me in Delhi.' Meera concluded.

Karmar looked at Ranbeer. 'And Bharadwaj? What did Tiwari tell you about his conviction?'

'I am told that the police are investigating more on him. But in the meantime he is likely to be sentenced to seven years of imprisonment for stealing Panicker's book and the encyclopaedia and for inciting theft and injuring a student.'

'Have you not told Tiwari about what we already know of the think tank and the sacred text? And, what did he have to say about Bharadwaj's involvement with the pelvic bone menace?' Karmar asked.

'I have and he believed every word. But he told me that none of those things fall within the purview of law. I mean there is no evidence to prove or even suggest that Bharadwaj had killed any of the women whose bodies had been found floating on rivers. And like we know, it is more likely that these bodies were of already dead women.'

'I must say I am amazed at his unflinching quest for the twelfth tantric text,' Kamakshi exclaimed.

Ranbeer looked pensive and shrugged his shoulders before replying. 'The cops have found reams of literature on black magic in his house. The man seems to be interested in all the archaic rituals that were practised in the Indian and African subcontinent.'

There was a long pause that Meera interrupted. 'Well, from whatever we have gathered, it is evident that Alex was trying to oust Venkatesh and Vijaylakshmi from the undercover network that they have been envisaging... and it seems likely that he would have partnered with Bharadwaj instead but...maybe Bharadwaj had his own secret ambitions. Maybe, he was planning to eventually doublecross Alex.'

'And establish his own cult of black magic. I guess he would have been quite formidable...don't forget that he was secretly initiating the young group of Aghors under Chet Singh Ghat,' Maya added.

Karmar smiled brightly. 'I wish the cops abundant luck in their investigations. And now we need to celebrate this victory. Let's have a small party at the café tomorrow night. I'm leaving for Rome day after.'

Everybody welcomed the suggestion.

Baccha adorned the entrance of Everest Café with strings of fairy lights.

Suchit and Gauripradа had arrived to be part of the celebrations. The main dining area was rearranged in buffet style.

'Where is Ranbeer?' Everybody started asking.

'He told me he will be back within an hour…oh here he is,' Meera pointed to the entrance of the dining hall.

Ranbeer was all smiles as he entered. 'I realised today that there is one bit of the puzzle that we hadn't solved. So, I went searching for the answer and got it.'

'What are you talking about?' Karmar asked.

'Well, we do know how Powell and Bharadwaj came to know of the existence of the sacred text. But we still didn't know how Venkatesh and Vijaylakshmi came to know about it. And, I somehow knew that only one man on the planet could provide the answer.'

'Who?' Half a dozen voices chorused.

'The clairvoyant. I went straight to his den before sunset and asked him if he remembered the man who had inquired about Limar Singh. He said he could describe him.'

'And his description told you it was Venkatesh?' Baccha was impressed.

'Yes. It had been a hot day and the man had folded his full-sleeved shirt. So he had even spotted his tattooed arm.'

Everyone smiled.

'Cheers to all the resounding successes of this mystery!' Baccha shouted excitedly from the centre table.

They all flocked near him and uncorked a bottle of champagne.

epilogue

It was the fall of 2015. A lot had changed in Ranbeer, Kamakshi, Meera and Maya's lives. Apart from winning the coveted category of Best Discovery by IDA, Ranbeer's documentary had bagged several awards at Cannes. He was busy delivering lectures on the nuances of documentary filmmaking in leading communication institutes.

Meera's thesis had caused an unprecedented stir in the global research fraternity. After *New York Times* and *The Times of India* carried her full-page interviews, she started receiving teaching offers from various Indian and international universities.

Maya and Alok had divorced. Alok had refused to give her alimony.

'Doesn't matter. I am glad that my adventure did a lot of good to him. Who would have imagined that this very poaching nexus was responsible for the dwindling count of spotted deers and Indian rollers on account of which, several forest officers including Alok, were being implicated in corruption charges by the higher authorities. After this nexus has been exposed everything against them is cleared,' she had told Arvind.

Arvind and Maya were set to marry soon. He too had bagged several awards in his field and was now working on a prestigious assignment with the Royal Society for the Protection of Birds. The findings would influence policy making on owl conservation at the international level.

Even Baccha and Suchit had prospered. Everest Café's popularity was soaring as Meera and Ranbeer had mentioned it in the course of media interviews. Almost everybody visiting Banaras made it a point to have at least one meal at Baccha's restaurant.

Suchit took charge of Sakhat's shop and started retailing an array of white goods like handicrafts, linen and homemade pickles.

As Kamakshi thought over the events of the last three years she smiled to herself. 'Kashinath was right when he said that sometimes personal misfortunes lead us to big missions. History will always remember our part in discovering India's most powerful tantric text.'

She was sitting in a secluded corner of Assi Ghat at the brink of twilight. The medley of temple bells in the vicinity translated to inspiration for a dream that she had long cherished—of writing a novel. She closed her eyes for a few minutes to invoke the blessings of the divine.

The first line that she penned in her diary read: *Holiness does reign in the unholy bastions of our self-righteous moral guardians.*

It was getting dark and difficult to see. As she got up to walk towards Everest Café, Kamakshi felt a strange, almost ethereal light filtering into her consciousness. It was telling her that she must start writing *The Mystic Sinners* for this was a story that the world deserved to read.

Acknowledgement

The Mystic Sinners would have forever remained a dream if the higher powers had not facilitated its journey through the unflinching support of my family and well-wishers.

Perhaps I can never thank my mother adequately for believing in my dreams. When I started writing, the strongest encouragement came from her. Her encouragement and support carried me through all my 'not so confident' moments. I hope that every time she holds this book she is reminded how incredibly important she really is to me. And, it is here that I feel a little moist-eyed for my father could not live long enough to even see me starting out on the journey of writing a book. He was an avid reader, particularly of Indian authors and would have been so very proud of me today. Baba, I know you are blessing me from above and I also know that you would have been the first one in the world to preorder *The Mystic Sinners* on Amazon.

Boromahi, my aunt, has been nothing short of a parent in my journey. For it is in her beautiful South Delhi apartment, surrounded by greenery that I wrote this book. There could have been no better place in the world to write as I believe that her love and blessings manifested in the energies of the house—energies that made words, lines and chapters effortlessly flow out of me.

My brother and sister-in-law too have been incredibly supportive. To be honest, my brother believes in the success of *The Mystic Sinners* more than me and despite her own challenges, my sister-in-law had quietly transferred some money into my account saying, '*Didi,* use this for your promotions.'

I am indebted to my grandmother for the special prayers that she utters in her puja room every morning and evening for my book. I would like to tell all my other aunts (*Chotomahi, Boropi* and *Chotopi*) that I am very touched at their belief in me and grateful for their blessings.

I thank my best friend, Himika Chaudhuri for it was she who meticulously read my manuscript at the stage where I required objective feedback. I am grateful for her support and encouragement all through my journey. My maid Sheela *Didi* too has been an amazing support in this long journey. Incidentally, (without my permission) she has already told all my neighbours that I have written a book. Her enthusiasm to see the book in print has touched me beyond words.

Everything of consequence that has been created or crafted in this world has had the blessings and guidance of a Guru. And for me, that Guru has been none other than Dipankar Mukherjee, who heads Readomania. Dipankar, if you had not given me your insights and inputs during the stages of manuscript revision, this book would have never shaped out the way it has. I am indebted to Indrani Ganguly (Managing Editor) and Rima Kar Ghosh (Senior Editor). While their feedback and suggestions during the stage of development editing translated to an enormous fillip for the book, their commitment and dedication towards perfecting my book has endeared them to my heart for forever. Dipankar, Indrani and Rima, I really hope you know how much all three of you and Readomania mean to me and always will.

about the author

Proyashi Barua is a Delhi-based content writer and consultant from Guwahati. An alumnus of Symbiosis Institute of Media and Communication (SIMC), she has worked for about fifteen years in the communications and media industry including *The Times of India, Hindustan Times,* and an international foreign trade magazine where she served in the capacity of an assistant editor.

An avid reader, movie buff and travel enthusiast, Proyashi loves children and dogs. She also has a keen interest in learning about the probable causes that led to the extinction of some important ancient and medieval civilisations. Astrology, numerology and music are some pastimes that fill her soul. This is her debut novel.

Proyashi can be contacted at proyashi.barua@gmail.com